17039

The Television Dramatist

The Television Dramatist

Plays by

LEO LEHMAN
PETER NICHOLS
JOHN BOWEN
JACK ROSENTHAL
DENNIS POTTER

Selected and introduced by

Robert Muller

Paul Elek

Published by PAUL ELEK LIMITED in 1973
54-58 Caledonian Road
London N1 9RN

MADE AND PRINTED IN GREAT BRITAIN BY
THE GARDEN CITY PRESS LIMITED
LETCHWORTH, HERTFORDSHIRE SG6 1JS

CONTENTS

INTRODUCTION

As I write this—not in the summer doldrums but at the start of an excitedly heralded 'New Season'—I have before me the current issues of *TV Times* and *Radio Times*.

I search for the week's drama output:

BBC TV is giving us a Thirty-Minute Theatre by Rayner Heppenstall and a revival of Bernard Shaw. On the commercial channel there is only one new play—by Terence Rattigan. That's it. No Sunday Night Play, no Wednesday Play, no Play of the Week, no Television Playhouse. Only if you look diligently will you find further examples of television drama concealed as 'Series' or 'Serials', or 'Adaptations'. Where have all the TV playwrights gone?

In introducing this personal choice of television drama, I seem to be in a position of writing a valedictory. The Great Days of the television play are past. But then Great Days always lie in the past. The Golden Age is never the present. The tragedy of the television play, however, is that even its past glories have to be taken on trust. Unlike old movies, which can be reclaimed from vaults, and old theatre plays, which can be borrowed from libraries, the television play usually sinks without trace after one showing, or—at most—two. It literally vanishes. To save a few pounds, the television companies wipe the tapes on which plays are recorded; they don't even bother to keep old scripts in their files.

No wonder that the television playwright, who begins his career with the usual hope of winning some small piece of immortality, grows weary with disillusionment over the years. For it is decreed: in order to win recognition from his peers he *must* make the sideways jump to the theatre, the cinema, or the world of 'literature'—*even if his best work is done for the small screen.* His novel may have been read by two thousand people, while millions watched his television play. No matter: the television play does not qualify for serious consideration.

The television dramatist is a dangerous clown. If he writes one play after another—as most of us do at the beginning of our luminous futures—he is warned against 'over-exposure' or—more dangerously—encouraged into channelling his energies into more lucrative and allegedly popular 'series' work. If he rations himself to a single play a year (in the theatre a respectable output by any standards) he is considered 'written-out'. (Also, he starves.)

The question that he dare not ask—and no television executive will do the asking (or answering) *for* him—is: 'How many plays can I write over a span of, say, fifteen years, without repeating myself, or becoming exhausted, or wearying my audiences? Thirty? Fifty? A hundred?'

There is no pension for writers who have 'chosen' television drama as a career, and Guild Awards aren't edible.

This bizarre productivity problem is not the only enemy of a television playwright's promise. We are slaves of fashion. This year's Golden Boy is invariably next year's Has-Been. The Headline Wonder of the sixties is—come the seventies—asked to spell his name over the telephone. Yesterday's Great Director humbly writes to ask if he could direct your work. The boy who, last summer, brought you coffee at rehearsals, sits behind a big desk when the leaves turn golden, and doesn't return your telephone call, probably because—as he will tell your agent—your work 'doesn't swing for him'.

Remember that television is organized like an industry: the writer only exists as a member of a creative team. Your script is at the mercy of your interpreters. May I be forgiven for this heresy, but *no television writer has ever got anywhere without the help of a good director.* He is rendered powerless without an imaginative producer (rare bird) who will commission a play on the basis of a hum-and-haw over a cuppa. He is done for, if lumbered with a story-editor who cherishes Louis B. Mayer fantasies; or with a director who is 'doing' your script because he needs the money and hopes to ingratiate himself with his bosses by keeping costs low and technical demands uncomplicated; or with a hardened executive who tells a writer who has never had any trouble in keeping the attention of an audience of ten million people 'to remember the fishmonger's wife in Rochdale, old son'.

And in listing these human obstacles, I have not even allowed for the television companies' PR departments, who will always push serials and series rather than what is scathingly called the 'one-off' play. Or the press, which—in these matters—has allowed itself to become the executive arm of Public Relations.

Ten years ago, a television play would without exception get notices in the dailies and quality Sundays. Today it is possible—and I quote a real example—for a respected playwright to have four plays transmitted over a period of six months, without getting *one* notice in the national press.

And yet the single television play—like the novel, against which the dice are similarly loaded—survives. And if I had been asked to choose fifty fine plays instead of a mere five, I could have done so, without lowering standards of quality.

In making this personal choice, I have followed my own tastes, which favour originality of theme and individuality of treatment rather than political orthodoxy or technical experimentation. I have also tried to find fitting examples of the various modes that are open to the television playwright: the entirely studio-made play, the play which blends studio-production with filmed inserts, and television drama wholly shot on location.

I have not favoured the work of successful drama-
tists, but it may be significant that the writers who
remained after the final sifting are all adept at writing
novels, or for the theatre, or for the cinema; i.e. the
professionals.

I salute the five survivors—but dedicate this selec-
tion to the others—the ones who toil invisibly in
Brecht's 'darkness', obstinately working on in the most
abused, most debased, most exciting medium ever
invented by man.

May my pessimism be confounded by the publication
of a further collection. Preferably before the single
television play becomes a legend of the past.

October, 1972   ROBERT MULLER

LEO LEHMAN

End of Story

Preface

LEO LEHMAN was born in Poland in 1926. His television plays include: *The Common Room, Thirty Pieces of Silver, A Reason for Staying, Late Summer Affair, Song of a March Hare, Freedom in December, I Don't Like You, Lovers of Florence, Girl With a Difference, The Cold Heart, Are You by Yourself?, Surface of Innocence, Quartet at Sheila's, Floating Man, Do You Remember the Germans?*

'I wrote for television because it was there. And because I was a dramatist. It is true that the theatre was also there, and, had I been acclaimed in it, it is likely that I would have written much more for it, and less for television. I don't think I would have written for the cinema, regardless of circumstances, for, although I love the idea of a filmscript, the prospect of what some genius or other is going to do to it distracts me. I am too vain as a writer, and the writer's contribution to a film, and his control over it, have always seemed to me too slight to warrant all the misery. I like seeing other people's films, but will write my own plays.

'This then has been television's attraction: that, despite the necessary and often glowing part played by everybody else, the play behind the play, the writer's play behind the actor's and the director's and the lighting man's, is not lost. At the end of the day, it is still there, and—if memory fails—can even be fished out from the bottom of an old chest (Elizabethan, cured of woodworm, held together with iron clasps). There is something irreducible about it.

'On the other hand, the more usual outcome, the sudden death of the play, the ritual—or mere indignity —of it being wiped out, and the tape made ready for the next bit of folly, has never worried me. Indeed, I rather like the idea of it being there one moment and gone (for ever) the next. It almost raises art to the level of life. The pretensions of art to permanence, in any event, leave me unmoved. We are not going to be missed.

'Is there a contradiction in this unemotional attitude to the performance and the expectation, even if remote, of seeing the edition of my collected works on a top shelf in my country "dacha"? There may be. I hasten to add that I haven't got the "dacha", either. I am reminded of Lord Clark's distinction between the fixed and moving image, and his doubt whether the latter has any place in art at all. At first I suspected the validity of his contention, but am inclined to agree with it now. I think anything that moves is suspect.

'What, if anything, is a television play? Long ago, I held the belief that only a live performance ought to qualify, and that pre-recording, as it is called, was the road to ruin. Later, I shifted my ground trying to draw up imaginary boundaries between recording for television and film. It was always a losing battle: from the outset, the television play was destined to become merely a film, shot in a hurry with insufficient means. In other words, there is no such thing. How does it happen then that we have created, and continue to create, these myriad things without a name? I put my head on the block: the play ends with the rehearsal script. Beyond that—all is confusion. Anyway, it defies definition.

'May I say that these considerations do not take away one whit from the pleasure of seeing the skeleton of one's play become the flesh and blood of perform-ance? I love rehearsals. Occasionally, I make a contri-bution bearing on greater accuracy: it's that which concerns me most. Having had the good fortune to work with the best of all television directors—Joan Kemp-Welch, who directed *End of Story*—I have at times had the feeling that everything in a play matters. These are the best moments.

'Television, it seems to me, has been the dramatist's salvation: out of the blue, it gave him a platform, and at the same time subjected him to the salutary discipline of an audience. Anybody can be a genius. It made a professional of him. And let me dispel the *canard* that the pressures of television have been of a nature to thwart the creative spirit. We can only compare our situation with that obtaining elsewhere: by any criteria, our freedom has been quite extraordinary. If we haven't done better, the fault was definitely not in our stars.

'And yet, the dramatist on the studio floor is a morose fellow: he argues that the theatre confers higher prestige, the cinema greater riches, and practically every other form of writing greater durability. His wife and child, and agent, abet him. I take it with a pinch of salt: in our time, the principal opportunity of the dramatist has not been in the theatre, or the cinema, or the circus, but on the small grey screen in the far corner of the room: this is where our art has flourished. And if our creations disappear into the bowels of the night the instant the picture ceases—well, how wonderful to be confounded with the elements, to become part of the surrounding ether. Ether to ether. It seems appropriate enough.

'What of the future? I must admit, about the future I am not so sanguine. I think we have had the best of the old/new wine. I look back with a certain melancholy. For a host of reasons, I do not look forward. Maybe it's gone on for too long. No matter—and this is the surprising nature of the beast: I may be proved wrong any night of the week. No, on reflection, there is no end to it. *Dien Merci.*'

LEO LEHMAN

5

End of Story was first presented by Yorkshire Television on 25 September, 1969* with the following cast:

KEITH	*Peter Barkworth*
MAUD	*Mary Kenton*
GERALD	*Griffith Jones*
FANNY	*Lally Bowers*
FATHER	*Arthur Hewlett*
TOBY	*Sean Bury*
DEBBIE	*Katie Macleod*
RICHARD	*Tenniel Evans*
NURSE	*Ursula Hirst*
TERENCE	*Roland Curram*
JOHN BROOME	*Peter Woodthorpe*
LAURA	*Jennifer Jayne*
OLD MAN	*John Gill*
BARRY	*Keith Grenville*
SECRETARY	*Joanna Royce*
RITA	*Adelaide Necheke*
GEORGE	*Alec Ross*
AN ACTOR	*Donald Barkham*
WAITER	*Ray Marioni*
NEWSCASTER (film only)	*Roy Herrick*
DONALD	*Michael Harding*

Produced by Peter Willes
Directed by Joan Kemp-Welch

The play that follows is a marginally revised version of that originally presented.

*It was also produced by the Bayerischer Rundfunk, Munich.

Characters

KEITH BAILEY
MAUD
TOBY
DEBBIE
GERALD HASS
TERENCE
LAURA
FANNY
SECRETARY
BARRY SIMON
RICHARD
OLD MAN
JOHN BROOME
FATHER
NURSE
WAITER
A FEW OTHERS

Setting: London
Time: Spring, 1969

ACT I

1

Interior. Donald's study. Night.

(A melodramatic scene:

A writer with bushy beard and a wild eye is writing passionately. His pen races over the virgin pages.

Music on his tape recorder: A Bach fugue, pretty deafening, although it's obviously late into the night.

A bottle of pills by his side—empty—and a glass of water.

Suddenly, in the middle of a sentence, he stops. Stops the music. An owl hoots in the night. But he is not listening to anything in the outside world, only the thumping of his own heart.

He rises. He takes a few steps. Panic seizes him. He is trying to reach another little bottle of pills on a shelf, against a forest of books. He gets to it, but it is too late: his arms flail helplessly, the thing slips from his hand. He staggers, clutching the sides of the desk, cushioning his fall.

He is lying on the floor. His lips articulate feebly a woman's name. Rosebud? Twice. Three times. Then all is silence. We don't know if she has heard him.)

CREDITS

2

Interior. Suburban home. Day.

(Hall with telephone. Staircase. Open plan kitchen.

Also, a spanish type patio visible beyond it.

A toddler is yelling in a pen. Maud is arguing with a neighbour over the wall.)

MAUD: I am sorry if the ball's gone over again. I have told him not to throw it. I can't do more. Take the ball away from him.

(*At the same time, the telephone is ringing. A little girl—Debbie—answers it.)*

DEBBIE: Who? Daddy? Yes, I will call Daddy.

MAUD: What is it? Is it the butcher?

DEBBIE: No, it's for Daddy.

MAUD (*To toddler*): Will you shut up, will you shut up. What do you *want*? (*To son, Toby, returning with ball.*) If you do it again, I don't know what I am going to do. (*To daughter.*) Did you say it was the butcher? (*To son.*) Why can't you *read*, for a change? Have you done your homework? Oh, you can't still be on holiday . . . (*To neighbour.*) No, Mrs Gross, he is not going to throw it again. (*To son.*) You're not, are you?

(*Toby produces a pistol. This has the singular effect of rousing Bruce, the dog, which sets off the toddler again. Despair.*)

3

Interior. Upstairs. Day.

(*The cool of the landing. Debbie outside her father's door. She is about to knock.*)

DEBBIE: Daddy—(*She listens.*)

PECULIAR VOICES: I will plug you, Harry.

What?

That's better. What have you done with her?

10

Who?

Melissa. Where is Melissa?

Melissa?

Melissa.

(*Pause.*)

She's gone to Ben Akbar's.

Ben Akbar's? If he so much as *touches* her, Harry, you will never see Ben Akbar again. Take me to him.

Me?

Yes.

When?

Now

No.

(*Crunch.*)

He will kill me, Felix.

I'll come to the funeral.

(*Debbie walks in.*)

4

Interior. Study. Day.

(*Keith Bailey switches off his record player. He is a writer too, but his study is not in the least bit romantic. Photographs of* Action *cover the walls.*)

DEBBIE: Mr Hass for you, Daddy.

KEITH: Coming. Thanks. Modern technology . . .

(*He has an extension, of course, but it's dead, apparently.*)

DEBBIE: What are you writing, Daddy?

11

KEITH: She Was a Monster.

DEBBIE: Who for, the Bruisers or the Nice People?

KEITH: The Bruisers.

DEBBIE: Hooray. Can I listen?

KEITH: Yes, why don't you?

(*She stays behind. Switches it on.*)

VOICE: You hear me all right, Ben Akbar, *don't flinch.*

DEBBIE: Oh, Daddy, you're such a lovely actor.

5

Interior. House as before. Day.

(*Keith on the phone*)

KEITH: Hullo, Gerald? No, it's just those blasted people, they won't connect it. What? Donald? Dead? Oh, my God. When?

(*Maud, in the kitchen.*)

Shut up, darling. Donald's dead.

(*She didn't hear him.*)

Yes, all right. No, of course, you can't be alone. Yes, I'll come over, we will have lunch. Right. (*Puts down phone.*) Oh, my God.

(*Maud comes in.*)

MAUD: Look, the butcher hasn't turned up. Please go and get it for me. I've ordered it, you don't have to do a thing. I can't cope when they're on holiday. Everybody else is having a nervous breakdown . . .

KEITH: Donald's dead.

MAUD: Who?

KEITH: Donald. The writer.

MAUD: Wasn't he the one who came to dinner?

KEITH: Yes.

MAUD: Well, he wrote such awful morbid stuff. I'm not surprised. I am sorry. Car accident?

KEITH: No, don't think so.

(*Pause.*)

MAUD: Darling, will you please, get it now. I can't even get started.

KEITH: I am having lunch with Gerald. I'll have to put on a tie.

MAUD: You know, you are quite unfeeling, it's the truth. There she goes again. (*The toddler. Also, the ball has gone over again.*)

(*Fades.*) What did I say, he's done it again. I am sorry, Mrs Gross.

(*Debbie comes downstairs.*)

DEBBIE: Daddy, Daddy. It's super.

KEITH: What is?

DEBBIE: When he goes Oooah.

KEITH: Who?

DEBBIE: Ben Akbar.

(*Pause.*)

KEITH: My little girl, a very fine writer has died, a friend of your daddy's.

DEBBIE: Have I met him?

KEITH: Yes, he came here, once. He had a beard.

DEBBIE: Oh, I know. He brought us a box of sweets.

KEITH: Did he?

DEBBIE: They all melted.

13

KEITH: Ppflotch.

DEBBIE: They all got stuck to the bottom.

KEITH: He died last night.

DEBBIE: I don't think they were very fresh, do you?

(*Pause. He walks upstairs.*)

Oh, Daddy, you careless Daddy. You haven't put the phone back. (*She does it for him.*)

6

Interior. The patio (restaurant). Artificial day.

(*Gerald and Keith, at lunch.*)

GERALD: I loved him. Did you know I'd decorated his flat for him? But there you are.

KEITH: What was it?

GERALD: Heart. In the middle of the night. Hazel was asleep. She didn't hear him.

KEITH: It's terrible, we're all going. Larry. Ben. In the last two years, alone.

GERALD: It's the strain, you see. It's not cigarettes, it's the strain. Ah, dear. He was a monster, but I loved him. (*Pause.*) He has left me with a problem, though.

(*Keith looks at him.*)

It was to be a fantastic production. He didn't finish it.

KEITH: He didn't finish the play.

GERALD: No, he did not. Hazel says nothing can be done, nobody can read his writing. I tell you what it is, it's crab vinaigrette, and it's lovely. Try it.

KEITH: It looks very nice.

GERALD: Try it (*He gives him some.*) I am without the

third play for Autobiography. What am I going to do? This man is making faces at me.

KEITH: Who—

GERALD: The man over there. I don't know him.

KEITH: He is not making faces at you. He's got a nervous—what's the name of it.

GERALD: That's not a—yes, it is. Sorry, Keith. I thought he was some kind of clown. (*He relaxes.*)

KEITH: What are you going to do?

GERALD: Ask you.

KEITH: Hm?

GERALD: Keith, dear boy, we have known each other for—what—nine?

KEITH: More.

GERALD: Don't. I haven't been doing this thing . . . Yes, I have. You did an Inspector Fuchs for me.

KEITH: Yes.

GERALD: Beautiful job. And at least eight Robbers.

KEITH: Yes.

GERALD: Bury Her Alive. Six episodes. And the Noose.

KEITH: That was a mess.

GERALD: The whole thing was a mess. Wasn't your fault.

KEITH: And The Manchester File.

GERALD: Good God, I'd forgotten all about The Manchester File.

(*Pause.*)

And now I want you to do Autobiography, which is something entirely different. Each play is a life. In depth. Here is your chance. Write a masterpiece.

(*Pause.*)

15

KEITH: Did you ask Lionel?

GERALD: Hm?

KEITH: Tock.

GERALD: I did, as a matter of fact. He's doing a film.

KEITH: Michael?

GERALD: Yes. Yes. Michael's writing a stage play. The so and so.

KEITH: What about—Max?

GERALD: Hm? Max, unfortunately, is away. South of France. He wanted two thousand, anyway. I can't pay that sort of money.

KEITH: So it came down to me.

GERALD: You are the only hack writer, Keith, I would have dreamt of asking.

KEITH: You have such a bloody refined way of asking, what can I do about it?

GERALD: Have some more wine. (*He smiles.*) What it amounts to is, can you come up with something—it doesn't matter if nobody watches, as long as the boys upstairs get a couple of notices in the Sundays, and go back to the ITA and say, we did the Barry Simon play, we did the John Broome *and* the Keith Bailey—everybody switched off, and if that's not art what is?

KEITH: You're getting sour, Gerald.

GERALD: Am I? Yes, I am. Forgive me. I don't want to be here. I want to be in Italy. Near Sienna. About ten miles from Sienna. I know just the place where I'd want to be. What is that you're eating?

KEITH: You can see.

GERALD: May I try?

KEITH: Of course.

GERALD: Can't resist, you know. You're such a funny person, Keith. You're offended, what?

16

KEITH: Why?

GERALD: Because I've called you a hack. Are you going to do it?

KEITH: I am going to do it, yes. I am going to have a go.

GERALD: I have to have it by the middle of next month. I say, this is very good. What is it?

KEITH: It was the veal piccata.

GERALD: I should have had that, you know. Silly of me. Aren't you hungry?

KEITH: I love you, Gerald.

GERALD: I like to hear you say it.

KEITH: Please finish it. I don't want it. (*He hands him the whole plate.*) I am going to surprise you, Gerald.

GERALD: No, you're not. I know you can do it. How do I know? Flair. How do you think I have kept my job with twenty thousand mamelukes breathing down my neck? Will you have a brandy with the coffee, dear boy?

KEITH: Please.

(*Pause.*)

GERALD: He is, you know. He is making faces at me, this fellow. I am going to ask him why.

(*He is going to get up and have it out with the man.*

Keith is dreaming.)

7

Interior. Bedroom. Night.

(*Keith and Maud in bed. Gentle light music on the radio. They are both reading.*

17

He switches to a Haydn quartet. Maud looks up from her book. Wonders. But doesn't say anything, at first.)

MAUD: What are you reading?

KEITH: The journal of an Egoist.

MAUD: Oh. Who is it by?

KEITH: Stendhal.

(Pause.)

MAUD: I thought you were reading the Deighton thriller.

KEITH: I gave it up. *(Pause.)* Gerald's asked me to do a play for him.

MAUD: What about?

KEITH: What do you mean, what about? Everything and nothing. Do it to astonish the world.

MAUD: A play like Hamlet.

KEITH: Yes. This is the moment of truth. I am a writer. *(Irony? Yes and no.)* A play which is going to say what I've always wanted to say. Through all the Ben Akbars, the Brothers Montillados, the Senorita Ibita, and bloody Inspector Fuchs.

MAUD: But, darling.

KEITH: What?

MAUD: You have nothing to say—what?

KEITH: Everybody has something to say.

MAUD: I am fagged out. You are seeing to Sandra, tomorrow morning. Sorry. *(Pause.)* It's not going to make you miss any Bruisers, is it?

KEITH: It is. Three Bruisers.

MAUD: I am not giving up my holidays in Italy for this. I am not. I think Gerald should have his head examined.

18

KEITH: You know what you are—what I mind—the rest—what I really mind—you are crude. You have a crude mind.

MAUD: Darling, I am trying to be nice. You're not a writer, you are not a *script*writer. Donald was a writer. You can't do the other thing.

KEITH: It's all the same—thing.

MAUD: Oh, oh, I am so sleepy. And you irritate me. (*Pause.*) Nothing happens in our lives. What do you want to write about? You can't invent these things. If nothing happens to you, there it is—you have nothing to say. It's as simple as that. You think up all those marvellous places. I mean, if you ever went there, or met some of those people—you'd die. I honestly believe you'd die. I am being mean, hm? Don't mean to. I have a headache. Toby fell off his bicycle, this morning, did you know?

KEITH: Did he?

MAUD: And he tore his trousers, the ones I bought him last week. (*Pause.*) And the dog got out on the road again.

KEITH: Who let him out?

MAUD: I don't know who let him out.

(*Lights out.*)

Good night, dear.

KEITH: Good night, love.

MAUD: I love you, really. But Gerald is very naughty. He shouldn't do these things.

(*Music out. Silence.*)

What are you doing at the moment?

KEITH: I am finishing a Bruisers. And I was going to do The Riders of Hell.

19

8

Interior. Script Editor's office. Day.

(*Terence Riddle's exiguous office in TV Towers.*)

TERENCE (*To Keith*): I am afraid it means a rewrite ... I like everything. Except the denouement. The denouement has to have inevitability, and I don't see it. I am very sorry. I think it's too subtle. Frankly. Schumann goes to see Henrietta. She plays coy because of course she knows that Evangeli is hiding in the loft. She knows what Schumann is really after, and it is not Evangeli. Is it?

KEITH: No.

TERENCE: It's Gupescu. Schumann, incidentally, has left the car engine running. Why?

KEITH: Hm?

TERENCE: Because he's expecting Artman's signal.

KEITH: Yes.

TERENCE: Well, then. Couldn't we have a bit of a psychological situation here? Henrietta loves Gupescu. Forgive me for saying it, Keith, but I think you have forgotten about that. When she turns round to get the red hot poker—incidentally, it's damned hard to get a red hot poker on the screen. I wish you had thought of something else. Anyway—it doesn't sound quite right, does it? It sounds a bit passé to me, a poker. I know we're in the Middle East.

KEITH: Pair of scissors.

TERENCE: What? Yes. Pair of scissors would be better. It's not ideal, but it's better.

KEITH: She was sewing.

TERENCE: No, you see—again—sewing isn't the answer, either. I don't know, Keith, but it all sounds a bit pre Bond to me, what we have here.

KEITH: What about an electronic computer?

TERENCE: What about it?

KEITH: She was computing on this electronic computer, and as he comes in—you know, after he says: I can smell your perfume, I can smell Evangeli—she picks up this computer, and clocks him over the head with it.

(*Pause.*)

TERENCE: You're mocking, aren't you?

KEITH: No, I just feel hot. I feel uncomfortable.

TERENCE: Yes, it's pretty stuffy in here. You know, these windows don't open. They just don't open. Blast them. Yes, Rita?

(*Girl's head in the door, she is black.*)

RITA: Freddie Shaw wants the rewrite for Monday.

TERENCE (*To Keith*): Can you do it?

(*He can.*)

What do they care about truth? (*To Rita.*) Tell him he will have it when we are ready for him.

RITA: He won't like that. (*Rita gone.*)

TERENCE: You know, when I see a marvellous script before me, I don't want to see it acted by all those terrible sillies. I don't want to see it done at all. Butchers. Where were we?

KEITH: In Henrietta's hide-out.

TERENCE: That's right. Gupescu is in the submarine.

KEITH: Is he?

TERENCE: What? Of course, he is. You wrote it. What's the matter? (*Pause.*) Henrietta, cornered by Schumann, seizes hold of this—red-hot poker. The *threat* of violence, Keith . . .

KEITH: Gerald's asked me to write a play for him.

21

TERENCE: The Greeks have taught us that.

KEITH: Gerald's asked me to write a play for him.

TERENCE: What for?

KEITH: Nothing. I mean, a play. A single shot play.

TERENCE: Instead of Donald.

KEITH: How did you know?

TERENCE: Inspired guess. What about?

KEITH: I don't know yet. It's for Autobiography.

TERENCE: Yes. Hm. (*Pause. His face has fallen.*) I was going to ask you to do the Monks for me. You know I am doing the Monks, after this.

KEITH: Yes, I have heard about it.

TERENCE: Ah, but have you heard *where* we are doing these Monks? In Cyprus. They are *Greek Orthodox Monks*. It's going to be about the everyday life of Greek Orthodox Monks on a mountain top in Cyprus. Bags of locations. You won't be able to do it now, I suppose.

KEITH: Well, no, not immediately.

TERENCE: Pity.

KEITH: I am sorry.

TERENCE: Yes.

(*Pause.*)

KEITH: What?

TERENCE: Hm?

KEITH: Are you sore?

TERENCE: Sore? Good heavens no. Why should I be sore? I will tell you why I am sore. I am sore as hell at the idea that there is anything superior about the single shot play. I work myself into a neurosis here—

day after day—then up comes somebody like Gerald, with your prestige symbol written all over his airy fairy face. Do you know why—because he failed with the Hooded Monsters. He failed with the Hooded Monsters so they put him on to *Art*. And how did he get there, in the first place?

KEITH: Hm?

TERENCE: Connections. Parties. I don't go to parties. Do you? Corridors of Power. I spit—on your Corridors of Power. I sit here and deliver the Monks. But I will tell you, Keith, I care more about my Monks than he does about King Lear. Because I love television. And he uses it. His heart is elsewhere. His heart is in the *Theatre*. And I will tell you, moreover, that when he gets John or Barry or what's the chap's name—when these illustrious authors condescend—because that's precisely what they're doing—they're *condescending* to write for television—more often than not it turns out to be *crap*, and when you say, look, it doesn't make sense—because it *doesn't*—they turn round and say, ah, but it's great writing, don't you see? I don't. I don't see it at all. And I will say this to you, moreover, that if Shakespeare—and I know my Shakespeare, Keith— were alive today—I will hazard the proposition—that he would *not* be writing for your Aunt Fanny's Theatre, which is just about the deadest piece of hokum there is, or for films—because that's just a lot of *dwarfs* running with cameras—he would be writing for television. And I am not so sure that he wouldn't be writing the Monks.

KEITH: I don't.

TERENCE: What?

KEITH: I don't think he would be writing the Monks.

(*Terence smiles.*)

TERENCE: Well. Maybe not. (*The friend once more.*) What is it going to be about?

KEITH: Don't know yet what it is going to be about.

TERENCE (*Meant to be reassuring*): You think up ideas faster than anyone. Except Max. True. Max is fabulous. But Max is in a loony bin.

KEITH: How is he getting on?

TERENCE: He is getting on. But he is not getting out. I believe if Max had been around Gerald would have asked him.

KEITH: He did, apparently. He didn't know Max was ill.

TERENCE: Well, there you are. He doesn't know anything, that man.

(*Keith is going.*)

You slog out your guts—you get all these writers—you look after them, nurture them: what happens: in rushes a precious bull of an elephant and tramples all over your china shop. Havoc. You will let me have it by Monday.

(*The rewrite. Keith nods. Rita comes in with tea tray.*)

RITA: Aren't you going to have a cup of tea, Mr Bailey?

(*He says no, thank you, pays her a dubious compliment.*

She laughs, because she has a sunny disposition.

Keith goes.)

TERENCE: Mad. Mad. He's going to fall down and break everything. And who's going to pick him up? I am. Biscuits?

RITA: Ginger nut.

(*He drinks his tea.*)

TERENCE: Autobiography. Autobiography. (*He muses.*)

9

Interior. Laura's. Day.

(A shaggy room, kitchen and bathroom.

He lies with his head in her lap. She is knitting, deftly, mittens for somebody else's child.)

KEITH: I am asking myself, what is my life? What can I say about it? I can think of a hundred plots. But has my life got a plot? I am seized with an awful timidity. What am I going to write about? I have invented a thousand characters. But not one of them, Laura, I swear, not one—was observed. Bits of them were. Bits. But when I think of you or Maud or myself —I wouldn't know where to begin. My hands fall off. Off. Look. I am lying here. My life's uninteresting. To me. So how could it be of interest to anybody else? (*Pause.*) Actually, I think, most people are hopelessly ordinary. What makes them extraordinary is just the energy they put into it. It's pure Chekhov, isn't it? What bothers me about *him* is that he should have been bothered. The doctor in the Three Sisters says— he just sits around, this doctor, doesn't do a damned thing—he says, to somebody's enquiry: no, I haven't got married. Life has rushed by so fast. There hasn't been time.

LAURA: You're lucky.

KEITH: What?

LAURA: You've got married. You've managed to get three children out of her.

KEITH: Here we go.

LAURA: You've kept them supplied with toys and cereals. And you have a dog. I don't know what you're complaining of.

KEITH: I wasn't.

LAURA: You have a marvellous life.

25

KEITH: Yes.

LAURA: Well, of course. All this great Yogi Bear family, and me, what more do you want?

KEITH: Look, I don't want—I was talking about *playwriting*, fiction.

LAURA: What do I get out of this arrangement? Fiction. You couldn't have chosen a better word.

KEITH: I am thirsty.

LAURA: Hm?

KEITH: Have you got any squash?

LAURA: Yes, it's in the fridge.

(*He gets up, fetches it.*)

Yes. Here I am. I am like a stooge I am. Come ten o'clock you rush home not to offend her by staying out all night. I mean, you really are having it both ways, aren't you? Without formal danger.

KEITH: Formal? What's that?

LAURA: Oh, shut up.

KEITH: What's got into you? I was lying here, perfectly contented.

LAURA: Of course you were. Why should you be *dis*contented, for God's sake, hm? You hop round here when you feel like it. I think you just want to get away from the noise.

KEITH: What—

LAURA: The children. The dog. Her.

KEITH: Oh, blast.

LAURA: That's right, spill it on my carpet.

KEITH: It's just water.

LAURA: I am not a bitch. I hate hearing myself. Love. Where is it getting me?

KEITH: What do you want?

LAURA: God, if I weren't out of work half the time, you wouldn't see me for dust. You wouldn't see me, that's all. (*Pause.*) I mean, it doesn't even feel sinful —it doesn't feel like anything.

KEITH: There you are. How can I—I can't. I can't write about you. Us. It would sound like nothing on earth. This is what she says. That is what I say. Trivial.

LAURA: Trivial?

KEITH: Hm?

LAURA: It's my life's blood, you bloody egoist.

KEITH: All right. I'll do it.

LAURA (*Tigress waking*): If you put me in one of your wretched plays, I'll cream you. Physically. I'll assault you. You don't know me.

KEITH: Not one of my wretched plays. *The* play.

LAURA: I wasn't meant for this kind of existence. I want to get married.

KEITH: Am I stopping you?

LAURA: Yes. I don't want to be an important actress. I just want to get parts. Am I getting them?

KEITH: You are getting a few.

LAURA: It's not enough.

KEITH: You're getting about as much as you're worth.

LAURA: You sod.

(*She hits him. He hits her. They fight.*)

KEITH: Look. You'll injure me.

LAURA: I don't care.

KEITH: It'll show. Stop it.

LAURA: Ohrrr, it's all you care about. Let it. You

27

know what—if she finds out—if she hasn't by now, she's a blind mouse, anyway—but if she does—do you know what *you*'re going to find out—that she doesn't care. How do I know? Because I wouldn't. I don't. I don't give a fig. Darling, I love you. Please marry me. Leave her. You've been with her fifteen years.

KEITH: Thirteen.

LAURA: It's unlucky.

KEITH: What?

LAURA: Sweetheart.

KEITH: What?

LAURA: It's such a hot day. We should be by the sea. For God's sake. Let's go away.

(*Silence.*)

KEITH: You know, adultery is the chief preoccupation of serious drama. Isn't it amazing?

LAURA: Art transforms reality. It doesn't repeat it.

KEITH: I want to make love to you.

LAURA: Let's go to the pictures.

KEITH: All right. No. I have work to do.

LAURA: Can't you find a part for me in the new play, the tart on the corner, for God's sake? I have no pride.

KEITH: Well, I do.

LAURA: You're sweating a lot, aren't you?

KEITH: It's the heat.

LAURA: Mm. It's not nerves.

KEITH: Yes, all right. It's nerves.

LAURA: Give me a kiss. You know, I met this actor chap, he says they're *giving* parts away in that film.

KEITH: Whose film?

LAURA: John Broome's.

KEITH: John Broome.

LAURA: What's the matter?

KEITH: Well, there you are. Nobody can resist money.

LAURA: He says he likes writing films.

KEITH: Who am I to contradict him?

(*She kisses him.*)

LAURA: I know you're good. I am not trying to pull you down. She may be. I am not.

10

Interior. Agent's office. Day.

(*Baroque Place.*

Secretary (Maureen). Door.

Laughter within. And voices, one male, one female.)

FEMALE: He didn't, he didn't, he didn't.

MALE: He did. He did. He did.

FEMALE: It's a *riot*.

MALE: I wasn't going to tell him.

FEMALE: He wouldn't, surely.

MALE: What?

FEMALE: He wouldn't. He wouldn't. He wouldn't.

MALE: He would, you know. He would.

FEMALE: They're all a lot of *pimps*.

MALE: They're not, you know.

KEITH (*To the secretary*): Who is it?

SECRETARY: Barry.

KEITH: Barry Simon?

SECRETARY: Yes. I hate typing these letters.

KEITH: Somebody else said no.

SECRETARY: Everybody's saying no, just now.

KEITH: Well, everybody's saying no in the summer.

SECRETARY: Not to you. We sent you another cheque, this morning.

KEITH: Yes. But that's funny stuff.

SECRETARY: I prefer it, honestly. I really do.

KEITH: I am doing an Autobiography, though. I don't know if you knew.

SECRETARY: How exciting. Barry's doing one.

(*A bout of laughter from the other room, the door swings open. The agent—Fanny—and Barry come in.*)

FANNY: Oh—what are you doing here?

KEITH: Well, I am your client.

FANNY: Was I supposed to see you?

SECRETARY: Yes, you were, Fanny.

FANNY: Oh, all right. What do you want?

KEITH: Your love, Fanny.

(*She laughs happily.*)

FANNY: Have you met Barry? Barry, this is Keith. Keith, this is Barry. Barry's off to New York. Broadway.

KEITH: Aren't you doing an Autobiography?

FANNY: My dear, he's dashed it off. It's all done. He wouldn't spend any time on crap like that. Don't know what he did it for in the first place, my darling.

KEITH: Money.

FANNY: Don't be bitter, dear. Barry doesn't do things for money.

BARRY: Don't I?

FANNY: Yes, you do, sometimes, don't you? Oh, you bastard. You mustn't be such a bastard. He is a bastard, isn't he?

BARRY: See you one of these days, Keith.

KEITH: Yes, I'd like that.

BARRY: Call you when I get back. Bye, Fanny darling.

FANNY: Bye, darling. Bye. What do you want to see me about?

KEITH: Plays.

FANNY: How boring. There must be something else. Oh, all right. Never mind. Come in.

(*Her room is feminine, piled with bric-a-brac.*)

Look what Barry gave me.

(*Impressed? Hardly.*)

What do you want to ask me?

KEITH: Whether I ought to do it.

FANNY: Why not?

KEITH: Because I am afraid to make a fool of myself.

FANNY: Well, it doesn't matter. Nobody's going to watch. You think people are just waiting to see you make a fool of yourself. They don't. They couldn't care less. They'll all be in the cinema, that evening. Or watching the man in the moon. It doesn't matter.

KEITH: It does. To me, it does. Does nothing matter?

FANNY: Kierkegaard matters. Buddha matters. Christ. No. Perhaps not. Buddha matters. Don't be daft, dear. Nobody gives a damn.

KEITH: Thanks.

31

FANNY (*Opening door*): What time am I seeing Mr Puttifer?

KEITH: Oh, God, you make me ill.

FANNY: Let me tell you about Mr Puttifer. He is the sweetest man. He runs a circus. In Sweden. Now the circus matters. I cry in the circus. I don't cry in the theatre.

KEITH: I am writing this for television.

FANNY: You've said it, dear. Mr Puttifer trains acrobats. He has a school for acrobats. God, you writers are boring. You can die swinging from one of those things. You can't die scratching a piece of paper. I don't know why you do it.

KEITH: We do it in order to keep you, darling.

FANNY (*Laughing*): You thought I wouldn't appreciate that. I do. Have a cigarette. How's that lovely family of yours?

KEITH: Fine, thank you.

FANNY: Then you have something to hang on to, hm?

KEITH: Yes, dear.

(*Pause.*)

FANNY: What's the trouble, Keith?

KEITH: You frighten me.

FANNY: I will tell you a secret. I am frightened myself.

KEITH: Of what?

FANNY: Of the Doctors. (*She lights cigarette, greedily.*)

11

Interior. His house (*bedroom*). *Night.*
(*A frosted bathroom door, ajar in any case.*

He has only just come in.)

MAUD'S VOICE: Robert Schildkraut called. It's about the Nice People. Frances has an abortion that's all right, but you must not use the word abortion, and there must be some doubt that it *could* have been a miscarriage. But you must not use the word miscarriage, either. Except in an emergency. I don't know what that means. And he said you may have to cut out Virginia altogether. He thinks she's pregnant.

KEITH: Who?

MAUD: The actress *playing* Virginia. Oh, I can't remember these idiotic messages. I think I am doing jolly well. The dog's got run over.

KEITH: What?

MAUD: It's all right. The car went over him, but the wheels didn't. He just had an awful fright. (*Pause.*) I am pleased you're not so terribly late. Where have you been?

KEITH: Oh, just fooling.

MAUD: Will you give me my towel—it's on the radiator.

(*He does so, without thinking.*)

MAUD: Isn't it a funny world?

KEITH: Yes.

(*Pause.*)

MAUD: What did you do all day?

KEITH: I walked along the Thames, and thought.

MAUD: You don't usually do it.

KEITH: No, I did it today.

(*Pause.*)

MAUD: I am feeling less bothered, for some reason.

33

KEITH: That's good.

MAUD: Are you going to work late? The telephone bill came.

KEITH: Mm.

MAUD: God. It's fantastic.

(*He walks out of the bedroom.*)

12

Interior. His study. Night.

(*Toby is reading in the study, a script. Keith comes in.*)

KEITH: What, aren't you in bed yet?

TOBY: No, I wanted to read your script—it's really great. (*Looks at it.*)

KEITH: Did you like the M1 sequence?

TOBY: Yes, yes, I thought it was fantastic. Mrrrrrr.

KEITH (*Pleased*): Go on, go, before mother catches you.

TOBY: Greg said I could go with them to the Club for the day.

KEITH: Yes, why don't you?

TOBY: It's about thirty shillings.

(*Pause.*)

KEITH: Is that why you stayed up?

TOBY: No. I wanted to read your script.

KEITH: Why do you tell fibs? You're always telling fibs.

TOBY: I'm not. I prefer Asimov because there's more to it. But your stuff's good, too. Really, Dad. Harry likes it.

KEITH: Harry?

TOBY: Harry Mort.

KEITH: You said he was stupid.

TOBY: Well, he is a bit. But his father likes it, too. They watch it together.

KEITH: Harry and his father. (*He gives him two pounds.*)

TOBY: Thanks, Dad.

(*He kisses him.*)

Goodnight, Dad.

KEITH: Goodnight, darling.

(*Left alone, he picks up a book, the Stendhal. Silence. He sits in his chair.*)

(*Reads*) 'To pass my leisure hours in this strange land, I should like to write a memoir of what happened to me on my last journey to Paris which began on 21st June 1821 ... I confess that the courage to write would fail me had I not the hope that one day these pages will appear in print and be read by people dear to me, such as Madame Roland or Monsieur Gros, the geometrician ... What kind of man am I? Am I intelligent? Have I wisdom as well as spirit? My whole heart's desire was to write a work of the imagination round a love affair that took place at Dresden in 1813, in a house next to mine. But the duties of my post constantly interrupt me ... When I take the pen again, my thoughts no longer please me, I am displeased with everything I had been thinking. To which a sage would reply that one must conquer oneself. I would reply: It is too late, I am forty years old ...' (*He puts the book down.*)

(*Her voice, from the other room.*)

MAUD: Are you coming?

(*Keith gets up.*)

END OF ACT I

35

ACT II

13

Interior. House (living room). Night.

(Newsreel shots on their box fill the screen, our screen.)

NEWSCASTER: Bihar, India. Although there was some rain here, last week, it has come too late to remove the threat of famine, due to the appalling drought which has been afflicting the State of Bihar in the last six months.

(Pictures of lethargic people, emaciated cattle.)

The road to the State's capital is littered with the carcasses of domestic animals, the inhabitants' most prized, and often only possessions.

KEITH: Now that—that, you see: I can feel passionately about that. I do. But that's about all. What can I do about it? Add captions to the pictures? *(He and Maud watching the film.)* And anyway, who's the villain? Nobody—All this sorrow and no one to blame —what does one say about that?

NEWSCASTER: In Paris a Source close to the Ministry of Foreign Affairs has reiterated France's disappointment at the outcome of the present talks. It is thought that despite British assurances French attitudes have in fact hardened recently.

KEITH: Yes. Yes, I could cry with rage. France is the threat to world peace because of her untamable Chauvinism. No writer is saying that. I am. And France, despite appearances, is more dangerous than Russia because she is more unstable. A life of de Gaulle, the hero misunderstood. I could do that. But the research, my God the research.

NEWSCASTER: More trouble in the Middle East. Plans

for the redevelopment of Jerusalem have led to fresh protests . . .

KEITH: Up the Jews . . .

MAUD: Darling, you'll waken the children.

KEITH: We are not neutral in thought, word and deed. What's wrong with Western civilization, it's the only one there is.

NEWSCASTER: A resolution is to be put down at the United Nations Assembly.

KEITH: Fair is foul, and foul is fair. But the world is not fooled.

NEWSCASTER: In the Commons, the Minister of Transport . . .

(*Keith switches off set.*)

KEITH: I can't bear it. (*Takes out a record.*) You see it's not that I am devoid of ideas I can think boldly. But how to make the point.

MAUD: What are you going to play?

KEITH: Fidelio.

MAUD: Play the Dungeon Scene.

KEITH: No, the Overture.

MAUD: I adore the man.

KEITH: I am seeing my brother tomorrow.

MAUD: What about?

KEITH: I don't know, money I should think.

(*Beethoven. Keith conducts.*)

14

Interior. Cafeteria. Studio. Day.
(*Brothers at a counter. Teas. Evening Standard.*)

RICHARD: Mildred's got so fractious, I can't anymore. I am not going to try for ever.

KEITH: Is Sally pleased?

RICHARD: Well, yes, Sally's pleased, why shouldn't she be?

KEITH: Are you going to marry her?

RICHARD: Eventually. God, can you imagine how long it's going to take, before Mildred lets me go?

KEITH: Do the kids know?

RICHARD: They know a bit. They don't know everything. (*Pause.*) Lousy tea.

KEITH: It's hot.

RICHARD: Yes.

KEITH: Don't be such a misery.

RICHARD: Everything's gone wrong. Honestly. Including Gilpin.

KEITH: I didn't know.

RICHARD: I can't get a penny out of Gilpin, any more. Not a cent.

KEITH: He's got fed up.

RICHARD: Yes, I suppose you could say that. He thinks a solicitor's office ought to be making a profit after six months. He's an upstart butcher, it's all he knows about. The result is I am broke.

(*Pause.*)

KEITH: Mildred's got money.

RICHARD: Hm? Mildred's money has been the mirage of my life. What do you do about that?

KEITH: Hm?

RICHARD: I am not likely to see the colour of Mildred's money.

KEITH: She has very blue eyes, hasn't she?

RICHARD: Very? No, hardly. Half blue. Blue with dots.

KEITH: Oh, my dear, dear brother, we are in a mess.

RICHARD: I am in a mess, not you. You're making a mint.

KEITH: Sure. The taxman's making a mint.

RICHARD: Well, I've told you what to do about that. (*Pause.*) I am honestly thinking of going back to Rab's.

(*An old man's head between them.*)

Yes?

OLD MAN: Have you finished with this paper?

RICHARD: Yes, I don't want it.

OLD MAN: Thanks.

KEITH: Go ahead.

OLD MAN: Has it got the two thirty?

KEITH: I don't know.

OLD MAN: What time did you buy it?

KEITH: What? I don't remember.

OLD MAN: Sometimes they have them, sometimes they don't.

KEITH: Yes.

(*Old man moves off with paper.*)

I suppose you will find it difficult again this month?

RICHARD: What?

KEITH: Paying your share for Father.

RICHARD: Practically impossible. I think he should be moved.

KEITH: Did you go and see him?

39

RICHARD: I am going tomorrow.

KEITH: I thought of going tomorrow.

RICHARD: In that case, I'll go next week. God, it's just the same situation as with Mother.

(*Keith shakes his head.*)

KEITH: I always felt—with Mother— weakness, disintegration—it's a woman's prerogative. It's much worse for Father.

(*Pause*).

RICHARD: Do you think it's worth keeping him there?

KEITH: Where would you want him to go?

RICHARD: I think he'd get just as good care, elsewhere.

KEITH: I don't.

RICHARD: You're prejudiced.

KEITH: Actually, you're probably right. But I still don't want to do it.

RICHARD: Why?

KEITH: Because he'd be hurt.

(*Pause.*)

RICHARD: Falsely.

KEITH: What?

RICHARD: Falsely hurt.

KEITH: Don't know what that means.

RICHARD: You know very well. He's always had a false sense of values.

KEITH: I don't think that's got anything to do with it.

RICHARD: Do anything with what?

KEITH: He would be hurt because he'd think we didn't care.

40

RICHARD: Well, I can't go on paying at the moment, it's too bad.

(*Pause.*)

KEITH: That's all right.

(*Pause.*)

RICHARD: I'll start again as soon as I can. (*Pause.*) What are you up to, these days?

KEITH: I am trying to find something meaningful to write about.

RICHARD: What's the matter, running out of ideas?

KEITH: No. Something that would have meaning. For me.

RICHARD: What for?

KEITH: Hm? To astonish myself.

RICHARD: You could make a packet in films, why don't you?

KEITH: Because nobody's asked me. Everybody's been about to ask me, but nobody's actually asked me.

RICHARD: That thing you had on, the other day, was pretty good.

KEITH: I wouldn't want to anyway.

RICHARD: Why, are you too good for it? (*He looks at him.*)

KEITH: Yes. No. I am trying to do something else.

RICHARD: You *run* away from fortune. You run away from everything.

KEITH: I love you, brother.

RICHARD: Hm?

KEITH: I love you.

15

Interior. Laura's room. Night.

(*He in the room, she in the kitchen, clearing up.*

He reads, she knows the part by heart.)

KEITH (VERSHININ): . . . I never talk about these things, normally. It's odd, but you are the only person I dare complain to. Don't be angry with me, I have nobody but you.

LAURA (MASHA): What a noise the wind's making in the stove. What a noise. Just before Father died, the wind howled just like this.

KEITH: You really are a wonderful creature. It's dark in here, but I can see your eyes.

LAURA: There is more light over here.

KEITH: I love you. I love you. I love your eyes. I love the way you move. I dream about the way you walk.

LAURA: When you talk like that, I can't help laughing, although I am frightened at the same time. Stop saying it, please. No. No. Do go on. Say it. I don't mind . . .

KEITH: Someone's coming. Let's talk about something else. (*Change of voice, Tuzenbach.*) I have a triple barrelled name—Baron Tuzenbach-Krone-Altschauer —but, in fact, I am a Russian. I was baptized into the Greek Orthodox faith, just like yourself.

(*She comes in, they are laughing.*)

16

Interior. Corner of club. Night.

(*He and Laura by themselves.*

Music. Hubbub of voices.)

KEITH: Everybody thinks I get mad because nobody takes a blind bit of notice—never has—of anything I've done. I couldn't be more pleased. When my things go on, I just hope that none of my friends will be watching. Admittedly, when I find out that nobody has, I am mortified. This place is full of people like me.

LAURA: You're not, are you? You're not going to marry me. And you're thinking—oh, God, I know what you're thinking—she doesn't expect me to, either. Well, I do. I am exhausted being your bloody futile mistress. I want to get married—to you, if I can, because I love you—but even that doesn't matter, in the end.

KEITH: Look, don't talk so loud.

LAURA: Yes, that's all you worry about, not to be embarrassed in front of all these other bums. Well, let me tell you—Keith, what do you want from me? How long is it going on for? I suggest you tell me. Here. Now. I want to be considered. You are not considering me.

KEITH: Shhh.

LAURA: I'm browned off. That's John Broome.

KEITH: Where? So it is. The light of the North.

LAURA: All right, if you are a John Broome, at least—you can say, I've put my women in my plays—or I've put my hatred of women in my plays. They all hate women. I tell you—you are all the same—writers—you all want to be homosexuals.

KEITH: Do you know him?

LAURA: I know the actor with him. You think I don't know anybody, wrong.

(*The great man and his acolyte.*)

ACOLYTE: Hullo, darling.

43

LAURA: Hullo, darling. This is Keith Bailey.

ACOLYTE (*Introducing*): John Broome.

BROOME: Hullo.

KEITH: Hullo.

LAURA: Isn't it nice, Keith, you've wanted to meet him.

BROOME: What do you do, then?

KEITH: I am a writer.

BROOME: What do you write?

KEITH: Rubbish, mostly.

BROOME: Mind if I sit down, nowhere to put your arse down. And the beer's awful. George. You've brought me here, George.

GEORGE: Yes, all right, John, I'll see what I can do.

BROOME: We want draught. We don't want any of this muck. That's the trouble with the country: bottled beer and overcrowding. Look at it. (*To Laura.*) What do you do? (*He sits with them.*)

LAURA: I am an actress.

KEITH: She's a very capable actress.

BROOME: Yes. Hate show business.

LAURA: You live off it.

BROOME: What?

LAURA: Show business.

BROOME: Maybe. Hm? Every little dolly you meet has to be an actress.

LAURA: I don't get you.

BROOME: Why do you have to be an actress?

KEITH: She didn't say she had to be an actress.

44

LAURA: I bloody well wish I weren't.

BROOME: Who wants it?

LAURA: What? I don't want it.

BROOME: For God's sake, why can't you say, I am a woman?

LAURA: Hm? Who . . .

BROOME (*To George, returning*): Haven't they got any?

GEORGE: No, John, they haven't got any draught beer.

BROOME: Sub-grotty, bourgeois establishment. Let them shut off that row, at least. (*Music.*) George.

GEORGE: What?

BROOME: For Chris' sake, we're having a conversation.

GEORGE: Yes, all right.

BROOME: Less noise.

GEORGE: I'll ask them.

(*Broome smiles. George turns again.*)

BROOME: I hate this country. It's eaten right through. The South is, any road.

KEITH: Not the North?

BROOME: No, that's a bit better. They still have their hands scarred, up there, the old people. And their backs. From what the Tories did to them. In the South, everybody's a Tory. Ten million Selwyn Lloyds. (*To George, returning.*) Are they going to shut it off, or not?

GEORGE: Well, I've asked them, John. (*Sits.*)

BROOME (*To Keith*): I tell you where to go to, if you want to be a writer—everybody wants to be a writer, it's a disease—like actresses—South America. I was in Mexico, last year.

KEITH: For the film festival?

BROOME: Hm? For the ... Smart pants Willie, aren't you? Is that your name?

KEITH: Bailey.

BROOME: Willie, the literate child of the Coca-cola civilization. English edition. Do you know what this country is—a thieves' paradise. You can tell a thief in Bolivia, you can't here, they're all wearing pin-stripe. And do you know the one thing that can save you— I've given up rowing in pubs, it's not nice—proletarians do that—a smashing lot of Red Guards to come down from the Welsh hills, or wherever Red Guards come from, and pick it clean. That's what it wants. Take the place apart. Spare Buckingham Palace, though. We want to keep the peepshow, don't we? (*Music stops briefly. Silence.*) That's what happens to nice chaps from the North, who came down to London —grammar school teachers—every one. With my teeth, you understand. With my grotty teeth. I was an artist, once. I only turned to plays when they invented the Royal Court. But the pinky boys have got in there now. The pinky and perky boys. (*Music on again.*) It's a brothel, this country, for the castrati. Here they roll.

GEORGE (*Returning*): It's all right, John, they're going to turn it down.

BROOME: It's not good enough George, you must assert yourself. (*To Keith and Laura.*) Do you despair, Willie? I despair. At fifty thousand a year. What's your rate?

GEORGE: He said they were going to.

BROOME: Say sorry to your friends for this interruption, George.

GEORGE: Come on, John, come on.

BROOME: We're not coming on ever again. A Carnaby Street ponce with a flick knife in his eye, that's what they're after, today. (*He gets up, sways.*) Bye bye, dolly.

46

GEORGE: Come on, John. We're going to Ugo's. You must have something to eat.

BROOME: I am not hungry.

GEORGE: Well, I am. I am going to collapse if I don't have something to eat.

(*Broome turns back.*)

BROOME: Look after the filly, won't you? Oh, Christ. (*He spills the beer. Moves round the table to mop it up.*) When did you last know despair? Friday?

KEITH: Saturday.

(*Broome shrugs. Lurches out. Silence.*)

My God.

LAURA: What?

KEITH: He's a museum piece.

LAURA: I thought he was rather nice. (*Pause.*) Oscar Wilde was.

KEITH: What?

LAURA: A poet and a talker.

(*Keith gets up.*

A couple brush past them. The young woman knows Laura. She is with Barry Simon.)

KEITH: How was Broadway?

BARRY: Oh rum, rum.

(*The couple move on.*)

KEITH: Sweet smell of success. Let's go.

LAURA: Where?

KEITH: We'll just walk, shall we?

LAURA: Yes, all right, I'd like that.

KEITH: Waiter. (*He leaves the change on the table.*) I'll have to take something, tonight.

LAURA: Do you have a headache? Must you?

KEITH: What?

LAURA: Never mind.

(*He is threading his way out. She stops him.*)

KEITH: I don't know, love, I don't know.

(*An eager young man at his elbow.*)

YOUNG MAN: Hullo, Keith, seen my latest epic?

KEITH: No, not yet.

YOUNG MAN: You didn't miss much—It's mediocre.

KEITH: I don't believe it.

YOUNG MAN: They mucked it up as usual. John Broome was here a moment ago.

KEITH: Yes, I know, I talked to him.

YOUNG MAN: He's like an old movie.

KEITH: Yes, maybe.

(*A girl friend meanwhile to Laura.*)

GIRL FRIEND: Sheila's coming over later. Why don't you stay for a drink?

(*Laura turns round unexpectedly.*)

LAURA (*To Keith*): Would you mind?

KEITH: If you want to—I have work to do. But if you want to. (*He is desolate, tries not to show it.*)

(*She nods her head.*)

See you, darling.

LAURA: Bye.

GIRL FRIEND'S FRIEND: What will it be?

LAURA: Oh. Vodka and tonic, thanks.

(*Suddenly he is walking out.*

She sees him through a crowd of faces.)

48

17

Interior. Bedroom. Night.

(*Maud asleep. He comes in silently, lights a bedside lamp. Begins to undress. She is looking at him.*)

KEITH: I thought you were asleep.

MAUD: I wasn't.

(*Silence.*)

KEITH: What's the matter?

MAUD: The baby's got measles.

KEITH: Oh, Christ, no. I am sorry.

MAUD: Sorry about what? You won't have to look after him.

(*Silence.*)

KEITH: I saw my brother, he's stony again.

MAUD: Is he?

(*Silence.*)

KEITH: What's the matter?

MAUD: Nothing.

KEITH: Now, look, please—

MAUD: What?

KEITH: Hm?

MAUD: It's half-past two.

KEITH: So what?

MAUD: You've been with that bitch again.

KEITH: Hm?

MAUD: I know. I can smell.

KEITH: Don't be vulgar.

(*Silence.*)

MAUD: What's happened to our marriage?

KEITH: Nothing. Nothing, nothing has, nothing will.

(*Silence.*)

END OF ACT II

ACT III

18

Interior. Hospital room. Day.

(*His father in bed.*

Keith and nurse.)

NURSE: He's going to have his tea soon, aren't we?

FATHER: What?

NURSE: We are going to have our tea soon, aren't we?

FATHER: Yes.

NURSE (*To Keith*): Is there anything you need, Mr Bailey?

(*He shakes his head.*)

He's a bit surly at the moment, but that's because he's just woken up. (*She goes on her business.*)

(*Keith sits down.*)

FATHER: Silly cow.

KEITH: Who?

FATHER: That one.

KEITH: I thought you were fond of her.

FATHER: The bell.

KEITH: What?

FATHER: Do you know where she puts it for the night?

KEITH: Where?

FATHER: There. So I can't reach it.

KEITH: I don't believe you.

(*Pause.*)

FATHER: And she opens the window.

KEITH: Which?

FATHER: There's a dreadful draught.

KEITH: Then you must tell her to shut it.

FATHER: People come and stare at me, sometimes, at night.

KEITH: Hm?

FATHER: She doesn't draw the curtains, you see.

KEITH: But it's on the fourth floor.

FATHER: They must have ladders, then.

KEITH: You must have dreamt it.

(*The old man frowns heavily. Silence.*)

Are you more comfortable?

FATHER: I've still got that pain. And I get thirsty. I get very thirsty.

KEITH: You can reach it, can't you? (*The jug.*)

FATHER: She shoves it away at night, that's another thing.

KEITH: Why should she do that now? For God's sake, be reasonable.

51

FATHER: She does, that's all. The little black one's all right.

KEITH: What?

FATHER: There is a little black one, she's all right.

KEITH: I haven't seen her.

FATHER: No, she comes weekends only. (*He takes a sip of water. Puts it back. Silence.*)

KEITH: How's the leg?

FATHER: It's never going to heal, I'll never get out of here.

KEITH: It takes time, your bones are not what they were.

FATHER: I am going crazy in here.

KEITH: Oh, for God's sake, Dad—Dad—what do you want?

FATHER: I want to get out of here.

KEITH: Would you like to change wards?

FATHER: What?

KEITH: Be with other people, I thought.

FATHER: What, in a general ward? (*Pause.*) Is that it?

KEITH: Hm? I didn't say ... I thought for your own good.

FATHER: I've been paying for thirty years. I've got the papers. Where are my papers? I bet they're not here now. I've been paying the Blue Cross for thirty years.

KEITH: It doesn't cover it.

FATHER: You're not keeping me here.

KEITH: It doesn't matter.

FATHER: I am not going into a general ward.

KEITH: There is no question of it.

(*Silence.*)

FATHER: How are the children?

KEITH: Very well, thank you.

FATHER: Are they coming on Sunday?

KEITH: They might. I am not sure. They might be going to the sea.

(*Silence.*)

FATHER: When is Debbie's birthday?

KEITH: Twenty-seventh.

FATHER: I thought it was. I knew it was this month. (*The old man is trying to get at the night table drawer.*)

KEITH: What do you want?

FATHER: I've got something here.

KEITH: What?

FATHER: I've got some money in here.

KEITH: It doesn't matter. I can take it from the account.

FATHER: It's here. It's in that drawer there. It's in a leather bag. They've tried to force it open, but it wouldn't give. That's the key.

(*Silence. Keith takes the key, but it is useless. The drawer opens of itself. There is only a small purse there. Keith opens it. A few coppers.*)

Take three pounds. Buy her a doll. A Dutch puppet.

KEITH: You mean, dressed like a Dutchman.

FATHER: Hm? What did you think I meant?

KEITH: I thought made in Holland perhaps.

FATHER: Tulips and butter.

KEITH: What? (*He smiles.*)

FATHER: With baggy trousers. She'll like that. Amusing people. Met this Dutchman, met him on board ship going out. Van Hofen. Loved pancakes. He could eat six, seven, eight pancakes at one sitting. Your mother liked that ship. She had company there. He was a planter.

KEITH: The Dutchman.

FATHER: Yes. He was a planter out there. That was the year Richard was born. She was pregnant on board.

KEITH: Hm.

(*Silence.*)

FATHER: Richard all right?

KEITH: Yes, he's all right.

FATHER: Unhappy boy. Does she still give him so much trouble?

KEITH: Who?

FATHER: Felicity.

KEITH: Mildred. No. I don't think so. (*He walks round the bed. He looks out of the window.*) You have a nice room. And you get the sun here.

FATHER: Yes.

KEITH: I thought you were going to say no.

FATHER: No. It's a nice room. Hm?

KEITH: That it's not a nice room.

FATHER: No. It is.

KEITH: Dad—

FATHER: Hm?

KEITH: I can't—

FATHER: Can't what? (*Silence.*) I get it in the evenings

here. (*He means the sun. Silence.*) Has the sale gone through, yet?

KEITH: Which?

FATHER: The cottage.

KEITH: No, it hasn't gone through yet.

FATHER: When that's gone everything will be gone. (*Silence.*) What are you writing about, these days?

KEITH: I am just wondering what to write about.

FATHER: Write a comedy.

KEITH: Yes, all right.

FATHER: People want to laugh.

KEITH: Yes, Dad.

FATHER: I am glad you came. I thought you were coming yesterday.

KEITH: I couldn't manage yesterday.

FATHER: I am glad you came today. Old Harry came yesterday.

KEITH: Well, there you are, why didn't you tell me?

FATHER: Nothing to tell. I think it was yesterday.

KEITH: What did he have to say?

FATHER (*Pause*): When old Harry goes, that's the end. There's nobody else.

KEITH: There's Aunt Penelope.

FATHER: She lives in Scotland.

KEITH: No. She doesn't, she lives in Surrey. So what?

FATHER: I thought she lived in Scotland. Listen . . .

(*The nurse outside with trolley.*)

(*Urgently.*) Come nearer. I want to tell you something. Open that drawer again.

KEITH: There's nothing in it.

FATHER: You have to bribe these people. So that they don't take the bell away. You have to give her something. Give her five bob.

KEITH: She wouldn't take it. You imagine these things.

FATHER: You think you know everything. A writer. She'll take it.

KEITH: I can't.

(*Nurse enters.*)

NURSE: Here's your tea. (*She rattles trolley up to the bed. Serves him.*)

KEITH: You see, how nice she is to you. He imagines you don't like him.

NURSE: Oh, we have our ups and downs, we have our little ructions, but we understand each other, don't we, Papa? Look what Mrs Parma has sent you, today, a chocolate cake.

KEITH: It's a lovely chocolate cake.

NURSE: Oh, yes, we get our bad days. Well, you can't wonder, being all alone in here.

KEITH: Yes, I thought he'd be better off with others.

NURSE: Of course, he would. But he's an obstinate old bird, aren't you, dear? (*To Keith.*) Would you like a cup of tea, Mr Bailey?

KEITH: No, thank you.

NURSE (*Only for Keith to hear*): What are you going to do about it, then?

KEITH: I don't know.

(*She carries on, is going.*)

Nurse.

NURSE: Yes?

KEITH: Ehm. I don't know. You are so kind. I thought of bringing you a box of sweets, but that's silly, isn't it? (*He gives her a note.*)

NURSE: Thank you very much. He gets a bit confused sometimes, it's the morphine. That's the effect it has on old people. (*To old man.*) You have a good son, haven't you—a very nice son indeed. Cheer up, Papa, we'll soon have you dancing again. I think he looks better today.

KEITH: Yes, he looks much better, I thought.

NURSE (*Pats old man*): Now eat up all that nice cake. Don't forget I'm always here, when you want me. All you have to do is go buzz-buzz. (*She goes.*)

FATHER: She took the money, didn't she?

KEITH: Yes.

(*Silence. Keith sits by him.*)

FATHER: The little black one's nice ... I once ...

KEITH: Hm?

FATHER: Long time ago—I must have been twenty-two, twenty-three ...

(*Silence. Keith is wordless.*)

Your hair's going grey.

KEITH: Where?

FATHER: Here. You're going grey.

(*Silence. Keith makes a move, as if to go.*)

Don't go yet. (*The old man eats his cake.*)

19

Interior. Open kitchen. Day.
(*Sunday lunch with the children.*)

MAUD (*To Toby*): Eat properly. Hold your fork . . .

KEITH: What's the matter with him?

MAUD: Debbie can hold her fork properly, why can't you?

DEBBIE: Yes, look, that's how you hold it, isn't it, Mummy?

TOBY: Oh, you—you're brilliant, aren't you? Beggar.

MAUD: Shut up, Toby, will you?

TOBY: Oh, really.

KEITH: Can't we have lunch in peace?

MAUD: What's the matter?

KEITH: Do we have to yell at each other, at the table?

MAUD: I am not yelling. You are.

KEITH: Oh, don't go on.

MAUD: It's not civilized enough for you.

KEITH: What?

MAUD: The life we lead.

KEITH: I didn't say . . . Yes, it could be. It really could be.

DEBBIE: What's civilized?

KEITH: Hm?

MAUD: Books and records.

TOBY: The Beatles. The Monkees. I am a Monkey.

DEBBIE: So am I.

(*Bit of a row.*)

MAUD: Stop it, you two.

KEITH (*Soothing it*): It's nice, anyway.

MAUD: What?

58

KEITH: The lamb. It's lovely.

MAUD (*To Toby*): How many times have I told you not to feed the dog at the table?

KEITH: Is it from our butcher?

MAUD: No, our butcher has let us down again.

KEITH: What's the matter with the man?

MAUD (*A smile*): I think he's having wife trouble.

KEITH: Don't wolf it.

DEBBIE: Sorry.

(*They eat. Keith looks out. Garden.*)

KEITH: It's a terrific day.

MAUD: Yes. Shall we go out this afternoon?

KEITH: I thought of digging up the tree, actually.

TOBY: Dad, you promised.

KEITH: What did I promise?

TOBY: Game of table-tennis.

KEITH: Yes, I did, you're quite right. All right.

DEBBIE: What about me?

KEITH: What about you?

DEBBIE: Aren't you going to play with me?

KEITH: All right. Half an hour.

DEBBIE: Three-quarters of an hour, Daddy.

TOBY: After the table tennis.

MAUD: After the washing up.

KEITH: After the catastrophe.

DEBBIE: What are you talking about? You are funny.

TOBY: What catastrophe, Dad?

KEITH: The Atomic war.

MAUD: Really, what for?

DEBBIE: Are children going to be killed in the Atomic war? They are, aren't they?

MAUD: Eat up your cauliflower. Nobody's going to get killed. There's not going to be war.

TOBY: How do you know?

MAUD: I have read my *Observer*.

KEITH: Mummy is being witty.

MAUD: Thank you, darling. It is actually a lovely day, couldn't we go for a swim?

TOBY: Oh yes, a swim, a swim, hooray.

DEBBIE: I don't want to go for a swim, I want to play with Fiona.

TOBY: A swim, a swim. Crunch.

KEITH: Nobody's said anything about . . .

MAUD: Stop it, everybody, please. You'll wake up Paul.

(*It's too late. They listen.*)

DEBBIE: Paul's awake.

(*Maud looks at him in silence.*)

MAUD: Just for once. Keith, please.

KEITH: What?

MAUD: Go and get him up, please.

(*Pause. He gets up*).

KEITH: All right, darling.

MAUD: Thank you. Keith.

KEITH: What?

MAUD: You wanted a big family.

60

KEITH: I love my family.

MAUD: Then bring him down and put him on your knee.

KEITH: Yes, ma'am.

TOBY: Yes, sir.

DEBBIE: Yes, ma'am.

(*He goes. Pause.*)

MAUD: Daddy's working very hard, and he has a lot to think about, at the moment. He's a wonderful daddy. You must not be all over him.

DEBBIE: No, Mummy.

TOBY: No, Mummy.

MAUD: That's right.

(*Pause.*)

20

Interior. Agent's office. Day.

(*Inner sanctuary.*

Fanny and Keith.)

FANNY: If you lead this kind of life, that's it. That's what you're going to write about. You all do.

KEITH: What other kind of life is there?

FANNY: Go out into the world and suffer.

KEITH: Honestly?

FANNY: Yes.

KEITH: Coming from you, darling.

(*She swivels in her chair.*)

FANNY: Scripts, scripts, look, mountains of them. God, if I see another play about a wife—the wife—and a mistress—the mistress—and how you're all being strangled by suburbia, poor wretches—I will scream. (*She has no pity.*) You get landed with all these houses and school fees and what not, and keep grizzling about it. I can't help you. It's not life that's ordinary. It's you, dears, you're the most ordinary generation ever. Darling, in the end—it's true, darling—the only thing you can feel passionate about is your income tax returns.

KEITH: John Broome included.

FANNY: What? Yes, of course, John Broome included. (*Pause.*) John Broome's just a big baby, darling.

KEITH: And Barry?

FANNY: Barry's a smart operator.

KEITH: And me?

FANNY: You're at the bottom of the heap, darling.

KEITH: Thank you, Fanny.

FANNY: It's dreadfully boring.

KEITH: What do you live by, Fanny?

(*She takes out a pill, two pills, from a little box.*)

What are these?

FANNY: I take some all the time. These are for my heart. I think they're for my heart. Do you know who put me on to them? Bibi Cremona.

(*Keith doesn't know him.*)

He's a professional cyclist. His real name isn't Cremona at all, it's Hetherington. And he has three fingers missing from his left hand. Three. He wrote this completely *illiterate* story, I couldn't sell it in a million years. But he's Tour de France, and all that. It's a whole world, darling. You can drive behind them in cars, lots and lots of cars. I'd love to do that, wouldn't you?

KEITH: Oh, Fanny, Fanny.

FANNY: What?

KEITH: I think you're great.

(*Pause. She is pleased.*)

FANNY: You know, last night, as I staggered upstairs loaded with scripts, I made myself a cup of tea, and I sat down, and I opened the first. And I dissolved.

KEITH: Why, Fanny?

FANNY: Because I suddenly thought, there is no end to it. None. (*Silence*). Gerald is a sweetie, isn't he?

KEITH: I am having lunch with him.

FANNY: What are you going to say?

KEITH: That I can't write it.

(*Pause.*)

FANNY: I think that's wise of you, darling. Keith, why don't you do something else? I wish I could.

KEITH: What? I can't cycle. I am too old.

FANNY: What about carpentry?

KEITH: It's all machine made, now.

FANNY: True.

KEITH: Fanny, in one word, what do you think I lack, talent, luck, gravity?

FANNY: Hm? Courage, dear. I think you lack courage. (*Her telephone buzzes.*) Remind me to show you that thing.

KEITH: Which?

FANNY: Cremona. (*She means his story. Phone.*) Hullo? (*To Keith.*) America. (*Phone.*) Hullo, Mr Finkenstein, you're an early bird. (*To Keith.*) Ask Maureen to give it to you. Bye.

(Keith goes. For a moment, he can still be seen in the half open door.)

3,000? I don't think he'll even look at it, my writers don't work for that sort of money... I don't want to discourage you, Mr Finkenstein, but the last writer I read for pleasure died a hundred years ago... No, the film rights haven't gone... Three thousand five? I might find somebody. What about... Keith Bailey? What? No... *Bailey*. You're a tease, Mr Finkenstein. *(Off phone.)* Maureen.

MAUREEN'S VOICE: What?

FANNY: Cigarettes.

21

Interior. Restaurant table. Day.

(The patio or not, it makes no difference.

Gerald and Keith (end of lunch).)

GERALD: I am sorry. I am sorry. I am sorry. I thought you were going to seize this opportunity. And do it. Bang. I would have been so proud of you. What were you protecting?

KEITH: My sanity.

GERALD: Tch. Tch. Tch.

KEITH: My life is a desert.

GERALD: Fanny has upset you, you mustn't let her upset you. She's going to her grave feathers flying, isn't she?

KEITH: You're full of death talk, Gerald.

GERALD: You are. I am not. She's going to outlive us all, actually.

KEITH: What are we talking about?

GERALD: I will tell you. We are talking about practical matters. I asked you for a script. You let me down. The good Lord, who's up there—he is, Keith, who do you think is up there, Lew Grade—has sent me a play, through the post, two days ago. From Terence.

KEITH: Terence?

(*Terence of the Monks.*)

GERALD: Yes, Keith. And it's divine. Not in a thousand years.

KEITH: What is it about?

GERALD: Himself. He dug in, and came up with a portrait.

KEITH: Portrait of himself as a dustbin.

GERALD: It is. It's sensitive, sad—it's very funny. He said to himself: I am not going to lie.

KEITH: He's incapable of it.

GERALD: Of what? All right, so he has lied. But attractively. With true finesse. I cried. I cannot tell you. Terence from six to eight. It must be the emptiest life on record. My dear boy, I went to see him this morning. Of course, he lives in this simply dreadful place. Terence, I said, I am going to redecorate it for you.

(*Pause.*)

KEITH: You know, we may be friends—and working together—but your poverty of spirit appals me. Your poverty of spirit is more than I can bear.

(*Stunned silence.*)

GERALD: I've offered you a job, you haven't offered anything.

KEITH: I am standing you lunch.

GERALD: Hm? Lousy compôte. They don't know what they're doing, here. I am glad actually.

KEITH: What about, Gerald?

GERALD: That you didn't write the thing. Awfully vulgar thing to do. Vision of truth.

KEITH: Terence has.

GERALD: Hm?

KEITH: He hasn't really.

GERALD: No, of course, he hasn't. But he's had a bash at it, the dear old thing.

KEITH: Will you have coffee, Gerald?

GERALD: No. Yes, all right.

KEITH: Waiter. Coffee, please.

WAITER: Black or white?

GERALD: White.

KEITH: Small black.

GERALD: The compôte was abominable.

WAITER: I am sorry, sir.

(*Silence.*)

GERALD: What are you thinking?

KEITH: I don't know. I was just thinking what started it all.

GERALD: What?

KEITH: Donald's death.

GERALD: Yes. He's been dead three weeks.

KEITH: Might be a million years. Might never have been.

(*Pause.*)

GERALD: What are you going to do now?

KEITH: What I've always done.

GERALD: You've lost weight.

KEITH: One day, you know, though.

GERALD: When?

KEITH: No, no. Leave me alone. I am not going to.

GERALD: Nobody's going to ask you again, dear boy.

KEITH: You know, I think we understand each other

GERALD: As long as we don't mention it. Hm.

KEITH: It's the cardinal mistake, isn't it? You must never say anything. Shhh.

GERALD: Nothing. Ever. It's too good for that.

KEITH: Oh, God.

GERALD: What?

(*Silence.*)

KEITH: I think if I did, I'd probably die.

GERALD: It's unlikely, you know. (*Smiles.*) Thank you, waiter. You know, that character over there, I do believe . . .

KEITH: What?

GERALD: I thought he was grinning at me.

KEITH: He's not. He's got one eye.

GERALD: I must get myself a new pair of glasses.

KEITH: We shall talk ourselves into the grave, Gerald, without ever saying anything.

GERALD: It's more civilized, you know. Waiter, you do, do really remind me of someone I met in Spoleto. Might it have been your brother?

WAITER: No. I have no brother.

KEITH: Pity.

GERALD: Keith.

KEITH: What?

GERALD: It's been lovely talking to you. I liked that. Of course, Terence's script, I am going to cast it with an all star cast. Everybody's mad about it.

KEITH: And the boys upstairs.

GERALD: My dear, the boys upstairs are going to have a fit. Shhh.

KEITH: Shhh.

(*Cut.*)

22

Interior. Landing upstairs. Night.

(*Children outside his door, ready for bed, listening.*)

VOICES (*As once before*): There's someone in there, I heard him.

How do you know?

I heard him, Schumann. Listen.

I tell you, nobody—nobody has been in that room since my brother died.

When was that, Gogo?

It was three and a half years ago.

TOBY: Shhh.

My God. There is, I tell you. There is.

It's a woman's voice, can you hear?

It's Henrietta!

DEBBIE: It's Henrietta! It's the Bruisers!

TOBY: Is it? Yes.

DEBBIE: Hooray.

Shoot the lock, Gogo.

Stand back.

(*A shot, second shot.*)

DEBBIE (*Running*): Mummy. Mummy.

MAUD: What's happening?

DEBBIE: Daddy's doing the Bruisers again.

MAUD: Thank God for that.

23

Interior. Study. Night.

(*Keith, expressionless throughout, listening to tape recorder.*

He has a gun in his hand—the one we heard on the tape —but it is Toby's.)

Henrietta, I found you. Who was it?

It was Jameson. I saw him in the window.

How could it have been, it's the fourth floor.

It was. It was. He must have brought a ladder.

Rubbish. Rubbish.

Start again.

Henrietta, my darling, I love you. I love you. I love you.

(*Pause.*)

I'm afraid.

PETER NICHOLS

The Gorge

Preface

PETER NICHOLS was born in Bristol in 1927. His television plays include: *Walk on the Grass, Promenade, Ben Spray, Ben Again, The Reception, The Big Boys, The Heart of the Country, Continuity Man, The Hooded Terror, When the Wind Blows, Daddy Kiss It Better, Hearts and Flowers, The Brick Umbrella.*

'The germ of this play/film/story was pitching the tent and cooking and eating the Sunday roast. What came before and after that was, as usual with me, a jigsaw of dimly remembered episodes, landscapes and people. I *did* tear my trousers in a public place and was too embarrassed to walk through the crowd; I chased a girl among the ferns of the Mendips; on the Bristol Downs, our Speakers' Corner during the war, we tormented the evangelists; one of my pets was a grass snake. Childhood excursions in the Morris Twelve were often to Cheddar Gorge, where we ooed and aahed at the Underwater Cathedral or the Alpine Village; where the restaurant's roof was a goldfish tank and its liquid light fell on a white piano.

'When the film was at last ready to be made, I was staying with my new family—wife and three children —on a friend's farm near Wedmore. The owner was directing a play in Israel and we had to keep the farm going, drink the milk and cream, eat the other produce, see the foxes didn't get the chickens and that two cows and their calves were in their sheds by nightfall. From the ridge behind the house we could look north towards Cheddar and the Mendips or south across the levels to Glastonbury Tor.

'Christopher Morahan, the director, stayed with us. The rest of the unit put up at a local hotel. These were

73

ideal filming conditions and Tony Garnett, the producer, was able to save us from the unwieldy industrial operation I'd already experienced on a feature film two years before. That, too, had been made entirely on location, but my memories are of futile script conferences in swank hotels, of long inexplicable waits, of queueing for thermal mugs of coffee and of trying to get in to see the rushes, usually without success. What came out of this mess was a travelogue with songs. *The Gorge* was almost as long and had to be finished in half the time. As there was almost no wet weather cover, the action being exterior, we depended on a month of sunshine and very nearly got it. Only once they had to pitch the tent in a barn and film by electric light while rain poured down the roof.

'As you will see from the script, this had to be a trusting partnership, more likely than usual because it would be the fourth time Christopher had directed from my scripts. A lot was left to him to accomplish in his own way, though what finally appeared was essentially a film of the script we had worked out together. The writer has always been taken seriously in television; in feature films, he had better grab the money and run. He won't get much else.

'The main reason for this is that very few original screen plays are done for the cinema, whereas television pours out new plays like tap-water. Film executives cannot read anything but balance sheets, but if you hold the cover of a book up to them, they might recognize it as a material property, a printed object they can buy. (Public libraries and film producers are the only customers for hard-back fiction.) So most film-scripts are adaptations. This has begun to change, though, as the film business tries to catch up with television by taking over its techniques and personnel and apeing its immediacy.

'But for playwrights The Box remains a happy medium. They are welcomed, adequately paid and respectfully treated. The work is enjoyable. Audiences of ten million may see the play. By the following week, of course, all ten million will have completely forgotten it, but you can't have everything. For lasting recognition, there's the live theatre (though there would have been problems in putting Cheddar Gorge on the stage).

'I suppose all my other television plays have been wiped to allow expensive videotape to be used again. *The Gorge* however is not a tape and one copy lies in the vaults of the British Film Institute, presumably as a record of British picnic customs in the mid-twentieth-century. An unforeseen outcome of the terrible afternoon when I tore my trousers.'

PETER NICHOLS

The Gorge was first presented by BBC television on 4 September, 1968,* with the following cast:

S T A N L E Y	*Neil Wilson*
L I L Y	*Constance Chapman*
M I K E	*Billy Hamon*
I V Y	*Betty Alberge*
J A C K	*Reg Lye*
N O R M A N	*John Woodnutt*
J O Y C E	*Hilda Braid*
C H R I S	*Elna Pearl*
C Y C L I S T	*David Webb*

Produced by Tony Garnett
Directed by Christopher Morahan

* It was later sold abroad to the television networks of five Commonwealth countries as well as to Scandinavia, Germany and Japan.

Characters

STANLEY, *50, heavily built, Bristolian.*

LILY, *Stanley's wife, 46, similar.*

IVY, *48, girlish, faultlessly turned out, prim.*

JACK, *50, Canadian, slight and balding.*

MIKE, *Stanley and Lily's son, 16, slim, serious. Slightly posher voice than his parents'.*

NORMAN, *42, dapper, dreamy, good-looking in a mousey way.*

JOYCE, *Norman's wife, 45, attempts elegance. Was once pretty. Bored manner.*

CHRIS, *their daughter, 15, pretty, direct.*

CYCLIST, *30-plus.*

EIGHT MOTOR-CYCLISTS (*four boys, four girls*), *all with strong Bristolian accents.*

A YOUNG MAN

PICNICKERS

HOME MOVIE

Stanley's house. Day.

(Sun rising behind suburban street, some time after dawn.

Pan over semi-detached, pre-war houses, all alike. Stop at one.)

Lounge. Night.

(Mike's face. A flash. Projector sound.)

HOME MOVIE

Exterior. Stanley's house. Day.

(The home movie is silent. We hear voices of the people watching but do not see them. Pictures of house from various angles. Milkman delivering.)

STANLEY: There we are then . . .

LILY: Home sweet home.

STANLEY: Sixty-seven.

LILY: Lovely colours.

JACK: Sure are.

IVY: Life-like.

LILY: Very natural.

IVY: You could touch it.

JACK: Sure could. Lilian—

LILY: What, love?

JACK: You want a cigarette?

LILY: No thanks, dear, I got a Mintoe.

JACK: You want a cigarette, Ivy?

IVY: I got a chocolate.

Lounge. Night.

(*Mike again.*)

JACK: Mike?

(*Mike nods.*)

HOME MOVIE

Exterior. Stanley's house. Day.

LILY: Anyone want a biscuit? Jack?

JACK: Huh?

LILY: Want a biscuit?

JACK: I got a cigarette.

LILY: Ivy?

IVY: What, love?

LILY: Want a biscuit?

(*The picture flickers to black and they all groan. Remains black.*)

LILY: Something stuck in the works?

JACK: Don't shoot the operator, folks, he's doing his best.

(*They laugh.*)

STANLEY (*Tense, harsh*): I switched it off. What d'you think I am—cheese at fourpence? Think I want to stand here working this while you lot pass the toffees round?

Lounge. Night.

(*Mike's face, close, when he strikes a match to light his cigarette.*)

STANLEY: Hullo, smoking again?

(*Mike inhales deeply.*)

LILY: Now, now—

STANLEY: There's a big boy. Smoking like that!

LILY: Give him a rest.

(*Pause. Mike ignores him.*)

STANLEY: All right. Only don't come whining to me when you get lung cancer. All got everything you want then?

LILY: Yes.

STANLEY: Right.

(*Film resumes. Close-ups of bedroom windows.*)

STANLEY: Notice all the bedroom curtains still drawn.

JACK: Tough it's not a talkie.

STANLEY: How's that?

JACK: Coulda had the sound effects. (*He snores.*)

(*The women laugh.*)

IVY: Good job somebody's got a sense of humour.

STANLEY: Talk about Christians awake, salute the happy morn!

LILY: Sunday morning. Can't we even have a lay-in Sunday?

STANLEY: I was up at the crack.

LILY: You always are.

STANLEY: I thought Jack wanted a comprehensive pictorial record.

(*Jack opens the front door and comes out to fetch the milk.*
He is wearing a tartan lumberjacket and trousers with carpet slippers.)

STANLEY: Some time later.

IVY: That's you, Jack.

(*Jack stands on the crazy-paved path and does arms outstretched, then arms - on - hips - knees - bend, acts crippled and has to use the wall to pull himself up again. Gets milk and goes inside. The women watching laugh.*)

STANLEY: Pity that. Acting the goat. Lowers the tone.

Lounge.
(*Mike.*)

MIKE: Very funny, Uncle.

JACK: You said it was okay at the time. I said I'll horse around a little and . . .

STANLEY: The lady of the house.

(*Back door leading to garden.*
Lily has come out in apron and thrown something about on the grass from a plate, apparently obeying orders from Stanley.)

JACK: . . . you said 'fine'.

STANLEY: Look! Lady of the house.

LILY: A picture no artist could paint.

IVY: That's you, Lil.

LILY: I've seen better dames in the pantomime.

82

STANLEY: What's wrong?

LILY: Fancy taking me in my apron. In the middle of doing breakfast.

JACK: You're way out of date. That's all the rage now.

LILY: What?

JACK: The kitchen sink.

(*In the film, Lily continues throwing something on the lawn.*

Watch it for some time.)

IVY: What you meant to be doing, dear?

LILY: Feeding the birds.

STANLEY: Throwing bread from a tray.

(*Mike again.*)

MIKE: Whose idea was that?

STANLEY: What's wrong with it?

LILY: I never feed the birds from one year's end to the next.

IVY: It's very natural though.

LILY: I never *have*.

STANLEY: You got to *move*. It's a film, not snaps.

LILY: The birds round here, you give them an inch, they peck your hand off.

(*In the film, garage doors. Mike moves in to open them. Mike wears woollen shirt and linen trousers. Resentfully he does as he is told.*)

STANLEY: Hullo! Rip Van Winkle.

LILY: Poor old Mike. He looks fed up to the back teeth.

STANLEY: Don't know what he's got to look fed up about.

IVY: I *thought* that was Michael.

STANLEY: Didn't stir his stumps till nearly eight.

MIKE: Nearly eight—on a flipping Sunday morning!

(*Different shot of garage, doors open. Large saloon car emerges, Stanley at the wheel. The car goes out of view.*)

LILY: There's the Green Goddess.

(*The camera remains on the garage for some seconds.*)

STANLEY: Tell the cameraman's changed, can't you?

LILY: Who was it?

STANLEY: Jack. I told you to follow the car round, Jack. What you stuck on here for?

(*Camera still on garage. Nothing to look at.*)

JACK: Never get the Academy Award now.

(*Mike's face laughing.*)

STANLEY: Come on, come on.

(*At last camera manages a shaky pan to follow the car and eventually finds it parked at kerb.*

Stanley standing behind it, is pointing, waving, shouting.

Light spills in and the picture goes white.

Aahs of regret from the women.)

STANLEY: Over-exposure. I told you to keep it out of the sun.

JACK (*Irritably at last*): You told me to follow the car. How d'you figure I . . .

MIKE: Don't argue with him, Uncle. That's what he wants.

STANLEY: Hold your tongue.

(Mike's face. Now angry.)

MIKE: I'm not sitting here to be shouted at. I don't want to see your doomy film anyway.

STANLEY: You stay where you are. Think I did it for my own amusement?

(Picture resumes. Front exterior of a semi-detached house, circa 1900, solid and ugly but in good repair.

Ivy comes down front path. Girlishly dressed, hair elaborately bouffant.)

IVY: That's never me.

LILY: Well, it isn't me.

(Ivy waves to camera. Gets into car.)

IVY: Well, I was all ready for once.

END OF HOME MOVIE

(See them all: Stanley and Lily front seat, Jack, Mike, Ivy back seat.

Car is passing through Sunday morning city streets.)

STANLEY: I should *think* so. You had twenty extra minutes.

IVY: Not like you to be late, Stan.

STANLEY: D'you think it was *me*?

IVY: Set the clock by you as a rule.

STANLEY: It was Rip Van Winkle held us up.

LILY (*Pleading*): Now, now—

IVY: Rip van Winkle?

STANLEY: Don't you know who Rip Van Winkle is? (*Laughs.*)

(*Mike, who has been staring sullenly forward between his parents bursts out.*)

MIKE: It's only half past nine now. What the flipping hell's it matter?

LILY (*Scared but still peace-making*): Now, now, don't fly off—

STANLEY: That the sort of language they teach you in the Sixth Form? Very nice.

MIKE: Just because you can't sleep the rest of us have got to get out of bed at some . . .

STANLEY (*To the car in front*): Make up your mind, madam!

MIKE (*Louder*): Just because you're a neurotic insomniac.

STANLEY (*Blowing the horn*): You trying to get me into an accident? You're . . .

MIKE (*Giving up*): Jesus Christ Almighty!

LILY (*Shocked*): Shush!

STANLEY: *What* did you say? (*Silence.*) Any more bad words from you, you needn't come. I'll stop the car and let you off. Got that?

(*Mike shuts his eyes tightly, slumps back. Others stare through windows disconcerted.*

Stanley's car crossing Avon at Cumberland Basin flyover.)

STANLEY: You got to realize, Sonny Jim, there's a lot to get through before the day's up. Uncle Jack's been away in Canada—how long, Jack?

JACK: Thirty-eight years, near enough. Went over when I was a kid around . . .

STANLEY: He wants to see all he can while he's here. Those red buildings on the left—everyone looking?

86

(*They all look except Mike.*)

STANLEY: Tobacco bonds.

LILY: Talk about the bricklayers' benefit.

IVY: Ought to pull them down.

STANLEY: On your right—

(*The heads turn as at Wimbledon.*)

STANLEY: River Avon and Clifton Suspension Bridge.

IVY: The tide's out.

LILY: Never seen it in.

(*Stanley's car climbing Dundry Hill.*)

LILY: School, children crossing.

STANLEY: I'll read the signs, you point out the views.

LILY: Something to see, is there?

MIKE (*Bored*): On the left.

LILY: What?

(*Everyone looks but Mike.*)

MIKE: View.

STANLEY: Over Bristol.

IVY: Aah. Wall in the way.

JACK: Just too late, huh?

LILY: Too late, too late, shall be the cry. Arnold the ice-cream man's gone by.

STANLEY: Shame.

IVY: Who's for another toffee?

LILY: No. Have one of these.

(*View of them all later, chewing with difficulty. All but Mike.*

The sound is amplified on the track.

Mike shuts his eyes against the noise.)

HOME MOVIE

(Wells Cathedral west front. Group posing. Jack, Ivy, Lily.)

LILY: Wells Cathedral.

STANLEY: Buzfuz took this. Sonny Jim. *I'm* supposed to be in it.

LILY: You must be off the edge.

JACK: Guess you couldn't get him in, huh Mike?

STANLEY: Don't know why not. Look at all that space the other side of you.

(Mike's face smiling.)

LILY: Perhaps you stood on the wrong end.

(Pictures of the west front in detail.
Slow.
Pans up, down and across.)

IVY: It's pretty of the church.

LILY: Nice of the West Front.

STANLEY: This is where I got the camera back.

(New shot of group now walking across, including Mike. We pan with them. They go inside, Jack removing cap. The picture goes black. Everyone Aahs.)

STANLEY: Inside the nave. I said at the time it was risky. Still. Worth trying.

LILY: Nothing ventured, nothing gained.

STANLEY: Shot it slow on purpose to let more light in.

(Picture resumes with the group walking by the moat, this time considerably faster than life.

Mike roars.)

JACK: Boy, oh boy!

88

STANLEY: Forgot to switch back.

JACK: Hurry, hurry.

(*Mike sings chase music. Jack laughs. Swans swim as though mechanized.*)

LILY (*Her courier's voice*): The moat round the Bishop's Palace where the swans ring the bell when they're hungry.

IVY: We couldn't stay to see that.

STANLEY: No. Lost enough time already.

(*Group walking fast away from water.*)

JACK: So long folks. Got to run now.

(*Women laugh.*

They go through an arch at the double.)

END OF HOME MOVIE

Stanley's car.

(*Few moments without dialogue.*)

LILY (*Reading*): Please drive slowly through village.

STANLEY: How much time have we lost?

LILY (*Checking watch against itinerary*): About fifteen minutes.

STANLEY: Too long at Wells. Only snag with dawdling about. We'll be a bit pushed for Glastonbury. What d'you say, Jack? Give Glastonbury the go-by?

JACK: You're the boss.

STANLEY: I've *seen* it. Make up your own mind.

JACK: Well—what *is* it?

LILY: Like Wells Cathedral but all in ruins.

JACK: That right? Bomb damage?

(*Mike laughs through his nose. Stanley nearly chokes himself laughing.*)

STANLEY: Dear, oh dear, oh dear.

MIKE: No. Henry the Eighth had it pulled down.

IVY: That's a natural mistake. We haven't all got the time to keep up with history, Michael. It's rude to laugh.

JACK: You and me better go into the corner together, Ivy? What d'you say?

IVY: Pardon?

JACK: With a dunce's cap?

IVY: Oh, yes.

LILY (*Reading*): Glastonbury is rich in popular legend.

STANLEY: Lily read out all the gen and then we needn't cram it in.

JACK: Give it a miss, huh?

STANLEY: Go another time.

(*Mike smiles at Jack.*)

LILY: Joseph of Arimathea came soon after the Cruci-fixion bringing the Holy Grail used by Our Lord at the Last Supper—

IVY: Who's for a Mintoe?

JACK: Anyone want a cigarette?

LILY: —which was later to be woven so inextricably into the elaborate pattern of Arthurian legend.

(*Pause.*)

STANLEY: Main thing is the Gorge.

IVY: We don't want to miss the Gorge.

Cheddar Gorge Road.

(Some of this may be aerial, but mostly it is from the ground upwards giving an impression of the depth of the ravine and the wildness of the rocks.

Silence for the first time.

Follow a hovering crow or hawk.

A stream, a falling rock, a cave mouth.

Look closely at gorse and heather. High shot of Stan's car coming down Gorge. Their point of view of passing scenery.)

STANLEY: Here's the famous Cheddar Gorge.

JACK: Sure is steep. That's really what you call phenominominal.

IVY: How's that again?

LILY: Phenomenal. The pee is silent as in bathing.

(The car goes down the gorge. They look out of the window at the cliffs.

High shot of car, pan off to crag or bird. Shock cut to the traffic jam around the entrance to the caves. Noise of cars and coaches very loud, people shouting instructions, warnings, jokes. Motor-bikes rev up, horns sound, ice-cream vans ring out 'Lilliburlero' and 'Greensleeves'.

Stanley's company struggle along the narrow street, pressing themselves against the walls and rocks to give room to passing vehicles. They talk or shout to each other, but nothing can be heard above the din.

See:
The veteran car museum beside the petrol station
The cheese cottage
The shop beside the waterfall sending off fresh cream
The boutique
The entrance to the caves, turnstiles clicking, customers patiently queueing on the pavement

The Stone-Age tableau
The ice-cream parlour with its glass roof
Shops selling pottery jars in the shape of yokels
    marked 'Oi be oop frum Zummerzet', urinating
    dolls, Beatle ashtrays, 'genuine severed heads',
    pokerwork mottoes
A slot-machine for horoscopes.

Stanley arranges Lily before a row of cottages, taking
his shot from the far side of the road to get enough in
the viewfinder. See the shot.

Lily walks into the garden. She approaches a party of
plaster gnomes gathered at a wishing-well. Crowds of
people press in and out of the garden.

Traffic blurs the foreground.

Mike's face fills the screen, unsmiling. He says some-
thing.)

LILY: Dear, oh dear. Convict Ninety-nine.

(*Mike manages a frozen smile, then tries to wave the*
camera away. He turns and walks out of shot.)

STANLEY: Not exactly the life and soul, was he?

(*Series of four shots against the same background:*
three people eating ice-cream cornets.

(1) Lily, Jack, Ivy
(2) Lily, Stanley, Ivy
(3) Jack, Stanley, Ivy
(4) Jack, Stanley, Lily.

END OF HOME MOVIE

(*Mike on his own pressing miserably through the*
crowd. But he is attentive, looking about him as though
for something he expected. Stanley and the others are
not far off but he keeps his distance.

At last see what he's looking for.)

Chris comes from one of the caves. Zoom on her but she doesn't see him. She is chatting with Norman beside her.

Mike waves to her, follows her some way.

Stanley draws Lily's attention to Mike's wandering. They all move after him.

Jack has bought paper hats with legends on their brims. He gives them one each, has one for Mike, too.

Mike at last attracts Chris's attention. She waves to him. They are both trying to keep it a secret. She obviously can't get away from Norman but nods to Mike to follow them. He catches up with her as she loiters behind Norman.)

CHRIS: See you at the lead mine?

MIKE: What?

CHRIS: Shall I see you at the Roman lead mine?

(Mike shrugs.)

CHRIS: That's where you said.

MIKE: Yeah. You going there?

CHRIS: I'll try to make my parents go there.

(Mike is almost too bored to speak.)

MIKE: You'll see our tent from the road. We'll pitch it by the road.

(Norman moves towards them, frowning as he sees Chris talking to Mike. She joins him.)

NORMAN: Who's that you were talking to?

(Jack catches up Mike and gives him the paper hat. Because it's Jack, Mike can't bring himself to refuse.

Stan wants a picture so Mike is prevented from following. They force him to put on his hat.)

HOME MOVIE

(*Five shots of the paper-hat wearers, their messages very legible.*)

LILY: Kiss me quick.

JACK: Dead Legs.

IVY: Okay Toots.

STANLEY: Dream Boy.

MIKE: Don't be shy.

END OF HOME MOVIE

Lounge.

(*Mike flinches.*)

(*In a pub, still with their hats, Jack buys them drinks.*

A Welsh coach party sings and the drinking stops. Silence till the end then warm applause.

The bar is unbearably crowded and someone spills Mike's drink over him.

Mike goes outside and pushes through the crowd in the direction he saw Chris going. His stricken expression beneath the comic hat makes some girls giggle. He removes hat and throws it away.

See some more of Cheddar as he looks for Chris.

At the car park Mike goes on looking. See how every space is packed with cars.

At another place, Chris is looking for him. Norman and Joyce are getting into their car and Norman asks her to get in, too.

Mike sees her getting in and watches the car move into the stream of traffic.)

In Stanley's car.
(Between Gorge and Burrington.)

The adults all slightly drunk, just a little freer with their tongues, their paper hats more rakishly worn. After a pause:

LILY *(Reading road signs)*: Keep out . . . no parking . . . private land . . . trespassers will be prosecuted . . . keep faith with British farmers . . .

(Stan's car travelling through Burrington Combe.)

STANLEY: How's the enemy?

LILY: Ten to one.

STANLEY: Not bad.

LILY: Says here 'Picnic 1300 hours'.

(Pause.)

LILY: There's Rock of Ages.

STANLEY: That's not Rock of Ages.

IVY: You're right, Lily. Rock of Ages.

JACK: What *is* the Rock of Ages?

LILY: Where the fellow sheltered when he wrote the hymn.

JACK *(Looking through rear window)*: That right?

(Suddenly Lily sings in a clear contralto.)

LILY: Rock of Ages cleft for me
    Let me hide myself in thee.

(Ivy joins her.)

LILY AND IVY: Let the water and the blood—

(*Then Stanley. Now it sounds like the gang of drunken Welsh.*)

LILY, IVY, STANLEY (*Together*):
From thy riven side which flowed—

(*The car moves up the combe, their song receding with it.*
  Expanse of common heath with views of distant country.

Pan round to show how wild and uncultivated it is. Mike comes on. He looks about.

Stanley joins him, carrying itinerary on a clipboard, surveys the ground, stamping on the earth.)

STANLEY: Got it to ourselves, I see.

MIKE: Yeah.

STANLEY: So far. (*He squints expertly under his hand, assessing the terrain.*)

MIKE: We ought to go farther off the road.

STANLEY: What for?

MIKE: Get the shelter of the rising ground.

STANLEY: Shelter?

MIKE: From the wind.

(*Stanley tests it with a handkerchief.*)

STANLEY: Slight breeze but nothing serious. Any case, I got shields will counteract the draughts.

MIKE: Down there, we'd be farther from other people.

STANLEY: Farther from the car, too. Farther to carry all the gear. Might get behind schedule. We must get in another dummy-run or Uncle Jack will be letting us down on the continent. (*He looks about, makes note on board.*) Views well up to scratch. (*Walks a few steps.*) Here's the place.

MIKE: It stinks.

STANLEY: Don't argue with me, son, you're not half bright enough. (*Walks off to car.*)

(*Mike smiles.*)

(*The following sequence—making camp—in silence or to music.*

Begin on open heath.

Jack and Mike bring parts of the tent.

Stanley brings the rest.

Various stages in its erection: sorting out the jumble of parts.

Hoisting the canvas.

Hammering the pegs.

Fixing the guy ropes.

At the same time, Lily and Ivy bring out the furniture. One table and five chairs—and after that the kitchen equipment: a unit with a heat-proof top, a volcano water boiler, double propane burner, kettles, pans, a pressure cooker, polythene and cardboard boxes full of food. They put on pinafores.

Jack is unlucky—hammering a peg, he hurts his finger. Rushing to obey one of Stanley's orders he goes flying over a guy-rope.
Helping to unfold one of the chairs he squeezes his thumb.
In pain he is hardly stoic, he sucks his finger and shows Ivy the wound.

Mike brings from the car a box with a large cross on it. Stanley is at the car checking off his list of stores.

Mike arrives for more luggage and is given the aquajet, a bulbous rubber container, and a foot-pump.

Mike on the way back passes Jack going for more.

97

Lily is cutting open a polythene bag with a chicken inside it. She removes a smaller bag containing the giblets. She searches through the food and says something to Ivy, who helps her look.

Jack trudges back with two deflated lilos and a pile of newspaper.

Mike draws some water off the aquajet into the pressure cooker.

Lily and Ivy give up their search, Lily shrugs and drops the fowl into the pressure cooker. She puts it on a burner, closes the lid and drops on the valve.

Ivy meanwhile lays the table.

Stanley leaves the car with more canvas and poles.

Mike and Jack pump the lilos. Mike pushes them into the tent.

The tent is described by the makers as architecture in canvas and it has a porch, windows and inner bedrooms.

Stanley tests the wind direction with his finger, decides on a position to leeward of the main tent. Here he begins to erect the smaller tent, which is like a tall tepee.

Jack draws water from the aquajet meaning to squirt it into the volcano. He loses control of the hose and water is released over the furniture.

Ivy wipes it over with a cloth.

Lily sees the steam issuing from the pressure cooker valve. She closes it and turns over the hour-glass.

Ivy wrings out the dishcloth and pegs it on to a line.

Jack lights newspaper in the volcano. He tears up paper and feeds it in as fast as he can.

Lily cuts open a packet of frozen peas with a pair of scissors. She pours them into a can of water and puts it on the other ring.

Ivy takes a plastic vase from one of the boxes, drops a bunch of plastic flowers into it and puts it on the dining-table.

Mike is standing by the car while Stanley ticks off items on his list.

Mike looks hopefully at every passing car.

Jack is in trouble. The volcano is smoking profusely and he is stuffing paper into the heating chamber as fast as he can. This only increases the smoke.

See this from as far off as possible—from a hill or from the heath or even from the air.

A great cloud of black smoke issuing from the stove.

Zoom in to Jack's confusion as he tries to touch it and burns his fingers.

Ivy comes to help.

Mike arrives with washing up bowl and stand.

Stanley, at the car, looks about a good deal before producing the next article.

He waits for a car to pass and finally brings out a chemical lavatory.

Lily turns over the hour-glass.

Mike has erected the washstand.

Ivy and Jack now have the volcano under control.

Ivy puts out the paper napkins.

Stanley arrives at the smaller tent and puts the lavatory inside.

Lily opens a tin of potatoes and heats them in a pan. They are already peeled and the size of large marbles.

The hour-glass has run through again so Lily takes the cooker off the ring and Mike squirts water at it from the aquajet to cool it.

Stanley pulls the cork from a bottle of wine.

Ivy sets out wine glasses to each place.

Lily is browning the chicken in the open cooker.

Jack pours water from volcano into bowl and the three men wash their hands.

The ladies take off their aprons.

Close up of Stanley seated behind the table as his plate is served, loaded with chicken, peas and potatoes. He looks at his watch.)

STANLEY: Not bad. Not bad at all.

(Zoom back to show them all sitting at the table, starting their meal.

Back farther until they appear very small in a great expanse.

Close ups while they eat.)

LILY: My stomach thought my throat was cut.

STANLEY: Don't I get any stuffing?

LILY (*To Ivy*): I told you he'd know.

IVY (*To Stan*): Left behind. Now don't make a fuss.

STANLEY: Dear, oh dear.

LILY: I'm sorry.

STANLEY: What's a fowl without stuffing?

IVY: Personally I've never been that keen on stuffing.

JACK: Tastes fine to me, Lily. Chow's always better in the open air, huh?

IVY: D'you do a lot of eating in the open?

JACK: Me?

IVY: Over there.

JACK: Used to. More than now. When I was with the C.P.R. out on the Prairie. Used to have mostly Chinese cooks. Good plain food, you know? Velly good chop-

chop, Johnny. Great life, though. Plenty of fresh air. 'Less you seen it, you can't imagine it. The wide open spaces. Not a living soul for miles.

(*Pause.*)

IVY: I should hate it.

JACK: Pardon me?

IVY: When my husband was alive, he used to take me on these walks. Not a car in sight. I cried once. He said: 'Why, whatever's the matter, sweetheart?' I said: 'Walter, I don't like it, I like people.' He said: 'But, Ivy, it's beautiful.' I said: 'It may be beautiful, Walt, but I can't stand it.' I said: 'People are my life.'

(*Pause.*

Ivy pats the sides of her mouth with her paper napkin, then sips her wine.

Eating continues. Mike puts down his knife and fork.)

LILY: Had enough?

MIKE: Yes.

LILY: Thank you.

MIKE: Thank you.

STANLEY: Leaving that chicken?

MIKE: I don't like chicken.

LILY: He's ate a good deal.

STANLEY: I dare say if you were a starving Indian you'd manage it. (*Eats on.*)

(*Pause.*

Mike, looking at grass.)

MIKE'S VOICE OVER: Please let her come, God. But not for a minute. Not till they've finished swilling at the trough.

(*Norman's car driving through Burrington Combe.*

101

He pulls in beside Stanley's. Norman's is smaller, older.

Norman wearing neat sports clothes, Joyce beside him in a neat suit, smoking a cigarette.

Chris behind in a man's shirt and jeans.)

JOYCE : Somebody here already.

CHRIS : Mummy, honestly—

JOYCE: Listen to me, Christine. I sat about in that ghastly gorge because you and your father wanted to see the caves. Now enough's enough. The rest of the day I want a quiet sit and read the papers. What's the point of driving all this way to sit about in a crowd? We could have got a crowd in Bristol.

NORMAN: Not today. It's Sunday. Bristol's empty.

JOYCE: Mad! By the year 2000 the population of England will be doubled. People will be pushing one another into the ocean.

NORMAN: Don't give much for our chances. We'll be nearly eighty.

JOYCE : Don't talk about it.

CHRIS: This is great when you get off the road. Honestly.

JOYCE : Radios everywhere, I expect.

NORMAN: Let's see—shall we?

JOYCE : You scout around.

(Chris gets out, looks for clues in Stanley's car.

At Stanley's tent, they are now on the dessert—fruit salad and cream.)

STANLEY : Any more cream?

LILY : In the jar.

STANLEY : Pour us out a drop.

(*Passes dish back to Lily, across Ivy. Lily puts her own dish down.*)

LILY: Lie down and I'll breathe for you. (*She gives him cream.*)

JACK: The extremes of hot and cold, Mike, absolutely fantastic.

MIKE: Yes?

JACK: Some night, under canvas, you'd maybe leave your tent-flap open so's you could breathe, but boy! You'd be sorry.

(*Lily passes Stanley's dish back.*)

LILY: Excuse me retching, I just come off the boat.

STANLEY: Thanks, love.

JACK: Halfway through the night you'd get this god-awful stench so bad it would wake you up.

IVY: Nice subject for the dinner-table.

JACK: Sorry, Ivy, but you know what it'd be?

IVY: I'd rather you didn't say.

JACK: A damn great grizzly bear right there in the tent.

IVY: My Lord above!

LILY: I should die of fright.

STANLEY: So would Jack, by the way he backs away from cows.

(*He laughs, goes on eating. The others laugh slightly. Mike looks at Stanley.*)

JACK: Yea? Well—a cow—you—

MIKE (*Loud and harsh*): What the hell d'you know about it? You've never been farther than the bloody Isle of Wight.

LILY: How dare you speak like that to your father!

MIKE: Why not? Why doesn't someone ask him why he thinks he's better at anyone than everything else? I mean, everything than anyone else.

STANLEY: Come on, Sonny Boy, spit it out.

MIKE (*Shouting*): Shut your damn face, you great stinking bully.

STANLEY: He gone mad or what?

LILY (*Tense*): Hush! Strangers.

(*Norman and Chris have come from the road and have obviously seen the incident.*

No one looks up. They all go on eating.

Close-up Chris. She glances at Mike.

Close-up Mike. He stares at the ground.)

STANLEY: More Liebfraumilch anyone?

(*Norman goes back to the car and Chris follows him.*)

LILY: You'll apologize to your father—

STANLEY (*Loud, putting down dish*): Very nice. Got cheese and biscuits?

LILY: In the box.

STANLEY: Hope it's Cheddar? (*He laughs.*)

LILY: *Canadian* Cheddar.

JACK: Hands across the sea.

(*Lily laughs. Glad to have safely passed another crisis.*)

(*Norman sitting with his car door open, his feet outside. Chris standing by him.*)

JOYCE: I can smell it from here.

NORMAN: We don't have to sit near them.

104

JOYCE: Is there plenty of space?

NORMAN: Miles.

JOYCE: Enough to get out of earshot in case they've got a radio?

CHRIS: I didn't see one.

JOYCE: How can you *see* them? No bigger than a Prayer Book these days.

(*Washing up bowl at Stanley's tent.*

Jack and Mike are washing up and drying, while Ivy and Lily are preparing instant coffee.

Ivy puts a teaspoon of powder into each cup and Lily follows with a measure of water from the volcano.

Stanley has produced two more bottles.)

STANLEY: Liqueurs for anyone?

LILY: Cherry brandy for me.

IVY: D'you bring the Benedictine?

STANLEY: No. Cherry Brandy or Tia Maria.

IVY: Tia Maria then. (*She goes off to the cars.*)

STANLEY: Jack? Liqueurs with your coffee?

JACK: Swell.

STANLEY: Which?

JACK: Two fingers of Benedictine.

STANLEY: I said no Benedictine.

JACK: Whatever you got, swell.

STANLEY: Buzfuz?

MIKE: No.

105

STANLEY: No what?

MIKE: No, thanks.

(*Norman, Joyce and Chris now appear over the ridge carrying their chairs and one small bag. They pass the slaving family, nod politely, murmur 'afternoon'.*

Mike looks with ill-concealed interest at Chris's parents.

They settle some way off on the common.)

JACK: You'd like it there, Mike.

MIKE: What?

JACK: Still wide open for a young man. Fellows like you with an education. Still need young men, boy. White men. We got the menace from the West.

MIKE: What's that?

JACK: The little yellow fellers—Nippons, Chinese. They're biding their time, that's all. They were all fixed to take over British Columbia, you know that?

(*Mike shakes his head, confused and ashamed.*)

I got proof. I was walking along the street one day in Vancouver, minding my business, all of a sudden I meet these four Jap girls coming the other way. And they were so confident they were gonna take over B.C. d'you know they tried to bounce me right off the sidewalk? I stayed right where I was, boy. Velly solly, I here first. I just walked right on by, they had to move over. But if looks coulda killed, Zowie!

MIKE: Did they ever try again?

JACK: Mmm?

MIKE: To invade Vancouver?

LILY: Coffee up.

JACK: Sneaky. Can't trust 'em.

(*Ivy comes back from car carrying box of chocolates and a transistor radio.*

106

Chris's point of view. She sees the radio but her parents don't.

They have settled facing the opposite way, reading papers and drinking tea.)

JOYCE: Have you ever *seen* such a showy great tent? Lawrence of Arabia's not *in* it.

NORMAN (*Looking*): You surprise me.

(*Joyce laughs.*)

JOYCE: One almost wonders why they bother to come at all. If they bring their houses with them.

CHRIS: Why don't you stop criticizing?

JOYCE: Why shouldn't I criticize when something strikes me as vulgar and—tasteless and pretentious? I see they haven't brought the cocktail cabinet.

CHRIS: You're only jealous.

(*At Stanley's, Ivy passes round the chocolates and they eat and drink.*)

NORMAN: What's the other tent for? The dog?

JOYCE: That's what they'd call The Toilet.

NORMAN: Ah. The *smallest* tent.

(*They smile.*

Chris, sipping tea, looks at Mike, sipping coffee.

Close-up: exchange of stares.

Lily and Ivy suddenly disturbed by the buzzing of a wasp. A great waving of hands and pantomimes of avoidance.)

JACK: It's on *me*.

(*Jumping, he spills some of his drink over Lily. He runs off, again falling over one of the guy-ropes. Gets up again and runs some way off.*

Stanley has been opening the Red Cross box and now has a spray which he directs at the wasp, releasing a cloud of insecticide. Following it round, he squirts it into Mike's face.)

MIKE: Thank you.

(He begins coughing, throws coffee on the ground. Stands and begins to move off.)

STANLEY: Where are you going?

MIKE: Walk.

STANLEY: Exercise you want?

MIKE: Yes.

STANLEY: I've got a ball.

MIKE: I want some fresh air, too. *(He goes on to heath, some way from Chris's party.)*

(Close up of Chris, watching Mike go.

Jack rejoins the others, rubbing his leg.)

JACK: That bee sure had his eye on me.

STANLEY: That bee was a wasp.

JACK: That right?

STANLEY: Don't get many wasps in the Rockies, I suppose?

JACK: I thought it was a bee.

IVY: That spray's got a lovely scent.

STANLEY: Got rid of it anyway.

(Norman and Joyce suddenly stand, repeating the pantomime, thrashing about and dodging.

Stanley approaches with spray.)

CHRIS: Leave it alone, poor thing. No harm in it.

STANLEY: See if this helps.

(*Shoots at the wasp but Joyce gets a mouthful and coughs, closing her eyes.*)

STANLEY: I beg your pardon.

(*She smiles through her cough.*)

STANLEY: I think he's gone. Nasty things.

NORMAN: Thank you.

STANLEY: That and the wind. Only snag with a picnic.

NORMAN: Yes. Thanks very much.

(*Stanley smiles at Joyce. Goes back.*)

STANLEY (*To Lily*): Smart woman.

(*Lily gives Joyce a bleak stare.*

Meanwhile at Norman's pitch.)

JOYCE: Talk about pushing.

(*They settle again. Chris moves a few steps away.*)

CHRIS: I'm going off.

NORMAN: Where?

CHRIS (*Shrugs*): For a walk.

NORMAN: Shall I come?

(*Chris turns up her nose.*)

CHRIS: Not unless you want to. (*She looks at the grass.*)

NORMAN (*Huffy*): Why should I *want* to? (*He returns to his paper.*)

JOYCE: Don't go too far. In case they start that radio and we have to go.

(*Chris goes off in other direction from Mike's.*)

NORMAN: I only thought she ought to have someone with her.

JOYCE: Don't be an old woman.

NORMAN: Have you seen the way men look at her? She's not a kid any more. Suddenly she's a grown girl.

(*He looks after Chris.*)

(*Joyce drinks from her cup.*)

JOYCE: Ugh! That muck's in the tea. (*She throws the tea away.*)

On Blackdown amid the bracken.

Mike pushes through, looking back, taking his time. Chris runs after him.

HOME MOVIE

(*Lily and Jack throwing the ball to each other. Stanley has attempted to follow the ball in progress but never quite catches up with it.*)

LILY: What's this—a Band of Hope concert?

JACK: No. A missing Ball Competition.

(*Mike laughs. Action continues.*)

Nearly got a glimpse of it then, Stan. Guess that was a slip-up.

END OF HOME MOVIE

Stanley puts camera down, joins game. Jack throws ball to him but it goes wide to Norman's pitch. Stanley goes to retrieve it, Norman throws it to him with a smile.)

STANLEY: Thank you.

(*He catches it and throws it double quick at Jack, who attempts a catch but hurts his finger and crumples with pain. He rolls on the ground, nursing his finger. Stanley grabs the camera and turns it on Jack.*)

HOME MOVIE

(Jack gets up, still shaking and blowing on his fingers. He goes towards Ivy in the tent.)

STANLEY *(Voice off, laughing)*: Butterfingers!

(On the heath,

Mike is watching for Chris. He is very tense as he sees her coming.

He turns away, combs his hair.

Chris approaches and they stand near one another. She looks at him.)

CHRIS: Hullo.

MIKE *(Offhand)*: Hullo.

CHRIS: I was afraid I wasn't going to get here.

MIKE: I nearly didn't either. You know I've got this other woman in Portishead?

CHRIS: Have you?

MIKE: Well, I thought I might get him to stop there but then I thought on a Sunday there'd be too many grockels and trogs and car-owning day-trippers like him—so—

CHRIS *(Sorry for herself)*: You *said* you'd come.

MIKE: Didn't.

CHRIS: Did.

MIKE: I said I *might*.

(Goes to return comb to pocket. She reaches for it. She combs her hair. He stares across the heath.)

MIKE: Your old man looks quite young.

CHRIS: Forty-one.

MIKE: That's quite young.

CHRIS: Which one's yours?

MIKE: The one with the great bulging belly hanging

over his belt as though he was suffering from elephantiasis or something.

CHRIS (*Smiling*): Who's the other man?

MIKE: Mum's cousin. I thought he was all right but he's just as stupid a creep as the rest of them. He thinks the Japs are gonna slit his throat or something.

CHRIS: Is your mother the one with blonde hair?

MIKE: Christ no! That's Aunt Ivy. She's not really my aunt. She and Mum were friends together in the Napoleonic wars or something.

CHRIS: Is it a wig?

MIKE: No . . . and you ought to see her dressed up.

CHRIS: Isn't she dressed up now?

MIKE (*Laugh*): This is *casual*.

(*Ivy tending Jack's fingernail in the shelter of the tent.*)

JACK: Can't get used to those hard balls.

IVY: Anything to do with nails, you've come to the right person.

JACK: You have trouble with your nails?

IVY: Trouble? That barely describes it.

JACK: Calcium deficiency?

IVY: No. Dancing.

JACK: That right?

IVY: When my husband, Walt, and I first took up dancing I honestly thought I should never go through with it.

JACK: Ballroom dancing?

IVY: I used to come home crippled. I said 'Walt, I'm crippled' but he kept me at it and we began to win some championships. By then we'd both got the bug. Which reminds me. (*She turns aside to switch on radio —Victor Silvester's orchestra.*)

(*Joyce glares across.*)

(*Chris and Mike saunter along a path. Blackdown is high, clear, with views to the Bristol Channel.*)

CHRIS: Wasn't Cheddar fabulous?

MIKE: Grotty. All those thicks mooning about.

CHRIS: No, it's great. So funny.

MIKE: D'you mean that seriously?

CHRIS: Yeah.

MIKE: A commercialized slum. One of the country places city people are allowed to go and spend their money. Doesn't it ever occur to you that landowners keep the best of the country for themselves, and make a nice bit on the side by running bogs for people like Fat Stan?

CHRIS: Who?

MIKE: My old man.

CHRIS: I don't care . . . I think it's funny.

MIKE: I tried to put him straight. He said yes, everything's a rat-race these days, got to live with that, modern life's all materialism.

CHRIS: That's great! With that tent?

MIKE (*Grins*): Yeah. Not only the tent, either. Car, cine-cameras, all this kitchen gear. Then he tells me to think of the starving Indians.

CHRIS: So you didn't see the Fairy Grotto? That was a knock-out.

MIKE: The Fairy Grotty.

CHRIS: Great, really.

MIKE: I wish I could find it funny.

CHRIS: What's it matter?

MIKE: I wish I loved the human race.

(*Stanley and Lily are talking to Norman and Joyce.*)

STANLEY: I reckon when they've pitched and struck once more we shall be ready for the Continent. They still fall over one another a bit but you should have seen them when I first got them. Talk about an awkward squad.

LILY: Fred Karno's Army.

JOYCE: What part are you going?

STANLEY: We reckon to keep the average low—two-fifty, three hundred miles a day. No sense rushing.

LILY (*To Joyce*): France.

JOYCE: Oh, I envy you. Put me down—I often say this to Norman—put me down in some Boulevard bistro with a Pernod and I'll be happy all day watching the world go by. Whatever you say about the French, they've somehow never lost the art of living. I mean, where can you go in Bristol and sit on the street and watch the world go by?

(*Pause. They nod and think about it.*)

STANLEY: Where the French fall down is in their toilets.

(*Norman is not paying attention, staring after Chris.*)

STANLEY: You noticed, Mister . . . um?

NORMAN: Sorry?

STANLEY: I say, where the French fall down is in their toilets.

NORMAN: I've never seen them do that, no.

(*Stanley looks at him carefully.*)

STANLEY: Go through France—plenty of well-kept war-graves, rows of trees, not a decent toilet anywhere.

(*A new family arrives at the site bearing its furniture.*)

JOYCE: We're being invaded. Norman, might be a good idea to lock the car.

STANLEY: Very good. Mine's open, too. Coming?

(*He leads off. Norman follows.*)

JOYCE (*To Lily*): Do sit down for a moment.

(*As Stanley and Norman pass the tent we return to Jack and Ivy.*)

IVY: Well, in the end I saw the doctor. He turned round and said to me 'You've got ingrowing toenails, with all the dancing you're doing'. I said 'Well, certainly my feet are black and blue'. He said 'they will be, the way you're putting them through it'.

JACK: What'd he do?

IVY: He said he could cut the nails off but they'd grow again inside a year. But what they'd much prefer was cut out the nail-beds.

JACK: Jees.

IVY: Because it was affecting the root. I turned round, I said 'No blessed fear. Cut the nails off, yes, but you leave my nail-beds where they are'. Well, I mean, just picture me in peep-toed shoes and no nail-beds.

JACK: Damned right.

(*Chris and Mike have found some bramble bushes and are collecting berries in their hands.*)

MIKE: Notice the way parents and people like that chew all the time? Makes a noise of men marching in mud.

CHRIS: Mine smoke.

MIKE: Got to have something in their mouths. Just now they were drinking liqueurs with instant coffee. Makes me curl up.

CHRIS: What d'you mean?

MIKE: Liqueurs. So suburban isn't it? You just imagine someone really sophisticated seeing that. Scathing they'd be. Someone like Evelyn Waugh.

(*Pause. Chris lost.*)

CHRIS: What sort of thing would she say?

MIKE: Who?

CHRIS: Evelyn—who was it?

MIKE: Evelyn Waugh was a man. A novelist.

(*Mike laughs. Chris shrugs it off. Chris pricks her finger. Sucks it.*)

MIKE: Hurt it?

CHRIS: Made it bleed.

MIKE: I'd give you some of mine but I'm anaemic.

(*She smiles. They move from the bushes into the bracken again. Eating berries.*)

MIKE: I reckon you could live on berries.

CHRIS: You'd have to know where to get a balanced diet. We learn it in domestic science.

MIKE (*Scorn*): Domestic science!

CHRIS: What?

MIKE: Cheese straws. Stuffed tomatoes.

CHRIS: It's not.

MIKE: 'Tis.

(*They walk on. Pause.*)

MIKE: Another man and me, we're going round the world pretty soon. My best friend Trev. He's a genius.

CHRIS: Round the world?

MIKE: Or perhaps Europe. Turkey. Somewhere like that. Perhaps get a bike. Or hitch.

CHRIS: When?

MIKE: Soon as we've done A levels.

CHRIS: Just two men?

116

MIKE: Why not?

CHRIS: Just a waste, that's all. You want some girls. I've got a friend. Incredibly sexy.

MIKE: That's all women are any good for.

CHRIS: Well?

MIKE: Don't need to have them around all the time, just for that.

(*She suddenly knocks the berries out of his hand. He goes for her but she screams and swerves away.*

He catches her by one hand. She throws the berries into his face and escapes again.

He runs after her.)

(*At the roadside.*

Norman and Stanley grimly considering their vehicles. Another has been parked nearby.)

STANLEY: Stripped her right down yesterday.

(*Norman nods. They look at Stanley's car as though expecting it to say 'Thank you'.*)

STANLEY: Greased her nipples. Touched her up where she got scratched Tuesday night.

(*Norman nods again.*)

STANLEY: Thoroughly waxed her body. Like a dream today.

NORMAN: Yes?

STANLEY: Fingertip response.

NORMAN: I've got a little man does all that for me.

STANLEY: I wouldn't let anyone near her.

NORMAN: In three years I've had no trouble at all. Economical, nippy—

117

(*Stanley looks at Norman's car despondently.*)

STANLEY: Only snag with these is the cornering.

NORMAN: Oh, I wouldn't agree with that. In fact, she corners better than any . . .

(*Another car has arrived. Stanley looks.*)

STANLEY (*Breaking in*): Blimey O'Riley. Like Brand's Hatch. Come on.

(*Turns back to the picnic and Norman has no alternative but to follow.*

At the tent,

Ivy and Jack with dance music.)

IVY: D'you know, sixty per cent of the married couples in this country first bumped into each other on the dance floor?

JACK: That a fact?

IVY: Perhaps that's why you never took the plunge? Not being keen on dancing?

JACK: Oh, it wasn't that I never had no chances. I was a rolling stone, I guess, always movin' on. A maverick.

IVY: My husband was a terrible dancer on paper.

JACK: That right?

IVY: To look at him on paper, you'd have said he could no more learn to dance than fly. Shy. Suffered with his legs. Not at all the type. But I think it's the challenge, the sense of achievement. You'd find that.

JACK: You think so?

IVY: You'd find yourself being swept along by the mounting excitement of the championships.

(*Chris and Mike still chasing through the bracken.*

At the picnic site,

A sallow staring man of thirty or more is wheeling his push-bicycle across the grass from the road.

The latest arrivals are setting up windshields and beginning to serve their meal.

Cyclist looks about him but keeps moving.

He arrives at Norman's pitch, where the men have rejoined their wives. Stanley is the only one standing.)

CYCLIST: Good afternoon. I have a message for you.

STANLEY: Is it about the car?

CYCLIST:
The lips of a strange woman drop honey.
And her mouth is smoother than oil.
But her latter end is bitter as wormwood,
Sharp as a two-edged sword.

(Pause. Stanley, staring at him, out of his depth.)

STANLEY: Fair enough.

(Cyclist walks on. A few yards away he drops his bicycle on to the grass and begins unstrapping a banner from the cross-bar.)

LILY: Got a lot to say for himself.

(Chris runs down into one of the sudden potholes found on Blackdown.

She pauses, listening for Mike. Then goes on down and sits on the grass.

She suddenly stares at the ground near her.

What she sees: a snake sunning itself.

Mike appears at the top but she gestures him to silence, showing the snake.

Mike crouches quietly, watching it. He moves close and seizes it.

119

He sits on the ground, caressing its head.)

CHRIS: Is it an adder?

MIKE: Grass snake.

(*She sits beside him and smoothes the snake's head with her finger.*)

CHRIS: Aren't you handsome?

MIKE: I had one for a pet. I used to take him for walks.

CHRIS: What, on a lead?

MIKE: In my inside pocket. His head used to look out between my fingers and women used to fall back against the walls when they saw what it was.

CHRIS: Shall we keep him?

MIKE: No.

CHRIS: Why not?

MIKE: This other one, he lived in the garden in a glass tank. One morning he was missing. I reckon Fat Stan let him out. Next we heard our neighbours had found him and the man had cut him in two with a chopper. Then they remembered something about the halves of snakes joining up again, so they buried him in two parts at far ends of the garden.

(*Chris shakes her head at human folly.*)

You don't want him to come across thicks like that. Be killed perhaps—for no good reason?

CHRIS: Course not.

MIKE (*To the snake*): Goodbye, then.

(*Mike lets it go and it slithers from sight. He lies back on the ground, staring at the sky. She lies on her stomach.*)

CHRIS: Shouldn't think anyone could see us down here.

(*He picks off a fern shoot.*)

120

MIKE: They used to think if you ate the spores of ferns you'd be invisible.

CHRIS: That would be fabulous.

MIKE: Mmmm?

CHRIS: Nobody could find us and you could have me.

(*She kisses his face.*)

MIKE: I'm hellish tired.

(*She turns away, hurt. He begins caressing her hair.*)

(*Ivy and Jack are still in Stanley's tent.*)

IVY: You ought to take a refresher course while you're over here. Then, when you go back to Canada, you might bump into some nice girl and reach an understanding.

JACK: I don't *have* to go back. Nothing to keep me there. I had some luck with stocks and bonds, made out pretty good.

IVY: You need a hobby.

JACK: You can sure fix a fingernail.

IVY: I should think so. I was a nurse in the war. Soft centre?

(*He takes a chocolate.*

At Norman's pitch they are also passing round the sweets. The cyclist has unfurled his banner so that it hangs on his chest like an apron. It reads: God is not mocked. He clears his throat, begins loudly:)

CYCLIST: How goodly are thy tents, O Jacob,
         Thy tabernacles, O Israel.

(*Everyone startled.*)

STANLEY: Dear, oh dear, oh dear.

121

(*Ivy turns up her radio.*

(*Stanley is taking pictures.*)

HOME MOVIE

Picnic site.

(*Norman, Joyce and Lily sit drinking, toasting each other.*)

LILY: She was a bit of a lady muck . . .

STANLEY: I don't know.

LILY: Mutton dressed as lamb.

(*See the cyclist making an oration. He is in full flood. New tents going up.*)

STANLEY: Mike won't remember this. You'd gone off to do a bit of nature study.

LILY: No, Stan!

STANLEY: What's the matter?

(*Mike's face as he watches the film.*)

STANLEY: Went off bird-watching or something.

HOME MOVIE

(*Camera pans to show heath.*

END OF HOME MOVIE.)

The heath. Pothole.

CHRIS: I know—let's take our shirts off.

MIKE: What for?

CHRIS: Get tanned. This is a sun-trap.

(*Mike shrugs.*)

CHRIS: I'm going to. (*She takes off shirt. Mike lies*

back on the ground, staring at the sky, stripping leaves from a stalk.

Chris has a bra beneath her shirt. She too lies back on the ground.

Mike picks another stalk, looks through it at the sun, then turns to running it along her arm.

She shudders and moves slightly, opens one eye and looks at him smiling.

He turns slightly towards her, runs the fern across her chest.)

MIKE: What's that feel like?

CHRIS: Nice.

MIKE: Must be funny, being a woman.

CHRIS: What d'you mean?

MIKE: I often try to imagine what it must be like.

CHRIS: Having bosoms?

MIKE: Yea.

CHRIS: Another boy said that to me. He said if he had bosoms he'd lie in bed all day playing with them. I tried it one night.

MIKE: What's it like?

CHRIS (*Shrugs*): Boring. Like playing with your fingers.

(They both stare at the sky again.
Mike yawns noisily.)

At the picnic site, the newcomers are now seated and have begun gnawing their chicken bones and filling their mouths with lettuce.

CYCLIST (*Reading from Bible*): And the Children of Israel also wept again and said, 'Who shall give us flesh

123

to eat? We remember the fish, which we did eat in Egypt freely; the cucumbers, and the melons and the leeks and the onions and the garlic'.

(*Lowering Bible.*) And the salad cream—

(*One of the picnickers pouring salad cream from a jar looks up at him.*

The cyclist speaks to the sky.)

—and the chicken legs and the chocolates and the crisps. The fish fingers and the sweet tea. The motor cars and garden furniture. Oh yes, my brothers, in the day of wrath you shall remember Egypt right enough.

LILY: Proper Job's comforter.

STANLEY: Let's move to the tent. Bit farther off, at any rate.

CYCLIST: In that day, make no mistake, there shall be wailing and gnashing of teeth.

JOYCE: You mean all of us?

STANLEY: Can't stand that. Allow me. (*He picks up their things and walks them towards the tent.*)

(*Lily stares at Joyce coldly, then smiles as she meets her glance.*)

CYCLIST: In that day you shall find insurance claims shall not be honoured.

LILY: Come into the body of the kirk.

(*They move off.*)

JOYCE: Only thing is, I'm not too keen on portable radios.

LILY: I'll turn it off.

CYCLIST: Neither for motor car nor its contents, nor for messuage nor its contents, neither for the life of the father nor the mother nor the children. And for why? Look at the small print, brothers. Haven't you ever read what it says about the Acts of God?

124

(The eating people try to ignore him.

Norman follows Joyce, carrying a chair.

Ivy and Jack welcome the family back.)

CYCLIST: What do I hear you say? Oh yes, but he sent down Bread from Heaven? Yes, to the Israelites. But you're not the Israelites. You're not the Chosen Few. You're the Uncircumcized!

STANLEY *(Stern)*: Dear, oh dear, oh dear!

LILY: Bit near the knuckle.

(At the pothole Mike and Chris are close together. They speak quietly, intimately.)

MIKE: Soon as I've got A levels, I'll be off to London. Go to university. Share a flat with Trev.

CHRIS: Shall I put in for London, too?

MIKE: Can if you like.

CHRIS: I'd love to be there with you.

(She kisses him. He responds ardently but when it is over, they resume their previous attitudes.)

MIKE: How d'you know you're going to *get* A levels?

CHRIS: How do *you*?

(He shrugs.)

MIKE: My results in O levels. You haven't even done *them* yet.

CHRIS: You like to make out I'm a kid or something.

MIKE: Well—how old are you?

CHRIS: Fifteen.

MIKE: Well—

CHRIS: You're only sixteen.

MIKE: Nearly seventeen.

CHRIS: When?

MIKE: Christmas.

CHRIS: Perhaps I'm too young for you.

MIKE: I never said that.

CHRIS: You never say anything. About me. Tell me what you think I'm like.

MIKE: Oh, God, honestly—

CHRIS: Would you say I'm nice-looking?

MIKE: Yea . . .

CHRIS: Would you say I'm nubile?

MIKE: What?

CHRIS: Nubile?

MIKE: Don't suppose you even know what it means.

CHRIS: Yes I do.

MIKE: What?

CHRIS: Well-developed.

(*Mike laughs.*)

MIKE: Hah! You'll be lucky if you get O levels. In English anyway. Never heard of Evelyn Waugh. Don't know what nubile means.

CHRIS: What *does* it mean then?

MIKE: Marriageable. So yes, you are.

CHRIS: I *always* thought it meant well-developed.

(*Pause. Mike yawns. Chris turns away.*)

MIKE: You're well-developed, too, I think. For fifteen.

(*She smiles at him. He studies the ground.*)

The picnic site. Stanley's tent.
(*Ivy has switched off the radio.*
Lily and Joyce now sitting.

Stanley is pouring more liqueurs.

Close up of Norman, who turns from staring across the heath.)

NORMAN: If you'll excuse me. Nature calls. Little walk across the heath is indicated.

STANLEY: Why not use my toilet tent?

NORMAN: That's kind of you but I'll—

JOYCE: I should, Norman, and I'll follow you, so don't be long.

NORMAN: No, you go there, I'll commune with the gorse and heather.

STANLEY: Pointless, when the facilities exist.

JOYCE: Hurry up.

(Norman goes to the toilet tent.)

JOYCE: Perhaps we could have the radio on.

STANLEY: Quite. Switch on the radio, Ivy.

IVY: Only just been made to switch it off.

STANLEY: Dear, oh dear, oh Lord! *(He turns the radio on. Noisy bit from a popular aria.)*

JOYCE: Oh, this is gorgeous! Anyone share my love of opera?

IVY: I used to like a good play. Walt and I never missed a play. The last we went to was 'Murder in the Cathedral'.

JOYCE: Oh, yes.

IVY: Walt was fond of a nice mystery. But oh, what a let-down. Nothing but moaning nuns.

STANLEY: Tia Maria for Mrs—um—Lily, pass it to the lady.

(Lily glares at him, passes drink.)

127

JOYCE: Thank you. This *is* civilized.

STANLEY: And Ivy's.

(*Lily passes Ivy's across Joyce.*)

LILY: Excuse me retching, I've just come off the boat—

STANLEY (*Too late*): Sssh ...

(*Lily, made aware of her vulgarity, laughs. Joyce ignores her, passing Ivy's drink.*)

IVY: I shall be tiddley.

JACK: Things are hotting up around here.

JOYCE: My husband and I seldom drink after lunch. Before dinner in the evening perhaps, a sherry or aperitif.

STANLEY: Jack's.

IVY: I'm the same. I always say I can't keep anything intoxicating on my tummy before tea.

JOYCE (*Queenly*): D'you think it's to do with our infantile environment?

(*Ivy looks blank.*)

LILY (*Rising to the occasion*): More likely got some psychosomatic origin.

STANLEY (*Proud*): Hullo, Lily, swallowed the dictionary?

(*Lily laughs happily and exchanges an affectionate glance with Stanley.*)

JACK: How was that again, Lilian? Psycho ... ?

(*They all laugh.*)

LILY: Psycho-somatic. The pee is silent as in bathing.

STANLEY (*Too late*): Sssh ...

(*Lily is miserable at her loss of face.*

128

At the pothole.

Chris sunning her back, eyes shut.

Mike combing hair again. He sneaks a look at her, returning comb to pocket.)

MIKE: We shan't make plans. Trev never does. Just take off. All our gear in a rucksack. Not like Fat Stan, with all these three-piece suites. Might as well not go. Gotta get away from this materialistic desert.

(The picknickers look up as from the road appear three teenage couples wearing the current motor-cycle gear.)

STANLEY: Hullo then. What we got here—a swinging scene?

(Norman returning from toilet tent.)

NORMAN: Listen, Joyce, I'm going after Christine.

JOYCE: Oh?

NORMAN: I'm worried about her.

JOYCE: She's a big girl now.

NORMAN: Exactly—

JOYCE: She can take care of herself.

(The motor cyclists are taking up positions by the speaker.

One of them has a radio playing pop music.)

JOYCE: You may be right. This noise is awful.

STANLEY: Time we were pushing on, too.

(Norman and Joyce prepare to go.)

STANLEY: Got a lot to get through. Weston, Clevedon, Severn Bridge. Perhaps a dekko at the Wildfowl Trust. Don't want to miss that, eh, Jack?

(*Jack dozing, head nodding.*)

LILY: No answer was the stern reply.

CYCLIST: 'The Lord will smite with a scab
The crown of the head of the daughters of Zion.
And the Lord will discover their secret parts.'

YOUNG MAN: Aye, aye. Yer that, Nige?

(*At the pothole, Chris sits up and unfastens her jeans.
While Mike talks she removes them.*)

MIKE: I expect when we feel like it Trev and I will have
women round to the flat. Nothing permanent, I don't
mean. You could come round, if you wanted to, for
instance . . .

(*She has turned her front to the sun. Closing her eyes
again.*

Mike covertly surveys her.)

We're not interested in marriage—Trev and I. It's no
better than a mortgage. Like buying someone on the
H.P. Typical of the commercialism of this society.

(*The young motor cyclists are now lying, sitting,
sprawling in front of the speaker.*

*They fondle and kiss each other and after each en-
counter, tidy and comb their hair.*)

(*A tableau of disgusted elders* :)

IVY: Dirty little devils.

STANLEY: All part of modern materialism.

NORMAN: If my daughter carried on like that, I'd take
her across my knee, big as she is—

JOYCE: Shall we go?

NORMAN: Take her pants down—

(*Joyce leads off to the heath. Norman follows. Stanley is making to follow. Lily goes with him.*)

STANLEY: You coming?

LILY: I thought I might come with you.

STANLEY: No need.

LILY: Stretch my legs.

STANLEY: Please yourself.

(*He is brusque with her. She is subdued, following like the wife of a Bedouin.*)

(*At the pothole, Mike, fascinated by Chris's semi-nudity, talks to postpone action.*)

MIKE: Look what marriage did for Mum. Behind all those clichés you'd hardly know there's a good brain. But there is. Wasted by spending her life with that Philistine. She doesn't even love him. It's just become a habit.

CHRIS: Don't you *like* the sun?

MIKE: Yeah, course.

CHRIS: Take your clothes off then.

MIKE: When I want to.

CHRIS: Nobody can see us.

(*Mike swallows his fear and begins unbuttoning his shirt.*)

(*Stanley and Lily leaving the picnic, making for the heath.*)

LILY: Stan, love, what's the matter? What's Lily done?

STANLEY: What's Lily done? Lily's had a drop too much I should think.

LILY: If I have, you gave it me.

STANLEY: 'The pee is silent as in bathing'! To a woman like that!

LILY: I didn't think. Don't be cross.

(*She tries to put her arms round him.*)

STANLEY: All right, that's enough of that. I'll take a shot of you on that path. When I give the word, start walking.

HOME MOVIE

(*Lily walking on the heath. She stops. Camera pans to follow her gaze.*)

STANLEY: Look at that for colour.

LILY: Beautiful.

IVY: All the different tints.

(*The pan finishes with a long held view of the heath.*

Mike's face watching the film, stricken at the memory.

END OF HOME MOVIE.)

(*At the pothole, Mike's shirt unbuttoned but still on. Chris is sitting up now.*)

CHRIS: What's the matter?

MIKE: What?

CHRIS: Isn't there anything the matter?

MIKE: No.

CHRIS: Take it off then.

MIKE: What if I don't want to?

(*She sulks.*)

CHRIS: I bet if I was Pat Meadows you wouldn't be wasting time like this.

MIKE: Don't expect I would, no. From what they say about Pat Meadows.

CHRIS: Don't you *know*? You always seem to be going around with her.

MIKE: Anyway what about you and Issy Wickham?

(*Pause.*)

CHRIS: What about it?

MIKE: I asked *you*.

CHRIS: It's all over with Issy Wickham.

(*Pause.*)

MIKE: They say Issy doesn't finish with a girl unless . . .

CHRIS: Well?

MIKE: You mean, you really . . .?

CHRIS: Issy's very attractive, but—I don't *like* him. Not the way I like *you*. (*She caresses his chest.*)

(*At the picnic site, the young people are beginning to dance to the music.*)

CYCLIST: The changeable suits of apparel. And it shall come to pass that instead of a sweet smell there shall be stink—

(*One of the men blows a raspberry.*)

YOUNG WOMAN: Innee dirty?

CYCLIST: And instead of a girdle a rent and instead of well-set hair, baldness—

YOUNG MAN: Yer, sod off, matey, thee do give I a pain.

CYCLIST: And burning instead of beauty.

(*At the pothole, Chris has removed Mike's shirt.*)

CHRIS: You said you wanted me.

133

MIKE (*Defensive*): When?

CHRIS: Tuesday lunch-time. In the museum. (*She kisses his ear, his cheek.*) Didn't you mean it?

MIKE: Yeah. Course. I did. Tuesday lunch-time.

CHRIS: Don't you any more?

MIKE: Don't all the time.

(*Mike's face—as if watching the film—but with closed eyes.*)

HOME MOVIE

(*Norman and Joyce moving across the heath. They wave to camera as Stanley zooms in.*

END OF HOME MOVIE.)

(*Norman and Joyce as they were in film.*)

NORMAN: Same when she was little.

JOYCE: Same as what?

NORMAN: You never cared for her. What did you say?

JOYCE: Nothing.

NORMAN: I thought you spoke.

JOYCE: No.

(*Pause. Walk on.*)

NORMAN (*Imitating*): That wretched baby's made a mess on the drawing-room carpet.

(*Pause. Walk on.*)

JOYCE (*Imitating Norman*): I'll change her and clean her up.

NORMAN: Who's that meant to be?

JOYCE: You loved all that side of it.

(*Walk on.*)

134

(*At the pothole, Chris and Mike emerging from a kiss. She pushes him back on the ground.*)

CHRIS: I could eat you up. Don't you want me?

MIKE: Time's getting on.

CHRIS: Didn't you bring anything?

(*He seizes on this.*)

MIKE: No. Well, that's it. I forgot. Sorry. Forgot all about it.

CHRIS: Why didn't you say? I've got one. Issy Wickham gave it me.

(*Lounge.*

Mike's face staring as he watches film.)

(*The pothole. Chris reaches for her jeans. Mike gets up.*)

MIKE: Oh, Christ, women—honestly! (*He runs off.*)

(*Chris stares after him.*)

(*The picnic site.*
Cyclist singing. Motor-cyclists dancing.

Other family finishing puddings. New parties arriving.

Jack and Ivy happy amid the bedlam, sitting by their tent.)

CYCLIST: Guide me, O thou great redeemer, Pilgrim through this barren land—

IVY: I'm always afraid they're going to take advantage—being a woman alone.

JACK: The lodgers?

IVY (*Nods*): I remember one morning Walter brought my cup of tea into my bedroom and I said 'Walt, that new young man—'. He said 'Yes?'. I said 'I believe he's got a dog in there'. He said 'Never'! I said 'Well, if he hasn't he's been making some very funny noises in the night'.

135

(*Mike running from Chris, almost in tears.*

Chris following, as she was, trying to put her shirt on as she runs.

Mike crouches in the shrubbery to look back at her.

Chris stops to button her shirt, trying to catch sight of him.

Mike, moving on again, finds too late that his trousers are caught on the thorn of a bramble; rips a hole in the seat so that a flap hangs down.

He tries to tuck the flap in, hold it up, cover himself as best he can.

His face wet and dirty with tears.

Chris moves into an open path,

Sees Norman and Joyce coming some way off and ducks out of sight.

Mike holding trousers, also sees them, ducks.
He begins running at the crouch.
He stops to look up and find his bearings.

Chris sees him, he sees her. She waves.
He ducks down again.

She would follow but is on the far side of the path and now Norman and Joyce are coming.

Mike makes off again, retracing their tracks.)

NORMAN: All very well for you to call me an old woman . . .

JOYCE: You *are* an old woman.

NORMAN: But if I were a sexual maniac, frankly, I couldn't think of a likelier place for an afternoon's entertainment, what did you say?

JOYCE: Not a thing.

NORMAN: I thought you spoke.

JOYCE: Not a word.

(*They draw level with Chris*.)

(*Stanley's tent again*.)

IVY: When Walter went in, he found a dog, a cat, hamsters. Well, a zoo. Now, of course, no pets is one of my rules. Not because I'm not an animal lover, because I am, but with other people about you can't. So Walter had to tell him to go. But if I'd been alone, you see, he might possibly have turned awkward. Which is where I feel the need of a man.

HOME MOVIE

(*On the heath, Lily looking upwards, shielding her eyes from the sun.*

Pan up to follow her gaze.)

STANLEY: This might be good. See the skylark?

IVY: Can't say I can, no.

LILY: Bit too far away perhaps.

STANLEY: Climbing, climbing, chirupping away.

(*Pause*.)

IVY: It's nice of the sky.

STANLEY: Swooping down now.

(*Camera is attempting to follow the lark's fall. Land comes into view. Searches about for bird. Finally settles.*

STANLEY: I got it but it's not too clear.

(*Quite close, Chris rises from the undergrowth, her back to us, looking for her parents cautiously.*

She turns to face us.)

(*Mike's face watching the film*.)

137

IVY: Well, I never.

JACK: Some skylark.

HOME MOVIE

STANLEY: Never knew she was in the picture.

LILY: Those people's daughter.

JACK: What happened to her pants?

IVY: Slacks.

JACK: How's that?

IVY: We call them slacks.

(*Chris sees Stanley and ducks out of sight.*)

LILY: She looked a bit forward to me. Bit of a roving eye. Like her mother.

(END OF HOME MOVIE.)

(*Mike, running from parents, reaches the pothole where he lay with Chris. Finds his shirt and puts it on. Finds her jeans and pauses, listening.*

Climbs bank, sees Norman and Joyce coming that way. Ducks again, picks up the jeans and makes off in other direction.

At the picnic, one of the young men is performing tricks with the speaker's cycle.

The speaker is making timid attempts to get him off and one of the girls is trying to draw him into the dancing.)

JACK: You own the house.

IVY: Oh yes. Walter's life insurance paid off what was left of the mortgage.

JACK: I got my own place too. In British Columbia.

IVY: You live alone?

JACK: All on my lonesome. It's far too big.

IVY: I wish I could do without the boarders. I lack capital, you see. Capital to play with. What I dream about when I'm in a dreamy mood—you know?—

JACK: Sure. Kinda romantic.

IVY: Is acquiring property on a large scale. You only need a start. I suppose your house is worth a fair bit?

JACK: Yes, I guess so.

IVY: You must come and have tea one day.

JACK: I'd like that.

IVY: See my dresses. They fill two rooms.

JACK: That right?

IVY: And Walter's.

JACK: Walter's dresses?

IVY: Dancing suits. And shoes. What size shoe are you?

JACK: Eight and a half.

IVY: I thought so. Same as Walter.

(*They watch the scene.*

Norman amid the undergrowth. Joyce still on the path.)

JOYCE: I'm not dressed for that. I'll keep to the path.

(*Norman seen from level, suddenly plunges down into the pothole where Chris lay with Mike.*

Stanley and Lily have also taken to the rough. Stanley, seen from the level, plunges down. Lily follows into the pothole.

Stanley steadies Lily as she arrives by him. She pulls him over with her, embraces him.)

STANLEY: Steady on, what you doing?

139

LILY: Long time since you took me for a saunter on the moors.

STANLEY: Oh, come on, woman. Wasting time—

LILY: Where's the fire?

STANLEY: I'm looking for Michael.

LILY: He's not looking for us. And we're not booked at the Severn Bridge. Weston-super-Mare won't have the flags out. (*Tries to kiss him.*)

STANLEY: There's a time and place—

LILY: And this is it, wouldn't you say?

STANLEY: Marvellous what a drop of vino—

LILY: It's not only a drop of vino. It's how I feel. Sentimental.

STANLEY: That boy shouldn't be allowed to go running off wherever he likes. He's supposed to be out with us. Not often we see him and when we do he runs off. He ought to be made to show he's grateful.

LILY: Forget him. He's only a boy. D'you remember that day during the war—(*She pulls him closer.*) You took me down Snuffmills.

STANLEY: Can't remember, no . . .

LILY: Your tunic buttons got caught up in my snood.

STANLEY: Gone right out of my mind . . .

LILY: We'd had a drink. The sun was baking, it was in the July . . . you were hot that day, you wouldn't leave me alone . . .

(*Stanley gets up and moves some paces off.*)

STANLEY: What have I done wrong with Michael? I've no wish to fight with him . . . (*He is really asking her, hoping for an answer.*) I only want him to show he's thankful.

140

LILY: What for? A day out with the family? Something he doesn't want. He's got his own friends, he's not a boy any more.

STANLEY: You said just now he was. You said forget him, he's a boy—

LILY: I don't care. (*She cries.*)

(*Stanley stares, shocked.*

Chris arrives at the pothole where she left her jeans.

Finds that they're gone.

Mike, carrying the jeans, runs from Norman, popping up now and then to look for Chris.

Norman calls across the heath.)

NORMAN: Christine!

(*Mike finds himself at edge of pothole.*
Looks down to see his parents struggling on the ground.

Lily turns away crying, Stanley attempting to embrace her.)

STANLEY: Oh, come on, love—

LILY: Leave me alone.

STANLEY: Lily—

LILY: Don't touch me.

(*But Stanley still tries.*

Mike stands. Stanley sees him, stands, too.)

STANLEY: There you are.

(*Mike drops Chris's jeans behind a bush.*)

Where've you been?

(*Mike runs down into pothole. Stanley and Lily ill at ease.*)

141

We've been looking everywhere for you. It's time—

(*Mike ignores him, speaks to Lily.*)

MIKE: I've torn my trousers.

LILY: How d'you manage that?

STANLEY: Acting the goat?

(*Lily looks at his trousers.*)

MIKE: On a thorn.

STANLEY: When you going to learn to take a pride in things? Where d'you think the money—

LILY: Sssh. I can darn it.

STANLEY: Right. Let's be pressing on regardless.

(*Starts up the bank. Lily follows. Stanley goes out of sight.*)

LILY: Come on, Mike.

MIKE: Why?

LILY: Well—

MIKE: What?

LILY: Please your father.

MIKE: Please—him? Don't forget—I saw him—just now. Neurgh!

LILY: He's fond of you.

MIKE: Hah!

LILY: Really. (*Sees he won't believe that.*) Come on.

(*Mike glances to where he left Chris's jeans. Then goes on with Lily in other direction.*

As Mike climbs into the open, he looks about for Chris. Sees Norman and Joyce at a distance.

No sign of Chris.
Zoom in on Norman and Joyce.)

142

(*A new pothole with a cave: Chris running down. She crouches listening to her parents, talking above.*)

JOYCE: My stockings are ruined.

NORMAN: Thought you were keeping to the path. Christine!

(*Chris, staring up, backs against the bank. Sees cave opening and retreats into it.*

Norman appears at top of hole, runs down into it.

Joyce waves across the heath at Stanley. She comes to the edge of the hole, speaks down to Norman.)

JOYCE: Those other people are going. Their boy's with them.

(*Chris, inside the cave, listening.*

Norman sees the cave, moves closer to look. Joyce stands at edge.)

JOYCE: What are you doing in that hole?

(*Chris moves farther into the cave. She is then equally alarmed by noises seeming to come from deeper in the cave—dragging, heavy breathing, the falling of a stone, all amplified by the echoing passage.*

Norman stands outside the cave.)

NORMAN: Any sign of her up there?

JOYCE: No. We've missed her. She's back at the car by now.

NORMAN: Go back then. I'll go on looking here.

(*Chris in cave:*

The noises drawing nearer.)

JOYCE: What an imagination!

NORMAN: You haven't *seen* the way men look at her.

Here's a notice: Mendip Caving. In case of emergency—

(*Chris rushes from the cave.*)

CHRIS: Daddy! In there!

(*Joyce runs down bank. Chris goes to her. Norman turns to cave.*)

JOYCE: Where are your jeans? Who is it?

(*A young man emerges, dressed as a potholer. Takes off helmet. Blinks in the daylight.*)

POTHOLER: Afternoon.

(*Norman knocks him down.*

Chris screams.

At the picnic site, pop music very loud and several couples dancing, including Jack and Ivy.

The speaker has his bicycle and has wheeled it to a safe distance, near Stanley's tent. He is shouting at the dancers but Jack and Ivy hear it most.

Ivy is teaching Jack the steps, smiling when he tramples on her.)

CYCLIST: I say therefore to the unmarried and the widows, it is good for them if they abide even as I. But if they cannot contain, let them marry. For it is better to marry than to burn.

(*Stanley, Lily and Mike arriving near the picnic. No dialogue audible over the loud pop music, which is now incidental, not practical.*

Mike sees the canvas village, with a new family arriving with their gear. He refuses to go through.

Lily speaks to Stanley and Stanley argues but soon goes towards the car.

Mike looks back over the heath.

Chris and her parents coming along the path. Chris apparently explaining her state.

Stanley, on his way through picnic site to cars, speaks to Ivy and Jack, dancing.

Motor cyclists drink, smoke, pet one another.

Stanley returns, now carrying a mac.

Jack and Ivy packing up.

Mike walks back through camp with mac on.

Several of the cyclists notice this and laugh.

The cyclists try to interest their friends in the incident, but they are too intent on embracing, kissing, rolling over one another and combing their hair.

Chris and parents arrive.

Norman looks at the throng, tells Chris to wait out of sight and goes on through, taking Joyce with him.)

HOME MOVIE

(Jack, Lily and Ivy strike tent. The actual moment of collapse. Then pan round to a general view of the camp.)

END OF HOME MOVIE.

(At the roadside, Norman is in his car, in driving seat; wriggles for a few moments, then hands Joyce his trousers through the window.

She goes off with them.

Norman pretends nonchalance, lights cigarette, smiles at Mike in next car, wearing mac.

Stanley and party arrive with tent and load it into boot.

Chris walks through the picnic site wearing Norman's trousers. She helps Joyce carry their furniture back to car.

145

Cyclist rolls up banner, stows it, wheels his pushbike to the road.

Other cyclists bump and grind to the music.

Chris and Joyce get into their car.

Mike, alone in car, notes Chris's trousers. Elaborate exchange of glances between the aborted lovers. Mostly Mike can't meet her eyes.

Stanley and company arrive with last of gear.)

HOME MOVIE

(Joyce waves to camera as Norman backs the car out, Jack waving him on, walking backwards, finally falling over as he loses balance. Camera dwells on his fall and then moves off with Norman's car as it retreats through the combe.

Cyclist launches off.)

Lounge.

(Mike's face as the car goes.)

HOME MOVIE. *Burrington Combe.*

(Seen from front seat of moving car, a good deal of traffic coming.

END OF HOME MOVIE.)

(Stanley's car waiting on B road at a T-junction for a gap in the long stream of returning traffic. He sees one and swings across and round, as the next car quickly pulls forward to fill the gap.

Collision.

Stanley gets out, inspects damage, seeing that the other car is Norman's.

Norman remains in driving seat.

Stanley directs oncoming traffic for a moment, then asks Mike to take over.

Mike refuses, shakes his head, so Jack has to do it.

Ivy, Lily, Mike remain.

Stanley now asks Norman to get out, even attempting to open the door so that Norman has no choice.

Sees Norman's bare legs and allows the door to be pulled shut.

Norman has urgent conversation with Chris and Joyce.

Chris begins struggling inside car to take off Norman's trousers.

Jack directs traffic hazardously.

Mike, in nearside window, watches Chris's contortions on their offside mirror.

Stanley has fetched camera and begins to film the scene for insurance purposes.)

HOME MOVIE

The collision from various angles, almost stills.

Norman, in the driving seat, wriggling into his trousers.

END OF HOME MOVIE.

(Stanley and Norman meeting and arguing the case.

The women smiling at each other from their cars.

On offside, a police car arrives and a policeman takes over from Jack and tries to get the traffic moving again.

On nearside, the evangelist cycles swiftly along the inside of the stationary cars.

Mike and Chris look at each other from their seats.

Follow the cyclist in various locations.

Traffic jammed most of the way, but he goes comfortably through it, a blacksuited puritan—across the Avon, into Hotwells, back to the non-conformist city at the end of a good day's work.)

Fade out

JOHN BOWEN

Robin Redbreast

Preface

JOHN BOWEN was born in Calcutta in 1924. His television plays include: *A Holiday Abroad, The Candidate, The Essay Prize, The Jackpot Question, Nuncle, The Truth About Alan, A Case of Character, Mr Fowlds, The Corsican Brothers, The First Thing You Think Of, Silver Wedding, The Whole Truth, A Most Unfortunate Accident, The Waiting Room, A Woman Sobbing, The Coffee Lace, Now Lies She There, The Emergency Channel.* He has also written scripts for the following series: *Front Page Story, The Power Game, The Guardians* and *The Villains,* and adapted the Somerset Maugham story, *Flotsam and Jetsam.*

'I began the Introduction to *The Essay Prize,* my own first volume of television plays (it did not sell well: there was never a second) with the question, "Why Write For Television?" and the answer I gave was that a television play is the only way by which a writer can "share a kind of insight, a way of looking at life, an enjoyment of the complexity of human motives, the ambivalence of human behaviour ... with those many people who do not have the habit of reading books", far less of going to the theatre.

'Well, that is still true, but I was ten years younger then, and more easily swayed by my own rhetoric. The answer ignores the way television plays are sent out to this non-book-reading, non-theatre-going audience, as part of a continuous stew made up of items so diverse that they would be indigestible if anyone ever bothered to digest them. But the audience in general does not digest them. No effort is required of it, hardly even the effort of choice; no response is expected. The stew—your play, bobbing about in it—is received, excreted and forgotten. Nourishment is not a consideration.

'Indeed, the stew-givers, both of the BBC and the commercial companies, often try to exclude even the possibility of nourishment. This play, *Robin Redbreast*, was first commissioned as a "suspense" play by the Series Department of the BBC and rejected. The producer is a kind and intelligent man: he was distressed to have to reject a play he admired, but the "close inter-relation between the fertility rite and the church festivals" would be too much, he wrote, for "the Powers-That-Be". Something taught in school sixth forms all over the country would be "too much" for the BBC Series Department. Luckily Graeme McDonald, who produces *Play for Today* for the BBC Drama Department, heard of the play, read it and instantly took it on.

'Worst is the lack of a continuing life. All my novels except the last are out of print, but they are still borrowed (freely in every sense) from libraries. Dedicated amateurs win prizes at Drama Festivals with plays I wrote years ago. Films are shown throughout the world long after they have been made, and end on that very television which shows a play once, perhaps (but only on the BBC) repeats it, then wipes the tape, and the play, already forgotten by its audience, even ceases to exist as an artefact. Dead. All other forms of art continue to exist after the act of creation and first showing, except the television play. Unless, as Pinter, Peter Nichols, John Mortimer, John Hale, Alun Owen have done—and I myself with this play—the writer reworks it for the theatre, and gives it a life after all.

'And yet . . . and yet. I say that, if I could afford to write only for the theatre I should do so, and certainly no television play could ever give author, actors and audience the real joy which is created when play, performance and audience come together in a threatre and all goes well. But there are ways of writing for television, ways of using images which, however I may free myself from realistic theatrical production, I can't match in the theatre. I admire naturalistic acting, and television can show it more closely than someone in whatever-shaped auditorium can see from six rows back. I say nowadays that I write television plays in order to buy time to write in other ways, but nobody writes only for money, and nobody would fret so about getting it right if money were the only consideration. There is still the possibility of excellence, and even if a television play ends up as a truffle in the stew, to be swallowed unrecognized by most, complained of by some ("What's this bit of coal doing in my stew?"), someone out there may yet know a truffle when he sees it, and savour it, and be glad.'

JOHN BOWEN

Robin Redbreast was first presented by BBC Television
on 10 December, 1970,* with the following cast:

N O R A H P A L M E R	*Anna Cropper*
M A D G E	*Amanda Walker*
J A K E	*Julian Holloway*
M R S V I G O	*Freda Bamford*
F I S H E R	*Bernard Hepton*
R O B	*Andrew Bradford*
P E T E R	*Cyril Cross*
M R W E L L B E L O V E D	*Robin Wentworth*

Produced by Graeme McDonald
Directed by James MacTaggart

* It was later sold to the New Zealand Broadcasting
Commission.

Characters

NORAH PALMER
MADGE
JAKE
MRS VIGO
FISHER
PETER
ROB
MR WELLBELOVED
A TELEVISION ANNOUNCER
A FREE-THINKING BISHOP } Voices
A LOCAL TELEPHONE OPERATOR } only
(In fact Mrs Gibbins of the
Post Office)

Settings: A Cottage in Warwickshire and two London
flats.

1

Interior. Madge and Jake's living room. Night.

(Madge and Jake are a married couple in their mid-thirties. He is a television producer. She works as fashion editor for an up-market women's magazine. They are old friends of Norah Palmer, whom they have been entertaining to dinner.

The room is furnished from Heals and Habitat. There is a Patrick Proctor aquarelle on the wall, and a print by Matisse, and maybe a small Frink head on the mantel.

There is a fire, burning smokeless fuel.

Norah and Madge sit together on the sofa, Jake in an armchair. All three have glasses of brandy.

But begin on a photograph of a manifestly unconverted country cottage. No other houses are in sight.

The landscape appears to be bleak.)

NORAH (*Heard*): That's the 'before' picture.

MADGE (*Heard*): It looks rather desolate.

NORAH (*Heard*): It's isolated, if that's what you mean.

JAKE (*Heard*): And the 'after'?

(Now we see them.)

NORAH: What?

JAKE: What it looks like now. After all the work.

NORAH: I haven't taken an 'after'.

JAKE: Oh!

NORAH: Well, it was Peter's camera, you know.

(Pause. Madge puts down the photograph.)

157

MADGE: My dear, you could always buy another.

(*Norah looks from one to the other.*)

NORAH: I've got very prickly, haven't I?

JAKE: Not really.

NORAH: That means I have. Well, I don't mean it. Not with you. Prickles are useful sometimes. Now I'm a single woman again, I'm always having to resist passes.

MADGE: Lucky you! I've been lusting after one of the window cleaners for weeks, and he never gives me so much as a flick of his chammy.

JAKE: I thought *I* might make a pass at Norah. I thought, next time you were out of the room, I'd sidle over for a quick cuddle.

MADGE: Go and get the coffee, you lecherous owl.

(*Jake goes.*

As he does.)

He already has, I take it.

NORAH (*Grins*): Not really.

(*Jake has gone.*)

MADGE: We were all single women once, love.

NORAH: I know. But it's different, Madge: You know it is. When you and I were young. . .

MADGE: Thank you.

NORAH: Younger. People made passes; of course they did. But we weren't fair game, then. An unattached woman of thirty-five is fair game. If I go out to dinner with someone or to the theatre, and then reject a heavy pass, he feels cheated, because 'I know what I'm doing', you see. And then I've just broken up with my feller, so I'm expected to be randy. Which God knows I am often. And living with Peter, well naturally I developed defences . . .

(*Jake returns with coffee and cups on a tray.*

Madge who didn't like him.)

MADGE: Yes.

NORAH: But they were only defences against *him*. So now we've broken up, I'm all soft and exposed.

JAKE: Like a little unshelled crab. Delicious.

(*He pours the coffee.*

Madge picks up the photograph again.)

MADGE: And you're really going to live in the cottage?

NORAH: I'm landed with it.

JAKE: Sell it.

NORAH: I don't want to.

JAKE: Then you're not landed with it. You want it.

NORAH: No, I don't want it, and I don't want to sell it. I'm sorry: I know that's silly.

(*Jake looks at Madge, and shrugs.*)

MADGE: Why couldn't Peter have kept it? If one of you had to buy the other out, it might as well . . .

NORAH: He didn't want it.

MADGE: You said *you* didn't.

NORAH: I hate waste.

(*Jake laughs.*)

Yes, love, yes. That's what kept Peter and me going for so long. I wouldn't cut my losses, and say, 'That's five years of my life down the drain. I'll start again.' So I kept working at it, and after eight years, he cut *his* losses. And it's such a waste! (*She begins to cry suddenly.*) Oh, blast!

(*Madge signs for Jake to go, but Norah stops him.*)

Don't go: I'm all right. I cry very easily nowadays,

159

THE TELEVISION DRAMATIST

and stop very easily. There you are: I've stopped.
We'll talk about the cottage. Anything.

JAKE: I'm not sure what there is to say about it.

NORAH: It's *there*: that's the most obvious thing. Four
miles from the village, a mile from the road. And I'm
going to live in it for a while. I've got to get used to
living on my own, as it seems.

(*Track in to the photograph again.*)

(*Heard.*) It's clearly a good place to start.

(*The noise of the waste-disposal unit is heard, and the
sound continues over to the next scene.*)

2

Interior. The kitchen of the cottage. Day.

(*Begin on the waste disposal unit.*

*Then we see Norah's hand, switching it off, Norah is
in the kitchen with Mrs Vigo, a village woman who
has been hired to come in and help with the cleaning.*)

NORAH: It's a waste-disposal unit.

MRS VIGO: What do you put in it, then?

NORAH: Well, not your hand is the most important
thing. It won't do bottles and cans, so we'll keep them
in a carrier bag, and I'll take them to Evesham whenever I go, and drop them in a litter-bin.

MRS VIGO: You reckon to live here, then?

NORAH: Why not?

(*Silence.*

Mrs Vigo looks away.)

You thought I'd just be using it as a weekend cottage?

MRS VIGO: It's not up to me to think. I mean, that's
your affair.

160

NORAH: No. please. I didn't mean to be rude, Mrs Vigo. You're right. Obviously I shall have to go back to London eventually, and take a job again, and just come here at weekends. But for the time being, I do plan to live here. And if you could come in ... two afternoons a week, say?

MRS VIGO: What job do you do, then?

NORAH: I'm a Script Editor.

(*Mrs Vigo doesn't understand.*)

I edit scripts. For television, you know.

(*There is a sudden scraping, rattling sound as if in one corner of the ceiling.*

Both look up, startled.)

I'm sorry. I don't know what that is. It's been happening lately.

MRS VIGO: It's mice, isn't it?

NORAH: Is it?

MRS VIGO: Fieldmice. They'm come in for the warm. No harm in that. (*She pokes suddenly at the sugar basin with her finger, disclosing a small brown stain on the sugar.*) That's right; you left that out last night I daresay; you can see the droppings.

(*Norah appalled.*)

As long as it's not rats. They'm vicious. (*She looks about.*) You don't get much company here, I reckon. I wouldn't fancy it myself.

3

Interior. Madge and Jake's living room. Evening.

(*Jake is pouring them both a glass of sherry from a decanter.*)

MADGE: She doesn't get *any* company, as far as I can see.

(*Jake brings the glasses.*)

JAKE: What does she do all day?

MADGE: Sits about. (*Takes glass.*) I hope she's not going to start drinking. (*Drinks.*)

Telecine 1: Exterior junction of made and unmade road. Day.

(*This is where an unmade road leads off the B-Road to Norah's cottage. It has a white-painted gate (always left open) and a box for letters on the gate. The name of the cottage, 'Flaneathan Farm' is painted on the box.*

Norah is taking a letter from the box. She locks the box afterwards, and walks down the road to the cottage (out of sight), opening the letter and beginning to read. She smiles at what she reads.)

NORAH (*Voice over*): No, I'm drinking much less than . . .

4

Montage. Videotape. Cottage interior. Day and night.
(*This is a montage of scenes inside the cottage.*

Norah's voice overlaps from the previous telecine, and overlaps the montage as a whole.

The scenes mix from one to another, and it might be an idea to slow down all the action, to try to get a drifting timeless feel.

The cottage interior comprises, on the ground floor, a kitchen, and a living room with an open stair to the

*first floor. The front door opens straight into the living room, and there is a side door from it to the garden.
The kitchen has been thoroughly modernized, and is divided by a partition into an eating and cooking area —double sink, fridge, very up-to-date electric oven and grill, storage cupboards in plenty.*

A scrubbed pine table in the eating area, set against a large window, looking out to the patio outside.

The living room has an ingle-nook, large wood-burning fireplace, beams, one wall of bare stone, the others white plaster, a deep sofa, two armchairs, T.V., bookshelves, a large window also looking out on to the patio. Since the cottage is set on a hillside, the patio itself is a paved area below the road by which one approaches. It has the cottage wall behind it, a garage wall to one side and a bank topped by a hedge on a third. It makes a kind of sun-trap.

Anyone standing on the drive leading down to the garage is above anyone sunbathing on the patio, and will have a hedge and sky behind him.

The bathroom (bath, bidet, w.c., washbasin: white plaster), and two bedrooms are on the first floor. There may be an attic above, which we never see.)

NORAH (*Voice over*): ... one does in London.

(*Norah is sitting at the kitchen table, writing a letter. She stops writing, and looks up, day dreaming.*)

Everything seems to be slowed ...

(*The bed, unmade.*)

... down. I sleep late. It's amazing how much one can sleep.

(*At the bedroom window, pulling the curtains and looking out. She is in pyjamas.*

Turning away.)

Twelve hours often.

163

(Back in the kitchen. Breakfast debris on the table. She gets up and goes into the living room. As she crosses from one room to the other, she feels something on her face, and puts her hand up to it. She turns to look at the corner of the wall by the door.

We see a spider's web, and go in close to the spider.)

I drift about the cottage.

(Might be larky to match mix to a clip from some old horror film, now on telly . . . some spider equivalent.

Norah is in the living room curled up on the sofa, watching telly, curtains drawn, fire blazing.)

In the evenings, I watch the telly, everything. Old films, Panorama, . . .

(Bring up sound sharply: voices chanting: 'Open the box. Open the box.')

. . . Michael Miles.

(Norah shrugs, and switches over. As she does so, there is the rattle which we already know is mice.

Sound of the mice in the corner.

Norah looks up in that direction.)

Did I tell you I have mice?

(Kitchen.

A beetle turned on its back on the window-seat.)

Insects. Everything.

(Norah picks up the beetle gingerly, opens the window, and drops the beetle out on to the patio.

She notices something on the exterior of the window-sill. It is a large striped glass marble, cut in half. Establish it. It should look a little like an eye.

Norah picks it up examining it curiously.

She shrugs, and puts it down on the partition dividing the kitchen area.)

164

Kitchen.

Norah reading, and eating a boiled egg.)

And I read a lot, of course.

(*Living room.*

Norah sitting in the window-seat, a rainy sky behind her.)

Indoors, when it's wet.

Telecine 2: Exterior. Patio. Day.

(*Norah sitting in a deck chair, reading:*)

And if there's the least bit of sun . . .

(*Fisher, standing on the drive, looking at her.*)

I'm out on the patio . . .

(*Back to Norah, reading.*)

. . . soaking it up.

FISHER (*Heard*): I wonder if I might hunt for sherds in your garden.

(*Norah is startled, and looks up.*

Fisher is a man in his late thirties. He wears boots and breeches, with a shirt and collar and a Norfolk jacket. Perhaps he wears a cap. He has rimless spectacles. He carries a stick . . . maybe it looks like a water diviner's wand. His accent is local, agricultural midlands, overlaid with the genteel. During this conversation we may be aware of Mrs Vigo, indoors, mopping the kitchen floor, preparatory to polishing it with Cardinal.)

NORAH: What?

FISHER: Sherds. One often finds them, you know, in freshly turned earth.

NORAH: Sherds?

FISHER: I have an archaeological interest. I'm a student of that, in my own time. Old things generally.

NORAH: I don't think there are any old things in the garden, but what the builders left . . . old beer cans and broken bottles mainly. But you're welcome to look.

FISHER: You haven't noticed anything yourself as you walked about? Some small sherd or other?

NORAH: I'm not sure I should recognize a sherd if I were to see one.

FISHER: It takes a trained eye. I was watching a programme on the television—Mrs Vigo tells me you have connections in that field . . .

(*Norah gives him a look over her shoulder at the kitchen window.*)

NORAH: Yes.

FISHER: It was about fishing for clams, a documentary programme. They spot the whereabouts of the clam by a small blow-hole in the sand. They have an instinct. It's the same with me. Roman pottery. Coins. Sherds of all sorts. I have *that* instinct. And that is strange, Mrs Palmer . . .

NORAH: Miss.

FISHER: Yes . . . 'miss': one likes to be sure. That is strange, Miss Palmer, because *my* name is Fisher, and yet I have never been to the seaside, nor any of my family. The Fishers have never been out of the village for hundreds of years. Except in time of war.

NORAH: I'm sorry.

FISHER: And what of the birds, Miss Palmer? Do they trouble you?

NORAH: I don't understand.

FISHER: Ah, you're confused, because of the rhyme. Sherds and birds; that is amusing. Sherds in the garden —as we hope—and birds in the house.

166

(*Norah looks at him warily, having begun to believe that he is barmy.*)

(*Explaining.*) Trapped. The cottage has been empty so long before you came. Women have always lived here, but not for some time, you see. I've frequently found birds, trapped inside.

NORAH: You've been here before?

FISHER: Indeed, yes; I get about. The birds would come in by the chimney, and be unable to escape. They'd beat against the windows, and after a while, expire.

NORAH: Most of the window-panes were broken when we . . . when I bought this cottage.

FISHER: Exactly. They should have known they had a way out, but being mere birds, didn't. That's what it means, you know, in the old tongue—'Flaneathan'— the Place of the Birds; that's its name.

NORAH: 'Flaneathan Farm'.

FISHER: 'Bird Place'. Or 'Place of Birds' as I prefer. You don't speak the Old Tongue, I suppose?

NORAH: If you mean Anglo-Saxon, not since Oxford.

FISHER: No, it's not much spoken. And never written, of course. I'll just take a look round, then, with your permission. (*He goes off, down the drive, behind the garage.*)

(*Norah rises and looks after him, bemused.*)

NORAH: Mind the nettles. (*Norah goes into the house.*) (*Pick her up in:*)

5

Interior. The kitchen. Day.

NORAH: Who's that?

167

MRS VIGO: That's Fisher, isn't it?

NORAH: Is he off his head?

MRS VIGO: No, he'm works for the Council, over to Evesham. (*She looks at the marble on the partition.*) You brought that inside the house, then?

NORAH: Yes. What is it?

MRS VIGO: Half a marble, isn't it? A glass marble, cut in half.

NORAH: Rather large for a marble.

MRS VIGO: They am large, that size.

(*Norah picks it up.*)

That's right. You hold it. Keep it warm. They'm like jewels. They like the body-warmth.

(*As Norah looks from Mrs Vigo to the marble. Then back to her.*)

FISHER (*Heard*): I'll be on my way, then.

(*Again Norah is startled. She turns to see him at the window.*)

You won't find anything in that garden earlier than the seventeenth century. Civil war trash.

NORAH: Mr Fisher, the garden is overgrown with nettles and dock, ground elder and convolvulous. You cannot possibly pretend to know whether . . .

FISHER: I've got the instinct, haven't I?

MRS VIGO: That's Fisher, isn't it? He'm got the instinct. Known for it.

(*Norah still has the marble clenched in her fist.*)

FISHER: You brought it inside the house, then?

(*Norah unclenches her fist slowly, to reveal the marble.*)

NORAH: How did you know it was outside?

FISHER: You wouldn't find that inside. It has to be brought in.

NORAH: Has to be?

FISHER: Looks like an eye, doesn't it? But it's only a marble, cut in half.

(*The rattle of mice again. They all look up.*)

I heard you had vermin. If I was you, I should take a walk through the woods. Up along the bridle path to the right, and back by the game-keeper's cottage: that's where I should go, if I was troubled with vermin. It used to be all oak round here, you know, but the Forestry, they don't like the old trees. Cut them down, burn them up, turn them into paper, and plant conifers: that's the Forestry way. You'll go far into they woods before you find an oak nowadays.

(*He goes. Norah looks after him.*)

NORAH: And what did he mean by that?

MRS VIGO: Oh, he'm a learned fellow, Fisher. You can't tell what he means.

Telecine 3: Exterior. Early evening. The woods and gamekeeper's cottage.

(*Norah walking through the woods. Background of bird song. She hears a noise... a distant regular* thwack! thwack! *She doesn't know what it is. She moves towards the direction she thinks it is coming from, uncertain.*

There is a clearing in the trees, where a cottage stands. In the garden of the cottage, a post has been set up.

What seems at first to be a naked man (though in fact he wears a black jock-strap and plimsolls) is striking at the post with the side of his hand, practising

169

toughening-up exercises: this accounts for the noise. The man is Rob.

Norah stops amazed.

Rob seems to sense her presence. He turns to look at her. He is an extremely good-looking man in his early twenties. Silence, broken only by bird-song.

Then Rob turns back to his exercises, striking at the post, ignoring her.

We see Norah, hurrying away! and the sound of the thwack! thwack! *fading into the distance. But this sound does overlap into the next scene, where it becomes the sound of a labourer, Peter, chopping logs.)*

6

Interior. The kitchen. Day.

(Mrs Vigo is washing-out drying-up cloths.)

MRS VIGO: Doing his exercises, wasn't he?

NORAH: I don't know, Mrs Vigo. Was he?

MRS VIGO: That's Rob. Karate. He'm known for it.

NORAH: Does he have to be naked?

(Mrs Vigo turns and looks at her, dead-pan, pause.)

MRS VIGO: Naked, was he?

NORAH: Well, he had something on ... But to all intents and purposes ...

MRS VIGO: Ah! What did you think to him, then?

(Pause.)

NORAH: I hope I don't understand you.

MRS VIGO: Stands to reason. If you'm got vermin, Rob's your man. 'You take the path by the game-keeper's cottage,' Fisher said. That's Rob's job, isn't it.

170

That's what he'm trained for. Rats, rabbits, foxes: that am skilled work, controlling them.

(*Rattle of the mice. Norah looks up.*)

You've not controlled them.

NORAH: They're only mice.

MRS VIGO (*Smiles*): That's right, vermin.

NORAH: I've been meaning to put poison down, as you know.

(*She looks out of the window. We see:*)

Telecine 4: Exterior. Patio. Day.

(*Peter, an elderly labourer, chopping logs with a two-headed axe.*

Looks up and gives her an oafish, gap-toothed grin, before continuing to chop.)

7

Interior. The kitchen. Day.

NORAH: I'm sure that man's mental. (*Bursts out, returning to the topic under discussion.*) Really I think Mr Fisher might have ... I mean there must be easier ways of getting in touch with ... One can hardly walk straight up to a naked man and say, 'Please get rid of my mice'. Isn't he employed by somebody?

(*Noise of chopping stops. Meanwhile:*)

MRS VIGO: Works for the estate, don't he?

NORAH: I'll talk to the Estate Office. I suppose it is quite a good idea to get a professional.

MRS VIGO (*Smiles*): That's right.

(*Norah is puzzled and worried. She looks out of the window again.*)

Telecine 5: Exterior. The patio. Day.

(*The axe, left stuck in the chopping-block. Camera move in so that we see the double-head.*)

8

Interior. Living room. Day.

(*Norah is giving Rob coffee.*)

ROB: You're an educated woman, aren't you?

(*This isn't a question, but an explanation of why he has said something.*)

NORAH: Yes . . . Yes, I am.

ROB: There's nobody educated around here. I was the only boy in the whole village to go on to Grammar School. The first in eight years. It's all in-breeding and inter-marriage around here. They're stupid.

NORAH: You don't have many friends, I take it.

(*Pause. He looks at her.*)

ROB: I don't have any friends.

NORAH: But at the Agricultural College . . .

ROB: I've left there, haven't I? I wouldn't make friends around here.

NORAH: Why did you come back?

ROB: You go where there's a job offered.

NORAH: One doesn't pick and choose? (*No reply.*) I mean, couldn't one apply to . . . Well, anywhere, any-

where in England? Or abroad? Somewhere under-
developed.

ROB: I would have gone to Canada, but I didn't have
the fare. I'm saving for it.

NORAH: Don't they have assisted passages for qualified
people?

(*Pause. He puts down his coffee cup, and stands.*)

ROB: You won't have any more trouble. You could of
put the poison down yourself, as a matter of fact.

NORAH: I've offended you. How?

ROB: It's harmless to human beings and they won't die
in the wall. They come out to die.

NORAH: It's asking questions, isn't it. I've been impertinent.

ROB: You should have had your pipes lagged properly
if you didn't want mice.

NORAH: Rob, please.

ROB: That's not my name.

NORAH: I'm sorry. They didn't give me any name but
Rob.

ROB: They call me Rob in the village. I answer to it,
to save trouble.

NORAH: Please sit down. I don't have any friends either.

(*Pause. He sits down saying.*)

ROB: My name's 'Edgar'. (*Small pause.*) I'm not qualified. I failed the finals.

NORAH: Let me give you some more coffee.

ROB: Thank you.

(*As she pours coffee.*)

NORAH: I do have friends in London, of course, but
I don't like them very much. My own life is in rather

173

a mess, Edgar. That matters at my age, but it's not really disastrous. I shall start again. And it won't take *you* long, you know, to save up enough for Canada.

ROB: What happened? (*Quickly.*) You don't have to tell me.

NORAH: I was living with someone for eight years, and it broke up.

ROB: Divorced?

NORAH: We weren't married.

(*Disapproval from Rob.*)

You don't approve: perhaps you're right. It seemed the best thing to us, but clearly it's ended badly.

ROB: It's not my business.

NORAH: Anyway, what I'm trying to say is, that because I thought I'd failed at something, and didn't know how to face people . . . because in my own case I found that people were either over-sympathetic, or really rather unscrupulous, or just simply uncomfortable at being with me . . . or I thought so, which probably made them so . . . anyway, I gave up my job and came to live here on my own. But I shall go back, and start again. I shan't waste the rest of my life.

(*Rob thinking. Pause.*)

ROB: I finished the course, you know. I wasn't thrown out.

NORAH: Can't you take the exam again?

ROB: I don't want to. They had no right to fail me. (*Pause.*) I don't mind if you call me 'Rob'. Everyone else does.

NORAH: Why?

ROB: I don't know. Can't remember. I was only six when I was adopted. Then, when I applied to Agricultural College, they wanted my birth certificate, and I found out what my name was.

NORAH: Who adopted you?

ROB (*Surprised she doesn't know*): Auntie Vigo.

(*Pause. Norah astonished.*)

NORAH: *My* Mrs . . . ?

ROB: She's got six of her own. I suppose the orphanage thought that made her suitable.

(*Sees Norah still can't take it in.*)

I mean, she got paid. It's not like being really adopted, you could say. I never called her 'Mum' or anything like that.

NORAH: Just . . . 'Auntie Vigo'?

ROB: She didn't stint me. Not for food or anything, or the uniform for the Grammar; it all cost money. She's all right. I don't remember my real mother.

NORAH: But you don't live with her.

ROB: No, I'm on my own now: I prefer that. She comes in, and cleans. (*Looks around*.) Just like she does for you. More like a servant in a way, than my Auntie. I don't belong down there, you see, not in the village. Now I've gone to college, it's raised me. I'm more like you, aren't I?

(*Pause.*)

NORAH: Yes . . . Just a minute.

(*She gets up and goes into:*)

9

Interior. Kitchen. Day.

(*She picks up the glass eye, and brings it back to:*)

175

10

Interior. Living room. Day.

NORAH: What do you make of this?

(*He takes it and examines it.*)

ROB: It's a marble, cut in half. One of thev—one of the large size. You don't see them often.

NORAH: You can't think of any reason whv I should bring it indoors?

ROB (*Surprised*): I don't know. It's pretty I suppose: the colours. I mean, you see things like this in the Sunday papers don't you. There was a girl I once went out with used to read *House and Garden*. An ornament.

NORAH: Would *you*?

ROB: What?

NORAH: If you found it on your window-sill, would you bring it inside?

ROB: Why would . . .

NORAH (*Impatient*): I don't know. If you did.

ROB: I'd want to know how it got there.

NORAH: But would you bring it indoors?

ROB: I'd throw it away, wouldn't I? I mean, it's no use to anyone. (*Smiles.*) But then, I'm not a woman.

(*Pause.*

Norah realizes the extent to which she is attracted to him. He notices this.)

NORAH: No, you're not.

11

Interior. Lounge. Day.

(A large jug with ice in it.

Tall glasses.

Madge and Jake are week-end guests.)

NORAH: He is quite extraordinarily dishy. I go around feeling like Lady Chatterley all the time, and having to hold myself in.

JAKE: Why bother, if you fancy him?

NORAH: Really, Jake!

JAKE: You're a free woman.

NORAH: People would talk, for one thing. As far as I can see, there's no privacy at all in the country. Whatever you do, wherever you go, everybody knows.

JAKE: If you're going to feel like Lady Chatterley, the woods are traditional. Some mossy glade, where you could feel the rough touch of the earth on your backside.

MADGE: Rough touch of the nettles, more likely.

NORAH (*A trace of unease at the conversation*): There are far too many people in the woods.

(Both are surprised.)

MADGE: People?

NORAH: One gets that feeling. Like being watched.

(Pause.

They are still looking at her, surprised. She becomes a little cross.)

Well, there *are* people; bound to be. Rob himself, he has a cottage there. And ... and ... forestry people. It's not a desert.

Telecine 6: Exterior. Woods seen from the cottage. Day.

JAKE (*Voice over*): It's not exactly Charing Cross Station either.

12

NORAH: I can't explain it. It's just a feeling.

JAKE: *I* understand. (*He finishes his drink and looks around.*) Pity! It's nice here.

NORAH: Now, Jake . . .

JAKE: No, I do know. I know exactly. You've begun to get that feeling, and it's no good. You'll have to sell up.

MADGE: Eh?

JAKE: There's a medical name for it, I expect. Something-or-other phobia. I'd lie awake all night listening to the voices.

NORAH: What voices?

JAKE: In the wind, my dear.

(*Madge doesn't understand, and is worried.*)

NORAH: It wasn't windy last night. How do you know there is a wind?

JAKE: There is, though.

NORAH: Sometimes.

JAKE: It comes down the hill, through the trees. It comes down that nasty little private road of yours, whipping in and out of the pot-holes. You hear the voices. Drunken voices, singing. Shouting things. Frightened women. A child— (*Shudders.*) Ugh!

(*Norah rises and picks up the jug.*)

178

NORAH: I don't hear any such thing. I'll get some more of this. (*She goes out.*)

MADGE: That wasn't very clever.

JAKE: Yes, it was.

MADGE: What are you up to?

JAKE: Good works.

MADGE: What good—

JAKE: It's not right for Norah, vegetating in the country. She ought to be back in town, getting on with the business of living. I want her to go off this place, and the sooner the better. Sell it. Or if she doesn't want to do that, she can keep it for weekends, and ask people to stay.

MADGE: Well, *we're* here.

JAKE: And whom else has she asked? Ever? I don't like being Norah's only friends. It's too much of a responsibility.

(*Norah returns with the filled jug.*)

And here's Lady Chatterley herself with a foaming jug.

NORAH (*Acid*): I put rather more lemonade in it this time.

MADGE: When are we going to see this gamekeeper of yours?

NORAH: I keep telling you; we're not on social terms.

JAKE (*To Madge*): Keeps him to herself. She won't show him to her friends.

NORAH: We're not on . . .

MADGE: Then I'd get some more mice, darling, if I were you. Harrod's Pet Department might send some up.

(*Pause.*)

NORAH: As a matter of fact, he has borrowed a couple of books.

13

Interior. The bedroom. Night.

(*Dark. Norah, lying in bed.*

We see her face in big close-up, eyes open. We hear the wind. Norah closes her eyes.

A change in the noise the wind makes. Overlaid is the noise of a disorganized drunken-sounding wordless singing.

Norah opens her eyes. Singing stops, and only wind is heard. It drops to nothing. She starts again. There is the distant call of an owl, the sound of a baby sobbing, then a scream, and then the wind drops and starts again.

Norah gets out of bed and goes to the window, looks out.)

Telecine 7: Exterior. The road to the cottage. Night.

(*Moonlight. All is quiet. The road seen as from an upper window.*

Wind still heard. No other noises.)

14

Interior. The bedroom. Night.

(*Norah shuts the window. The noise of the wind is less loud. She begins to go back to bed.*

There is a creak as she steps on a loose board. It startles her.

She gets into bed. There is the rattle we have learned

to associate with mice, as if from within an interior wall.

Norah switches on the bedside light, and looks about. Nothing out of place. The wind gets a little louder. She switches the light off.

Go in on her face. She closes her eyes. We begin to hear the noises in the wind again. And then a sudden sharp—)

Telecine 8: Exterior. The patio. Night.

(Thwack! as a log is cut in two by the big axe.

Then we see Peter, grinning and gibbering as in Scene 8, but more so.)

15

Interior. The bedroom. Night.

(Norah in bed, her eyes tightly shut. Wind noises. Distant laughter.)

Telecine 9: (a) Exterior. Patio. Night.

(Fisher stands on the drive. Instead of his spectacles, he has frames in which are painted eyes like the half-marble we have already seen.)

Telecine 9: (b) Exterior. The road leading to the cottage. Night.

(The road as we have just seen it, except that the figure of Fisher from the previous Telecine (a) lingers over it. As it disappears we hear the thwack! thwack! thwack! again.

Super over the Telecine:

Rob nearly naked, as we have seen him before, moving towards the camera.

He moves in, his two hands alternating in a sideways chopping movement.

Then we see that he has a knife in one hand. He ceases to make the chopping movement, and holds the knife before him, moving in closer and closer.)

16

Interior. The bedroom. Night.

(Norah opens her eyes.

She has frightened herself thoroughly.

Wind noise. She sits up in bed, and switches the light on again.)

NORAH: Blast that Jake!

(She takes a book from the bedside table, and begins to read, looking up once as the rattle is heard again, but quieter.)

17

Interior. The kitchen. Day.

(A kitchen knife is cutting the head off a dead chicken.)

MRS VIGO: You've not seen his weapons, then?

(Norah takes a moment to reassure herself that there is no double meaning, then:)

NORAH: No.

MRS VIGO: Souvenirs.

182

NORAH: Of what?

MRS VIGO: Gestapo. Storm Troopers.

NORAH: But Rob's too young to—

MRS VIGO: Writes away for them, doesn't he? Writes to the Body Magazines. They'm full of adverts for that trash. (*She pulls the innards out of the chicken.*)

NORAH: Can't the butcher do that?

MRS VIGO: Doesn't come from the butcher. She'm one of mine. Been hanging upside down all night. (*Scratches herself.*) Fowl and fleas, they go together.

NORAH: But, when I asked you to bring me a chicken I didn't mean you to kill one specially.

MRS VIGO: She'm gone broody. No use for laying. Wring her neck, slit her throat, hang her up; it's all she'm good for.

(*The rattle of mice. Both look up.*)

NORAH: They're back again.

MRS VIGO: Bound to be.

NORAH: Why? Rob put poison down.

MRS VIGO: Peter.

NORAH: Peter?

(*She looks out of the window to see:*)

Telecine 10: Exterior. Patio. Day.

(*Peter going up the drive with a wheelbarrow.*

He smiles and waves in his demented way.)

MRS VIGO (*Voice over*): Got no teeth. He'm all gummy, Peter. Known for it.

18

Interior. Kitchen. Day.

NORAH: What's that to do with the mice?

MRS VIGO: Eats his sammwiches in your shed, doesn't he? He'm can't manage the crusts. He leaves them lay. Encouragement to mice, that am, bound to be.

(*Pause. Norah controlled.*)

NORAH: Yes... well, I'd better ask Rob to have another go at them.

MRS VIGO: He'm coming to supper, as I hear.

NORAH (*Sharp*): From whom?

MRS VIGO: Pardon.

NORAH: From whom do you hear this?

MRS VIGO: Nobody.

NORAH: From Rob?

MRS VIGO (*Laughs*): No. Why would Rob tell me? That's private affairs.

NORAH: Yes. But someone told you.

MRS VIGO: You did.

(*Norah's face amazed denial.*)

Asking me to get a chicken. You wouldn't cook a chicken for yourself.

NORAH: Anybody might have been coming.

MRS VIGO: That's right. He'm bought some gentleman's cologne. Gunsmoke. Wilf Bulmore brought it in on the bus. Ninety p.

(*Norah defeated, about to leave, then turns to ask another question.*)

NORAH: Why do you call him Rob when his name's Edgar?

MRS VIGO: He answers to it.

NORAH: It's not his name.

MRS VIGO: Short for Robin.

NORAH: You don't like Edgar? As a name?

MRS VIGO: Got nothing against. (*She puts the chicken under the tap to clean the inside.*) You ask Fisher; he'll tell you about names. All the old names. He'm noted for learning. There's always one young man answers to 'Robin' in these parts—has to be.

19

Interior. Kitchen. Dusk.

(*That evening.*

Begin on three candles, lit in a china table-candelabrum.

Kitchen light is off.

Pull back to show the table, set for dinner for two.

Norah, changed into a linen dress from the shirt and jeans of the previous scene, places a red paper table-napkin on each side-plate.

Norah stands back and looks at the table.

Satie piano music on the gramophone is heard from the living room.)

NORAH: Yes, I think so.

(*She blows out the candles, and switches on the kitchen light. She looks at her watch and goes into:*)

20

Interior. Living room. Dusk.

(*No fire.*

Music now louder.

Norah switches on the standard lamp and goes on upstairs to:)

21

Interior. Bedroom. Dusk.

(Jump straight to Norah at the dressing-table.

The light on, looking at herself critically in the mirror. She decides that there are bags beneath her eyes, and that they show, and applies make-up.

She bares her teeth and puts on perfume.)

NORAH: Really, this is ridiculous.

(She starts to leave the bedroom, but stops herself. She is thinking. She turns, and goes to the bedside-table. She puts one hand out to open the drawer. She is still in doubt.)

Why not? If one fancies him. *(Opens drawer.)* Better be safe than thing.

(There is a small metal box inside of the kind used to contain a contraceptive cap.

Norah opens the box.

It is empty.

We see her face, unable to understand this. She begins to search through the meagre contents of the drawer.

All this time, the piano music has been heard faintly from below.

Now a knock from outside.

The front door is below the bedroom window.

Norah goes to the window which is open.)

Is that you, Rob?

Telecine 11: Exterior. Patio. Dusk.

(The outside light is on. Rob is looking upwards. He wears his blue suit.)

ROB: Yes. (*Looks at his watch.*) You said quarter-to-eight.

22

Interior. The bedroom. Dusk.

(Norah at window.)

NORAH: You're admirably punctual. I thought we'd have a drink on the patio before dinner if it's not too cold.

(She turns from the window and leaves the bedroom.)

Telecine 12: Exterior. Patio. Dusk.

(Rob looks about him, ill-at-ease, because he is in a social situation he is not used to.)

23

Interior. Living room. Dusk.

(Norah comes down the stairs.

Piano music gets louder.)

24

Interior. Kitchen. Night.

(Begin on the glass marble, then show that dinner is over.

187

Rob is talking. He has been talking for some time.)

ROB: That was the Waffen S.S. Like, they weren't police, you see. They were soldiers, the Waffen S.S. only they weren't part of the army. I mean, they still wore the S.S. uniform—you know, black with the death's head badge. And they had this independent discipline, quite separate from the army, because of being an élite, you see. A lot of the guards in concentration camps were Waffen S.S. They had the toughness for it.

(*Rob has been pronouncing 'Waffen' in an anglicized way.*

Norah now uses German pronunciation.)

NORAH: Isn't it 'Waffen'?

(*Rob looks at Norah, not understanding.*)

Isn't that how it's pronounced? 'Waffen' S.S.?

ROB: I don't know. I never heard it pronounced. I've just read about it.

NORAH (*Gets up*): Maybe we'd better go into the other room. It's more comfortable.

(*As they move, Rob continues.*

We can see from Norah's face, no longer turned to him, that she is almost dying of boredom.)

25

Interior. Living room. Night.

ROB: You can tell they were different from the Army because of the names of the ranks. They were all called 'Führers', right down to Corporal. That means 'leader' in German, 'führer' does.

NORAH: I know.

ROB: The Corporal was a Rottenführer. Then a Sergeant was a Unterscharführer and . . .

NORAH: You'll excuse me if I just nip upstairs for a moment.

ROB: A General was a Gruppenführer; that's a Lieutenant-General. A Major-General was . . .

NORAH (*Going*): I shan't be a moment.

ROB: Oh . . . That's all right.

NORAH: There's one downstairs as well. (*Pointing.*) You go through that door. Or you could always pee in the garden. There's nobody about.

(*Rob is shocked.*)

ROB: I'm all right, thank you very much.

(*Norah's face as she leaves.*

Rob about to settle himself. He seems to hear something. (Though the audience does not.)

Cocks his head, then decides it is nothing, and sits.)

26

Interior. Bathroom. Night.

(*Norah by the washbasin. Water in it.*)

NORAH: Dear God! To think I said I fancied him. (*She freshens her face with water, then she looks at herself in the mirror.*) You're middle-aged Norah Palmer. Two more hours chat about the S.S. and you'll be an old woman.

(*Faintly we hear the noise of a car.*

She lifts her head to listen.)

27

Interior. Living room. Night.

(Overlap the noise, a little louder.

Rob listening.

He gets up quickly, and goes to the window.

The noise stops.

He parts the curtains a little, looks out, but can see nothing.

He goes to the door, and opens it.

Norah returns, down the stairs.)

NORAH: Ah! You . . . ?

(Rob steps back into the room, quickly.)

ROB: No, I wasn't. I thought I heard something.

NORAH: What?

ROB: Like a van or something up on your road, up the hill. It's stopped now.

NORAH: The tractor comes down sometimes.

ROB: Not at this time of night, it doesn't. *(Closes door.)* I couldn't see anything, though.

NORAH: I'll get you a drink.

ROB: Not for me, thanks. I mean, I have to keep in condition.

NORAH: Yes, of course.

ROB: If two people are having a really interesting conversation, you don't need drink to keep it going.

NORAH: I think *I* do need a drink.

(As she goes to get one for herself, Rob says:)

ROB: Anyway . . . what it was, you see . . . the S.S. . . .

190

it was like an order of chivalry. Like King Arthur and the Round Table.

(*She looks at him amazed.*)

Mind you, they diluted it.

NORAH: Did they?

ROB: They let the police in. Merged them. In continental countries you don't get the same class of person in the police; the S.S. were dedicated men.

(*Norah closes her eyes.*)

Telecine 13: Exterior. The top of Norah's road. Night.
(*Moonlight.*

Night sounds.

A van, parked, no lights.

We see Fisher, sitting in the cab, beside the driver, Mr Wellbeloved.

As from Fisher's point of view we see the figure of Peter, walking down the path towards the cottage.

A nightingale begins to sing.

Wellbeloved looks at Fisher.)

FISHER: Nightingale.

(*We see the side of the Cab, and the inscription on it:*
'*H. Wellbeloved, Family Butcher.*')

28

Interior. Living room. Night.
(*Norah stifling a yawn.*)

ROB: The S.D. was the Security Service. They were

merged with the ordinary security in 1939 to form the R.S.H.A.

(*Norah yawns again.*)

NORAH: I thought it was military history you were interested in. I wouldn't have bothered to get you Michael's book on the Franco-Prussian war, if I'd known it was only the S.S.

ROB: I'm expanding my interests all the time.

NORAH: Ah!

ROB: Anyway...

(*Norah yawns again.*)

NORAH: I'm so sorry.

ROB: That's all right.

NORAH: I expect it's the air.

ROB: What is?

NORAH: Country air. It makes one sleepy. 'Known for it' as Mrs Vigo would say.

ROB: She's right. It does.

NORAH: I expect we're both ready for bed.

ROB (*Brightens*): Yes, I am.

(*Norah realizes that she has said the wrong thing, and decides to correct her error.*)

NORAH: Well, if you're sure you won't have a drink before you go...

(*Rob doesn't know how to take this. He thinks he knows why he has been asked to supper. Is he expected to make his willingness clear, or is this some middle-class game, in which one goes through the forms of taking leave, but ends up in bed? He decides to play for time, by answering the question.*)

ROB: No.

(*She is standing, waiting for him to stand. He is sitting, not sure what to do next.*

Pause.)

I mean, Yes thank you; I am sure. I don't drink much.

NORAH: We'll say goodnight, then, and thank you very much for coming over. I'm not really a lonely person, but it does make a pleasant change, cooking for someone else occasionally. (*A little joke to keep things cheerful.*) Besides the mice.

(*He gets up slowly. His throat is dry. He clears it.*)

ROB: I wouldn't think you'd have any more trouble. With the mice.

(*Norah moves away a little towards the door—which is also towards the stairs.*

Rob tries a smile, and takes a step towards her. She gives a little look behind her.)

I've never been upstairs in your house.

(*The situation is broken by a noise from outside the (still curtained) window: it is a booted foot knocking against something on the patio. Both react sharply to it. Then Rob goes to the door, opens it, and looks out. He sees nothing. Norah has moved up behind him. He turns back.*)

Can't see anything.

NORAH: There are always noises at night.

ROB: Yes. (*He steps back into the room, and closes the door.*)

NORAH: They don't mean anything. I should think you'd be used to them.

(*Pause. He looks at her, and decides that she is one of those women who needs an excuse for it.*)

ROB: You could do with a bit of protection, though, I dare say.

193

(*He moves towards her, and is stopped by.*)

NORAH (*Sharp*): No.

ROB: What?

NORAH: No, I don't need protection, thank you. And, Rob my dear, it's very kind and flattering that you should think of kissing me goodnight, but we really don't know each other well enough.

ROB: But I thought . . . when you asked me . . .

NORAH: No. That was not the idea. (*Smiles: tries to console him.*) I'm not a baby-snatcher, Rob. I must be at least (*momentary hesitation*) ten years older than you are.

ROB: I'm not a baby.

NORAH: Of course not. You're a very good-looking young man. I'm sure there are plenty of girls of your own age in the village who'd—.

ROB (*Sharp*): I don't have anything to do with them. I don't keep my body at its peak for them.

NORAH: Or for me, Rob.

(*Cut away to his face, hurt and angry. A moment's silence.*)

For yourself, perhaps.

ROB: Goodnight. Thank you for supper.

(*He turns, opens the door, and leaves. The door closes behind him. Norah left.*)

NORAH: Oh dear! Oh dear, oh dear, oh dear!

(*She begins to climb the stairs.*)

Telecine 14: Exterior. Norah's road. Night.

(*Rob walks angrily up the road away from the cottage.*

*Peter (who need not be recognizable) rises from a
hiding-place in the hedge, as Rob passes, and hits him
on the back of the head with a weighted stick. Rob
falls.)*

29

Interior. Bedroom. Night.

*(Norah gets into bed, and turns the light out. The
Nightingale is heard from outside.)*

Telecine 15: Exterior. Top of Norah's road. Night.

(Fisher and Wellbeloved in the cab of the van.

*Peter is outside. Peter has a bad speech defect, so that
it's hard to understand him, though Fisher does.)*

PETER: She'm . . . She'm . . .

FISHER: Gone to bed? (*Peter nods vigorously.*) All
right. (*He starts to leave the van.*) Turn the van round,
Henry, ready to go.

*(We see Fisher and Peter walking down the road
towards the cottage, their backs to us.)*

30

Interior. Bedroom. Night.

*(Moonlight. Curtain flutters in a small night breeze.
Norah in bed, asleep.*

*A noise is heard, a kind of fluttering. Then a collision.
Fluttering again. Collision.*

Norah wakes. First she listens. Then she sits up in bed,

195

and switches the light on. Noise heard again. She wonders what it is. She decides to get out of bed, and investigate.

As she reaches the door.

31

Interior. Living room. Night.

(The curtains have been drawn back. The room is dark, but moonlit. A fluttering shadow. A collision against the window.

Norah comes to the top of the stairs.)

NORAH: Hullo?

(Silence. She begins to come downstairs. At the bottom, she turns on the light. She sees something coming at her she screams, putting her hands to her face.

Telecine 16: Exterior. Patio. Night.

(The cottage, close to from the outside, light coming through the window.

Norah heard screaming.)

32

Interior. Living room. Night.

(Norah, still screaming, her hands to her head. Magnify the noise of flutter and collision.

Door opens quickly. Rob runs in. He grabs Norah, and pulls her down on the stairs, clear of the door.)

ROB: It's all right. It's all right, Miss Palmer.

(*Silence. If possible, something seen to fly out through the door. The presupposition of this whole sequence is that a bird has come down the chimney and been trapped, but clearly the bird itself must be faked.*

Norah held by Rob on the stairs.)

It's gone now.

NORAH: What was it?

ROB: Only a bird. They come down the chimney if you haven't lit the fire. Then they get frightened.

NORAH: *They* do!

ROB: You can't blame them. You thought it would get in your hair, didn't you? I've often heard that. Women being frightened of . . .

NORAH: I don't know what I thought.

(*Both of them realize that she is in his arms. He has confidence now.*)

ROB: You don't need to be scared, Miss Palmer.

(*He kisses her. Her response is delayed, then passionate. When their faces and bodies move apart.*)

NORAH: Fisher told me about the birds.

33

Interior. Bedroom. Night.

(*Norah is in bed:*

Rob is taking his shirt off, leaving his top bare. He flings it on a chair he puts his hands to his waistband to undo the button, then modestly intrudes, and he switches off the light. He will only dimly be seen, as he takes his trousers off. Meanwhile:)

NORAH: What were you doing out there?

197

ROB: I heard you scream.

NORAH: You'd been gone an hour, at least.

ROB: That's right. Somebody hit me over the head. I thought I heard a van earlier.

NORAH: Rob!

ROB: Poachers I expect. Nothing to worry about.

(*Bed creaks as he gets into it.*)

Harvest Festival tomorrow.

(*Bring up the sound of: voices singing, 'We plough the fields and scatter, the good seed on the land'.*)

Telecine 17: Exterior. A country road. Night.

(*The van of H. Wellbeloved, Family Butcher moves away down the road.*

Keep the sound of the Hymn as an overlap. Fade down the sound as we go back to:)

34

Interior. Bedroom. Dawn.

(*A little light through the curtains.*

Norah and Rob lying side by side, covered by television's obligatory sheet.)

ROB: What it was, you see, I could never think of anything to say. I always wanted to be able to hold a conversation, but there was never anybody to hold a conversation with until I got to College, and then I didn't know how to do it.

NORAH: What about that girl? The one you went out with who used to read *House and Garden*?

ROB: I only went out with her twice. That was the most I went out with any of them. I mean, just because I keep myself in condition, and all that . . .

NORAH (*Smiles*): At your peak.

ROB: It isn't enough, though, is it?

NORAH: Rob, my dear, you are good-looking. I said so, and I meant it.

ROB: It doesn't seem to make much difference if you can't think of anything to say. I mean, I have *had* girls: of course I have. But it was . . . it was like being collected.

NORAH: Ah!

ROB: Anyway . . . I read this article in the *Reader's Digest* about how you should specialize in one subject, because experts are always interesting. And I noticed there were these adverts in my body-building magazines for S.S. uniforms and weapons, and I thought, 'I'll specialize in that' because obviously a lot of people were interested in it.

NORAH: And did it work?

ROB: You're the first person I've been out with since. And we did hold a conversation, didn't we? Except at the end, when you . . . when you got rid of me.

NORAH: Never mind.

ROB: I thought you wanted me to seduce you, you see.

NORAH: Well, I did, in a way.

ROB: I expect I just missed the psychological moment to move things to a more physical plane.

(*He kisses her. Bring up sound: the dawn chorus of birds.*

Norah is beneath him.)

NORAH: Bloody birds!

35

Interior. Kitchen. Day.

(*Begin in close up on a boiled egg in an egg-cup. A spoon comes down on the top. A knife slices the top off.*

A tap heard at the window.

We see Norah (skirt and blouse) looking up, surprised.

We see Mrs Vigo at the window, dressed for church, and carrying a carrier-bag.

Norah is surprised to see her. She opens the window.)

MRS VIGO: I come to take you to church.

NORAH: But I'm an agnostic.

MRS VIGO (*Sharp*): Jewish? You didn't say you was Jewish.

NORAH: No. 'Agnostic' means . . . Well, it means one isn't religious. One doesn't go to church.

MRS VIGO: Well, you can't, can you? Parson only comes over one Sunday in four. He'm rides his cycle from Painsbury.

NORAH: Really, I . . .

MRS VIGO (*Overlaps*): Fisher says, 'If you don't come for Harvest Festival, Parson, you'm get no welcome here at all, and I'll do lay-reading.' Consequently, Harvest Festival we always has him, and he gets his dinner with Major Grange.

NORAH: I'm *not* religious.

MRS VIGO (*Ignores her*): Easter the same. We reckon to have him over then, but Christmas is another matter; we don't take much account of that. You'll need a hat. (*Holds up the carrier-bag.*) I brought one.

NORAH: Mrs Vigo, it's really very kind of you—

MRS VIGO: Decorations can't be missed. We'm known for them. Sheaves. Apples. Pumpkins big as your arse. I come up to fetch you. It'd not be kindly taken if you'm seen to spurn the decorations.

Telecine 18: (a) Exterior. Patio. Day.

NORAH: Don't I need a dress?

MRS VIGO: So long as you'm not wearing trousers, they won't reckon to put you out.

(*She takes the hat out of the carrier-bag. It is a straw bonnet with flowers on it. Norah takes it.*)

NORAH: Thank you.

(*She puts it on. As she ties it under her chin, her head goes up, and she sees something on the roof.*)

Oh!

MRS VIGO: What's the matter?

NORAH: The drainpipe.

Telecine 18: (b) Exterior. Section of roof. Day.

(*The drainpipe has come away from the wall.*)

MRS VIGO (*Voice over: clicks tongue, disapproving*): Careless!

Telecine 18: (c) Exterior. Patio. Day.

NORAH: Careless?

MRS VIGO: Come away, that has.

NORAH: But why? It was all right yesterday.

MRS VIGO: That's right. Come away in the night, must have.

(*Norah's face. She is trying to connect this with the other happenings of last night, but can't make a connection.*)

You can hear the bells. Twice a year they'm gets rung. Rope broke last year. Don't want to be late.

NORAH: No . . . All right . . . (*She puts on her bonnet.*) There was something I wanted to ask you about anyway. Something seems to be missing from the bedroom drawer. I wondered if you'd moved it.

MRS VIGO: What's that, then?

NORAH: Well, it's . . . it's er . . . a small . . . well, a cap. (*No, comprehension from Mrs Vigo.*) Not a hat, you know, but a . . . a contraceptive cap, in fact: a dutch . . . I mean, one uses . . . (*Still no comprehension.*) Oh well it really doesn't matter. (*As they go.*) I may have mislaid it somehow.

36

Montage of still photographs.

(*First the church tower.*

Sound: A single bell indicates that the service is about to begin.

Then a succession of pictures of Harvest Festival decorations—sheaves of wheat, apples and pears, eggs and cheeses, flagons of perry and bottles of home-brewed wine, then (more oddly) dead rabbits, a hare, pheasants.

Meanwhile we hear the Vicar's voice. He has a very pronounced Birmingham accent.)

VICAR (*Voice over*): And so, at this time of fulfilment of the country year, let our thoughts return to that one source from which all good gifts come from, and be we wise *or* foolish virgins, let us say, 'We shall keep our oil, for *thee*, Lord. Guarding and holding our precious seed, even in the dark days of winter, to bring it forth once more in the spring, when the green shoots pierce the earth, in praise of the only begetter of all our goodness.' And now to God the Father, God the son (*Fading*.)

Telecine 19: (*a*) *Exterior. Roof. Day.*

(*Peter on the roof, mending the drainpipe, overlap the Vicar's voice.*

Vicar's voice over, fading.)

NORAH (*Voice over*): What are you doing?

Telecine 19: (*b*) *Exterior. Patio. Day.*

(*Fisher is supervising from the ground. Norah has just returned from church.*)

FISHER: Mending your drainpipe, which has come away.

NORAH: Last night.

FISHER: As I heard.

NORAH: From whom? (*Polite incomprehension.*) Oh, never mind. (*Another tack.*) Peter's excused Harvest Festival, I suppose? Unlike me, he isn't expected to admire the decorations.

FISHER: He took part in the Worship, but did not remain for the sermon.

NORAH: And you?

FISHER: Oh, I'm a lay-reader, Miss Palmer.

NORAH: Is that an answer?

FISHER: Our parson, you see, is not an educated man. The merest Brummy, to tell you the truth. He takes his sermons from a book—'Holy Thoughts For a Holy Year', Evangelical Press, fifty new pence. But in rural areas, the church puts up with what it can afford. We don't complain.

NORAH: You feel you could do better?

(*Fisher smiles but does not reply.*)

Just as, perhaps, you can tell me how, on a quiet September night, the drain-pipe came away from the wall.

FISHER: I should say it was someone on your roof.

(*Pause. She is trying to take this in.*)

NORAH: Some man?

FISHER: Would find it easier than a lady. Some lurker.

NORAH: Why?

FISHER: Up to no good.

NORAH: A burglar? That's ridiculous.

FISHER: Perhaps you heard something? In the night.

NORAH: Nothing. Nothing at all happened last night except—nothing happened. (*Small pause.*) A bird came down the chimney.

FISHER: Ah! I said it was a place of birds.

Telecine 19: (c) *Exterior. Roof. Day.*

(*Peter has finished. He gives his daft grin and wave, and shakes the pipe to show it is secure.*)

FISHER (*Voice over*): It must have been a very large bird, Miss Palmer, to have dislodged your drainpipe.

Telecine 19: (*d*) *Exterior. Patio. Day.*

NORAH: It wasn't. Just an ordinary frightened bird.

FISHER: A nightingale perhaps? Or an owl? At that time of night. (*She can't answer.*) And nothing has been taken? Nothing missing at all?

NORAH: Nothing. Excuse me. (*She goes indoors. Fisher calls to the roof.*)

FISHER: Mind how you come down.

Telecine 19: (*e*) *Exterior. Roof. Day.*

(*Peter giving a thumbs up sign.*)

37

Interior. The bedroom. Day.

(*Norah comes in quickly. She goes to the drawer of the bedside table and opens it.*

The box is in there. Her fingers open the box.

The contraceptive cap is inside.

We see Norah's amazement. She takes the box out of the drawer slowly, and examines it.)

38

Interior. Madge and Jake's living room. Night.

(*Fire in the grate. The time is two months later—an evening in late November.*

Begin on Madge's face, as Norah speaks. Probably it is drinks time.)

205

NORAH: Something rather boring has happened.

MADGE: Yes.

NORAH: I appear to be pregnant.

MADGE: Appear to be?

NORAH: Am.

(*Pause.*)

JAKE: You've been having it off, my dear, with that young man.

(*Pause.*)

NORAH: Yes.

MADGE: But, Norah, how could you possibly come to—

NORAH: I don't understand it myself.

MADGE: You forgot—?

NORAH: No. It disappeared. For one night. And re-appeared the next day.

JAKE: What does she mean?

MADGE: Precautions, Jake.

JAKE: Oh, ah! (*Slight pause.*) But why should—

NORAH (*Sharp*): I don't know why anyone should do such a thing. The only possible reason is that someone actually wanted me pregnant, which is too stupid to consider seriously.

MADGE: But, Norah dear, even then . . .

JAKE: You didn't *have* to, did you?

NORAH (*Control*): I didn't have to, Jake. I didn't intend to. It happened.

(*Pause.*)

JAKE: May one ask how?

NORAH: I was frightened by a bird which came down the chimney.

206

JAKE (*Polite disbelief*): And fell into his arms.

NORAH (*Still controlled*). He had, in fact, left the house an hour before. I'd gone to bed. I heard a strange noise, and went downstairs. The bird was trapped. It flew at me. I screamed. He happened to be outside, and heard me.

MADGE: Happened to be?

NORAH: A passing poacher had hit him on the head, and knocked him out.

(*Pause. They are looking at her.*)

JAKE: Yes. Yes, of course.

NORAH: It also seems likely that somebody was on the roof at that time. The bird may actually have been put down the chimney.

JAKE: You think *he* ... thing ...

MADGE: Rob.

JAKE: Thank you. You think Rob did it?

NORAH: I told you; the whole thing's too fantastic to bear thought.

JAKE: You do think about it though.

MADGE: And you are pregnant.

NORAH: I said so.

(*Pause.*)

MADGE: You'd like us to do something about it!

NORAH: Thank you, Madge; I'm quite capable of finding an abortionist for myself. (*She sees that she has hurt them.*) Sorry! Sorry!

MADGE: Does he know?

(*Norah shakes her head.*)

JAKE: And you really think he may have ... well, planned ...?

NORAH: I don't *know*. Maybe he's telling the truth; I can't remember whether he had a bump on his head or not. As for the bird, it could have got in on its own—I didn't hear anybody on the roof—except that the drainpipe *had* come away. And Rob's not bright. I mean, it's such a complicated plot, if it is a plot. And he couldn't have got into the house to steal—anyway, how would he know where to look? How would he know I wasn't on the pill?

(*Pause. They are looking at her.*)

Yes, you're right; it's mad, the whole thing. There's no reason for it. He thought I wanted to be seduced. He even said it: 'I thought you wanted me to.' So why? Why? (*No answer from them.*) Anyway, I'm afraid I've gone right off him. To tell the truth I was never that much on.

Telecine 20: Exterior. Patio. Day.

(*A day in late November. It would be jolly if it were raining. In any case, Rob is wearing winter clothes. He comes to the front door and knocks. No reply. He goes to the kitchen and looks in. Nobody. He knocks again, looks up at the first-floor window, which is curtained, turns and goes disconsolately away, while:*)

NORAH (*Voice over*): I've been rather like the weather, I'm afraid—getting steadily colder since Harvest Festival—and once I found out I was expecting a little stranger, I just upped and left.

39

Interior. Bedroom. Day.

(*Mrs Vigo has been watching through a slightly parted curtain. She lifts it, to watch more openly as Rob is leaving.*)

MADGE (*Voice over*): And you won't go back?

NORAH (*Voice over*): Oh ... sometime. In the spring.

(*Mrs Vigo lets the curtain fall.*)

(*Voice over.*) At the moment, it's more important to find a job, and somewhere to live.

40

Panel with bell-pushes. Special shot.

(*This must be outside the main door of what is clearly a large apartment-block, since there are about twenty names, of which Norah Palmer is No. 16.*

Rob's finger presses the bell.)

41

Interior. Norah's apartment. Day.

(*Begin in close up on the glass marble, cut in half, which stands on the outer edge of Norah's desk.*

Sound of the loud buzz of the bell.

Then see Norah in close up answering the door-phone.)

NORAH: Hullo?...Who is it?...Hullo?...

(*But whoever-it-is doesn't answer. She shrugs and puts the phone back on its hook.*)

42

Special shot. Light indicator.

(*The indicator with lights which show that a lift is going up to the sixth floor.*)

43

Interior. Norah's apartment. Day.

(Norah is at the desk, typing. Now we shall see more of the room which is the 'room' of the 1 rm K & B, of her tiny rented flat. Christmas cards on the mantel and on the sideboard.

A knock at the door.)

NORAH: Yes?

(The knock is repeated. She goes to the door and opens is cautiously.

Rob is there, dressed in raincoat and tweed cap.

(Perhaps the door has a Christmas wreath on it, which we should now see.)

Rob carries a parcel. He is very distressed.)

ROB: You mustn't . . . mustn't . . .

NORAH: What are you doing here?

ROB: I came to tell you. I got the day off because it's Christmas. I came up by train.

NORAH: You'd better take your coat off, and sit down, I suppose.

(He comes a little way into the room, but doesn't take his coat off. He stands staring at her.)

Well, don't just stand there. *(She closes the door behind him.)* Do you want a cup of tea or anything?

ROB: You mustn't kill . . .

(She decides that he may be having some sort of breakdown, and retreats towards the telephone on the desk. She speaks more gently.)

NORAH: Sit down, Rob. I'm not angry. You took me by surprise. Just sit down; you'll feel better.

ROB: Don't kill my son.

(*Pause. She realizes what he is on about.*)

NORAH: Oh. Is that it?

ROB: Don't do it.

NORAH: How did you find out?

ROB: Auntie Vigo.

(*Pause.*)

NORAH: No point in asking how *she* knew I'm pregnant. Since she knows everything. Did she tell you I was thinking of an abortion.

ROB: She said you were modern in your thoughts.

NORAH: I'll make the tea. (*She moves to do so.*)

ROB: No.

NORAH: Now, Rob—

ROB: I only got a day-return. Then I had to find the way.

NORAH: A taxi would have known it.

ROB: I haven't the money for taxis. The train goes back (*Looks at watch*) in forty minutes. (*Pause.*) You won't kill him, will you.

NORAH: Rob, are you asking me to marry you?

(*Silently. Clearly he isn't.*)

No? Well, I wouldn't, even if you did. So what you are asking me to do is to bear the child, and then rear it, all on my own—an unmarried mother. That's what you took a day-return to ask me.

ROB: I'd help.

NORAH: Support him? When you can't even afford a taxi? Or would you send the money from Canada? When you get there.

ROB: You're the mother. Don't you want him?

NORAH: It. No.

(*Pause.*)

ROB: I'll take him, then.

NORAH: And why do you want 'him'?

ROB: It's my seed, isn't it?

(*Norah is angry. She slams her hand down on the desk. The half-marble falls to the floor.*)

NORAH: How dare you? How *dare* you come here, talking to me about your 'seed' like something out of one of your S.S. text-books? Do you think I want an abortion? I've never wanted a child, but that's a different matter to killing one, scraping one out, curetting it—all those *words*! What's inside me may look like a tadpole, it may not think, or breathe, or feel, but it's alive to me; it's part of me. I don't want it killed any more than you do. I'm thirty-five. Soon I'll be past the age to bear a child. I didn't think I minded that; I'd be a terrible mother anyway. But now I find I do mind, I do care, I do want this child almost as much as I don't want it, maybe more. And I'm mixed-up and really rather unhappy about it. But don't tell me what to do, Rob, because it may be your child, but it's certainly not your business.

(*Pause. He picks up the half-marble, and gives it to her.*)

ROB: You brought this with you, then?

NORAH: I found it in my suitcase when I unpacked. No doubt your Auntie Vigo put it there.

ROB: She's a strange woman. Known for it.

NORAH: Just tell me one thing, Rob.

(*He looks at her.*)

That bird that came down the chimney and frightened me:—did *you* . . .

212

(*He doesn't seem to understand her.*)

No? Well, I didn't really expect you to tell me if you had. Anyway ... when I come down to the cottage again, I want it clearly understood that, whatever I decide to do about the child, I don't want to see *you*. Seed is just seed, Rob; it doesn't give you any rights.

(*Pause. Rob produces his parcel.*)

ROB: I brought you a present.

(*She takes it, and unwraps it. It is a teddy bear.*)

Telecine 21: Exterior. Private road to the cottage. Day.

(*Norah in an open car, suitcases in the back. If possible, reverse shot to see the cottage itself, and Mrs Vigo standing at the door, waiting.*)

44

Interior. Living room. Day.

(*Norah, entering. Mrs Vigo follows.*)

MRS VIGO: You don't have to keep the baby. Nobody suggested that; you'm a busy woman, not given to motherhood.

NORAH: Indeed?

MRS VIGO: You can have him looked after. His father came from the orphanage, as *you* know.

NORAH: Aren't you being rather impertinent?

MRS VIGO: Good advice, that am, not cheeky.

NORAH (*Angry*): Has it ever occurred to you, Mrs Vigo, that I'm not obliged to employ you?

MRS VIGO: Can't do the cleaning, not by yourself.

First, you'm not used to the work, and second, you'm too heavy: And you won't get nobody else from the village to come, I tell you that.

NORAH: Because I'm a fallen woman?

MRS VIGO: Because *I* cleans here. (*Pause.*) I come up special to give you good welcome. So if you'm feeling like a cup, I'll make the tea.

45

Interior. Kitchen. Day.

(*Tea in progress.*)

MRS VIGO: I'll come up daily. You'm be needing to take things easy. No need to pay.

NORAH: Well, I don't know that I shall be staying all that long.

(*Pause.*)

MRS VIGO: You'm come here for the rest.

NORAH: For the weekend.

(*As Mrs Vigo doesn't seem to understand.*)

After all, I have a job again now.

MRS VIGO: You'm never working, seven months gone.

NORAH: It's only brainwork.

MRS VIGO: Can be done anywhere.

NORAH: Indeed, yes. Therefore, not necessarily here.

MRS VIGO: Easter'm in two weeks.

NORAH: Yes?

MRS VIGO (*Explains gently*): Here am your place, miss.

(*Norah looks at her, amazed.*)

In the winter, in the dark days, you go where you will. There'm no objection, no effort made to keep you. But now, come Easter, here am your place.

(*She gets up to take her cup to the sink.*

Norah half turns to watch her.

We see, and so does Norah, that there is another of the half-marbles on the partition.)

46

Interior. Bedroom. Night.

(*Norah in bed. Sounds in the wind.*

Norah sighs. She sits up, then gets up. Creak from the loose boards. Sounds become ordinary wind-noises.

She leaves the room.)

47

Interior. Kitchen. Night.

(*Norah comes in. Curtains are already closed. She switches on the light, and fills the electric kettle.*

She picks up the half-marble, and looks at it, curiously. Sounds in the wind begin to return.

She goes over to the curtains, and pulls them. The light spilling on to the patio reveals:)

Telecine 22: (a) Exterior. Patio. Night.

(*Rob standing there. He turns, and begins to move away quickly. Reverse shot to show Norah at the window, alarmed.*)

Telecine 22: (b) *Exterior. The road to the cottage. Night.*

(*Rob running away up the road.*)

Telecine 22: (c) *Exterior. Patio. Day.*

(*Camera movement: First Mrs Vigo, then Fisher, both standing still as statues, both listening. We hear the starter of a car, pressed several times but no noise of the engine.*

Norah appears from the lower end of the drive, as if from the garage.)

NORAH: The car won't start.

FISHER: We could hear you had difficulty.

NORAH: I suppose the petrol pump in the village doesn't run to a mechanic?

FISHER: Can you have flooded the engine?

(*She looks at him, controlling her temper.*)

The plugs would not be wet, since the car is under cover.

NORAH: Perhaps you'd like to try, Mr Fisher. You seem to know a lot about it.

FISHER: Oh, I'm not mechanical, Miss Palmer. I understand the language of machinery, but not the practice.

MRS VIGO: Fisher don't do driving. He'm leaves that to others.

FISHER: Mr Wellbeloved, the butcher, is our mechanic. With your permission, I'll ask him to step over. His wife will mind the shop.

NORAH: Thank you. It's a long way, I'm afraid.

FISHER (*Going*): Luckily I have my bicycle.

216

Telecine 22: (d) Exterior. Road to cottage. Day.

(Fisher riding his cycle, very dignified.)

MRS VIGO (*Voice over*): Fisher don't drive. He'm known for learning, not for driving cars.

48

Interior. Kitchen. Day.

(Coffee in the kitchen. Norah, Fisher, Mrs Vigo, Wellbeloved.)

WELLBELOVED: Crack in the distributor rotor, isn't there?

NORAH: I shouldn't know a distributor rotor if I saw one, cracked or not. The point is, can you fix it?

WELLBELOVED: You can't fix it. Her'm cracked.

FISHER: You would have to replace the part.

NORAH: All right. Replace it.

(Wellbeloved turns enquiringly to Fisher.)

FISHER: Miss Palmer wishes you to replace the part.

NORAH: How long will it take?

WELLBELOVED: No time.

NORAH: Good.

WELLBELOVED: When I has the rotor.

(Pause.)

NORAH: I suppose . . . a garage would have one?

WELLBELOVED: Could try to Evesham.

NORAH (*Stands*): You'd better use my phone. Try as many garages as you like. (*She goes out.*)

FISHER: Phone the garage, Henry. We must help all we can.

49

Interior. Lounge. Day.

(*Norah bringing her suitcase from the car. To her:*)

FISHER: Allow me to assist you, Miss Palmer.

NORAH: I don't know what you're doing here.

(*Fisher takes the case.*)

FISHER: Mr Wellbeloved is phoning the garage.

NORAH: Anyway, why should it suddenly go?... this distributor thing?

FISHER: Most things in cars go suddenly, Miss Palmer. An unconsidered crack in metal a weakness in a belt or pipe, a sharp stone in a tyre, a loose wire, all unnoticed for mile after mile, approaching ever nearer to the point of no return, and then—breakdown. It is the same with bicycles to tell you the truth.

NORAH: Yes ... (*Slight pause.*) It couldn't be induced?

(*Fisher is surprised.*)

I never lock my garage ... If there were somebody ... hanging about outside.

(*Mrs Vigo is now seen standing at the door.*)

FISHER: But why should anyone do such a thing?

NORAH: I don't know who. Could it be done?

FISHER: One would be bound to notice. To crack the rotor from the outside, as it were. With (*Camera on Mrs Vigo.*) scissors, say. It would be immediately noticeable to a skilled mechanic. (*He goes with the case.*) I'll just take this indoors.

MRS VIGO: He'm reads a lot, Fisher. Books of all sorts.

NORAH: What does the garage say?

MRS VIGO: Can't get it to Evesham. They'm have to go to Coventry.

NORAH: Well, that's not far.

MRS VIGO: Two weeks delivery.

(*Pause.*

Norah a little shaken.)

NORAH: I suppose one could take a train.

50

Interior. Living room. Night.

(*Norah on the phone.*)

NORAH: It's ludicrous. There's no station nearer than Evesham, and the bus only goes through the village twice a week . . . There *isn't* a taxi. At least, there isn't one in the village, and when I got the exchange to find me some taxi-people in Evesham, the number didn't reply . . . The car itself? Immobilized. They took the distributor thing away, though why should they bother, when it isn't any good—No, of course there's no reason to come back to London; I can work perfectly well from here, but that's not the point, Jake. I feel such a prisoner without the car.

51

Interior. Madge and Jake's living room. Night.

(*Jake at the phone. Madge in an armchair.*)

JAKE (*Hand over mouthpiece*): She says she feels a prisoner without the car.

MADGE: She wants you to go and fetch her, I suppose.

52

Interior. Living room. Night.

NORAH: Look, Jake, my dear, what I was wondering . . . If you and Madge *would* like a day in the country on Sunday . . .

(*There is a burst of very loud static.*

Norah tries to talk over it.)

I said if you and Madge . . .

53

Interior. Madge and Jake's living room. Night.

(*Jake holding the phone away from his ear. Horrible static. He tries again.*)

JAKE (*Shouting*): I can't hear. (*To Madge.*) She's working up to it. (*Into phone.*) That's better. There were ninety-seven Nigerians on the line . . . Hello, Norah? Oh gawd!

MADGE: Cut off?

JAKE: I'd better try the exchange, I suppose.

MADGE: I shouldn't bother. She's bound to ring again.

54

Interior. Living room. Night.

(*Norah jiggling at the phone.*)

NORAH: Hullo? . . . Exchange? . . . Hullo? . . . Hullo? (*She puts it down. Waits. Picks it up. No tone. She begins to press the receiver bar up and down, in an attempt to attract attention.*)

ROBIN REDBREASTegment>

55

Interior. Madge and Jake's living room. Night.

(*Jake at the phone.*)

JAKE (*Into phone*): I see. Thank you. (*Puts down phone.*) Out of order.

MADGE: There you are. I told you Norah would ring if she could.

JAKE: Well, what do you think? I mean, she obviously wants us to go out and get her.

MADGE: Yes, but she didn't say so. (*Sees he is still clearly undecided.*) Jake, love, when you consider how much bother the telephone usually causes, why be ungrateful when it does something convenient for a change. I mean she isn't really a prisoner, this is the twentieth century. If she wants to get away badly enough, she will.

56

Interior. Kitchen. Day.

(*Mrs Vigo washing out dishcloths at the sink.*

Norah very nervous playing with the half-marble.)

NORAH: My phone's out of order.

MRS VIGO: That's right.

NORAH: You know?

MRS VIGO: Used the box in the village this morning, didn't you?

NORAH: To report it. Yes I tried to get a taxi from Evesham at the same time, but the number didn't reply.

MRS VIGO: That's right, Mrs Gibbins said you had trouble. (*Norah: A look.*) At the Post Office.

221

NORAH: It's Mrs Gibbins, then, is it, who's been trying to get me the Evesham number?

MRS VIGO: That's right.

NORAH: Does it seem odd to you that for five days I've been trying, without any success, to get away from here? (*Mrs Vigo: No reply.*) It seems odd to me. I looked in at the butcher's this morning, but apparently the rotor hasn't come from Coventry. My car doesn't work, Mrs Vigo, my phone doesn't work, people put live birds down my chimney,

(*Sharp look from Mrs Vigo.*)

I can't open the window at night without seeing Rob hanging about outside, and I've begun to feel trapped, and decidedly nervous.

(*Pause.*)

MRS VIGO: He'm hanging about, then?

NORAH: Don't you know he is?

MRS VIGO: I don't reckon to know every bloody thing, miss.

NORAH: But do you know, and will you tell me, why I am being kept in this cottage? Waiting for something. Alone.

(*Pause.*)

MRS VIGO: If you'm lonely, you can ask Rob to come in, since he'm hanging about outside.

(*Pause.*

Norah realizes that she has been playing with the half-marble, and puts it down.)

NORAH: Don't bother to come here any more, Mrs Vigo. I can manage the cleaning for the short time I'm here.

222

57

Interior. Living room. Night.

(Norah writing a letter.)

NORAH (*Voice over*): I'm sorry if I sound hysterical. I'm alone here. I keep telling myself it's only imagination, but I've had proof now. Yesterday was one of the days the bus comes. I packed a case, and carried it a mile across the fields.

Telecine 23: Exterior Village street. Day.

(Norah takes her case to just outside the door of the General Stores.)

NORAH (*Voice over*): I waited by the stop.

(Three village women with baskets give her guarded nods and smiles.)

NORAH (*Voice over*): There were a couple of village women there already.

(Then they move away up the street.)

NORAH (*Voice over*): But they moved up the street.

(Norah looks about her, to make sure she's at the right place. Establish the Midland Red sign in the window of the shop.)

NORAH (*Voice over*): I don't know why. I was at the stop, outside the General Stores.

(Bus appears at the end of the street. It stops for the women and they get in . . . all in long shot.)

NORAH (*Voice over*): Then the bus arrived. It stopped up the street where the women were. They got in.

(Norah running, carrying the case.)

NORAH (*Voice over*): I ran towards it.

(*It goes past her.*)

NORAH (*Voice over*): It passed me without stopping.

(*Final shot of the bus disappearing.*)

58

Interior. Living room. Night.

(*Norah still writing.*)

NORAH (*Voice over*): There's something wrong, Jake. I don't know what it is. They're keeping me here for something making sure I can't get away before Easter. I'm afraid. Please, both of you, don't be rational about it. Make allowances, and come and get me, as soon as you can.

59

Special shot. Part of post-office counter.

(*A letter, face upwards addressed to Mr and Mrs Jake Summers, 41 Royal Crescent, London S.W.12.*

Establish the top left-hand corner, where the words first class and urgent are written in capitals.)

FISHER (*Voice over*): I think you should be very careful with this one, Grace. Just keep it a few days to make sure it doesn't get lost in the post.

60

Interior. Living room. Night.

(*Norah is by the fire. Concentrate on the fire, and the shadows of the flames. No other lights. She is watching television. Curtains drawn.*

Television announcer's voice is heard. Norah is hunched up, nervous, ill-at-ease.)

Announcer (Heard): ... with us now in the studio to discuss the real meaning of Christ's Passion in the nineteen-seventies. The panel consists of Malcolm Muggeridge, Lord Longford, the Very Reverend the Suffragan Bishop of Eatanswill, the Right Honourable Justin de Villeneuve and a doctor.

NORAH: No, I don't think so.

(She switches over: we hear the aria, 'He was despised and rejected' from the Messiah.

She hears a tapping at the window.

She reacts to it sharply, gets up, goes to the window, hesitates, draws the curtain, but there is nothing.

She goes to the phone, and picks it up, but there is still no dialling tone. She switches on all the living room lights, notices that one of the bolts on the door to the shed and ground-floor loo is not drawn: and draws it.

Rattle of mice. Then the phone rings. It startles her. She goes into:)

61

Interior. Living room. Night.

(She picks up the phone.)

NORAH: Hello? ... Hello? ...

(But the caller doesn't speak, she puts the phone down slowly.

A slight tapping noise again from the window. She opens the front door and looks out. Nothing. She closes the door. Then she locks it.

She looks back at the phone, and decides to try something. She goes to it, and picks it up. This time there is

225

a dialling tone. Magnify it, to make sure we know what it is.)

NORAH: Well, thank God for that.

(She dials the operator. Ringing tone. Then an answer.)

OPERATOR *(Heard)*: Can I help you?

NORAH: Yes, please. I want to make a London call.

(Connection broken. Dialling tone.)

Hello? . . . Exchange? . . . *(Dialling tone stops. No noise. Norah presses down the bar, but can get no tone. Slowly she replaces the receiver.)* I see. *(She returns to the television from which Handel can still be heard, and switches channels again.)*

ANNOUNCER *(Heard)*: Bishop?

BISHOP *(Heard)*: Well, I don't think that any serious Christian nowadays believes that Jesus Christ—if there was such a person . . . actually rose from the dead so that when tomorrow morning, we give the traditional Easter Greeting, 'Christ is risen' what we're *really* saying . . .

(Norah cuts him off by switching off.)

NORAH: Not even a good night for television.

(There is a knock at the door. Norah stares at it.)

Don't be stupid. There's nothing to be frightened of.

(Knocks again.)

And stop talking to yourself. You're making me nervous.

ROB *(Heard: indistinct)*: I know you're in.

(Norah goes slowly to the door.)

NORAH: Who is it?

ROB *(Heard)*: Rob.

NORAH: I'm sorry. You can't come in.

226

(*Attempt to open the door from outside. It rattles but does not open.*)

It's no use trying to open the door. It's locked.

ROB (*Heard*): Please ... please.

(*Pause.*)

NORAH: I'll switch the outside light on. (*She does so, and starts to go upstairs.*)

Telecine 24: Exterior. Patio. Night.

(*Rob standing by the door, illuminated by the light above it.*)

ROB: Let me in, let me in, please.

(*Sound of the upstairs window being opened. He looks up. Norah is at the window.*)

NORAH: I told you I didn't want to see you. Why have you come?

ROB: There wasn't anywhere else. Please let me in. I've got nothing to do with it.

NORAH: With what?

ROB: With any of it.

(*Pause.*)

NORAH: I'll let you in. (*She leaves the window.*)

(*We see Rob anxiously looking around him.*)

62

Interior. Living room. Night.

(*Norah unlocks and opens the door. Rob stays by the door.*)

NORAH: I'm a pregnant woman. You shouldn't be bothering me.

ROB: I got nervous.

NORAH: *You* got nervous!

ROB: It's very lonely where I live. You start imagining things. I wanted somebody to talk to.

NORAH: You could have gone to the pub.

ROB (*Suddenly angry*): I don't go to the pub. (*Recovers: placating.*) I'm sorry. But I'm not one of them; you know that.

NORAH: You'd better come in.

ROB: I knew you'd be here, but I telephoned first anyway.

NORAH: That was you? Why didn't you speak?

ROB: I couldn't think what to say. (*He closes the door behind him, and locks it.*)

(*She watches.*)

NORAH (*Carefully*): Isn't that for me to do?

ROB: What?

NORAH: Lock the door. It's my house.

ROB: Oh ... Yes. If you like.

NORAH: Why did *you* lock it?

ROB: You had it locked before.

NORAH: Yes ... Well, come in and sit down.

(*He does so. Both watch each other.*)

ROB: You aren't sitting down?

NORAH: I shall when I want to. I feel rather restless at the moment.

ROB: Nervous.

NORAH: I said 'restless'.

ROB: I thought you said you were nervous earlier. (*Begins to relax.*) I feel better now.

NORAH: I hope you don't think I'll ask you to stay the night.

(*Silence. Clearly he did think this.*

Norah begins to be a little scared again.)

Just because I'm ... (*Half-gesture to her belly.*) You have no rights here: don't think that.

ROB: I'm going to Canada next week. I thought you'd like to know.

NORAH: How did you get the money?

ROB: I was loaned it. Ticket bought for me.

NORAH: By whom?

ROB: Fisher.

NORAH: Why?

(*Pause: Rob uneasy.*)

ROB: I don't know.

NORAH: I think you do.

ROB: No.

NORAH: Something you'd done? Some ... service rendered?

ROB (*Indignant*): I'm paying it back. It's only a single fare. Sixty pounds. I'll pay all the money back.

NORAH: What had you done for Fisher to induce him to lend it to you?

ROB: Nothing. I told you.

NORAH: And how did you know my phone would work when you rang?

(*Pause: Rob doesn't understand.*)

ROB: Why shouldn't it work?

NORAH: It's been out of order.

ROB: How should I know that?

NORAH: Everybody in the village knows. It's been out of order for a week. Then you want to phone, and it works. Then it goes out of order again. It's out of order now.

ROB: I don't go to the village.

NORAH: But you know them well enough to borrow sixty pounds.

ROB: I didn't borrow. It was loaned. I never asked; it was offered.

NORAH: I want to know why.

(*Pause.*)

ROB: Makes no difference . . . It was that night . . . you and me . . .

NORAH (*Very still*): When the bird came down the chimney?

ROB: That's right.

NORAH: Sixty pounds. It seems rather a lot for a one-night stand. Especially when . . . (*She shakes her head trying to think.*) Was he watching? Listening? Getting his kicks that way? No, that's not why; it can't be.

ROB: I don't know what you'm on about.

NORAH (*Sharp*): 'You'm'?

ROB (*Angry: spaces it out*): You are on about.

NORAH: You mustn't pick up bad habits of speech from your Auntie Vigo. Who knows everything.

ROB: Look, if you want to know, I'm trying to tell you. The poachers that night—the ones that knocked me out. That was Fisher. He says he had to attack me. Compelled to it. He's respectable, Fisher, known for it;

he's a lay-reader. If it was to come out he'd been poaching, his reputation would be besmirched. He said.

(*Pause.*)

NORAH: You believe that?

ROB: Why not? Why else would he . . .

NORAH: You expect *me* to believe it?

ROB: It's the truth.

NORAH: If he hadn't told you he was the poacher, how the hell would you have known? (*Rob can't answer.*) Are you trying to make me believe that seven months later . . . when you hadn't the least suspicion . . . he came to you, and confessed, and then paid you sixty—

ROB: Loaned.

NORAH: —pounds to keep your mouth shut. Are you asking me to believe that?

(*Pause. Faintly a van in the distance.*)

ROB: He's a funny fellow. He's got his own ways.

NORAH: There's a van on the hill.

(*Both listen, nothing.*)

It's stopped now. (*Moves away from him towards the kitchen.*) Why did you come here tonight?

ROB: I told you: I was nervous. As if . . . people were watching me.

NORAH: What people?

ROB: I don't know.

NORAH: Village people?

ROB: Could be.

NORAH: You know what you said when you arrived? —'I've got nothing to do with it', you said. With what?

ROB: I don't know.

NORAH: You don't know much. They haven't told you much. Just enough to get you indoors.

ROB: 'They'?

NORAH: People?

(*Pause, Rob tries to laugh. It is not convincing.*)

ROB: You *are* nervous.

NORAH: Why are they keeping me here until after Easter? (*He can't answer.*) Why did the house have mice? (*A rattle: they both look.*) And has again. Because I would need *you* to get rid of them, Rob. And you're a very good-looking young man. Known for it. And I'm a woman without a man—sex-starved, as they say. And when I ask you round for the evening, Rob, why is it that I was robbed—what a jolly pun that is; I was robbed, wasn't I, in every way?

ROB: I don't know what you mean.

NORAH: No means of contraception. It disappeared, and reappeared the next day. But the night intervened. You intervened.

ROB: We made love, if that's what you mean. You know we did.

NORAH: No. We 'had sex'. Rather arranged sex. The bull was brought to the cow; that happens in the country. And it took a lot of arranging. Because I went off you, and sent you away—since you were boring me silly. (*She sees his face, hurt.*) I put you out, and went alone to bed. But then a bird came down the chimney and I was frightened, and you were conveniently nearby to rescue me, and after that—what could be more romantic? Except that somebody had been on the roof to *arrange* that romantic rescue.

(*Pause.*)

ROB: Not me.

NORAH: No, that wasn't your part.

232

ROB: I was hit on the head. By Fisher.

NORAH: What's your part now, Rob?

(*He rises, confrontation.*)

ROB: You're being funny with me, aren't you?

(*She backs away to the kitchen. He follows.*)

63

Interior. Kitchen. Night.

NORAH: I don't know what's in your mind exactly, I've heard of things. Every now and then there's a song and dance about it in the Sunday papers. Devil worship. Graves dug up. Churches ... desecrated. Blood ... stories of blood, always rather vague. I've never believed it happened seriously.

ROB: You're being funny.

NORAH: Why have you been keeping me here, all of you?

ROB: You're being funny. I don't understand half of what you say.

(*The knife we have seen earlier is on the draining board. Norah has been backing towards it, and now grabs it.*)

NORAH: Yes, I'm being funny. This is very sharp. Your Auntie Vigo uses it to cut the heads off chickens.

(*He gazes at her in horror. Then in his turn he backs away. She advancing, towards the door.*)

ROB: You're off your chump.

64

Interior. Living room. Night.

(*As Rob reaches behind him for the door-key, there is*

233

a laugh from outside. He jumps. Norah is only slightly affected.)

NORAH: Your friends are outside.

ROB: I've got no friends.

NORAH: That was your part, then. To get in, and let them in. I don't know why. It's easy to break a window. Perhaps an act of betrayal is part of the ritual. Don't try to turn the key. (*Locks the kitchen door.*)

ROB: Please.

(*Norah is pointing the knife at him, and has come as close as she thinks safe.*)

NORAH: Come away from the door. I don't know anything about killing people, but I know where the delicate hurtful parts are. You tell your friends that if anyone tries to get into this room, I'll make a mess of their prize bull.

(*She beckons him to follow, and backs towards the fire.*

Silence. As they go, the door handle is turned, and the door tried.

They are still while this is done, then move back again. She feels more secure with the fire behind her.)

Safer here.

(*The other door to the outside through the downstairs loo is tried, but Norah locked it earlier.*)

ROB: I don't understand any of this. (*Desperate.*) Look, I'm on your side. I don't know what's happening, but I'm on your side. (*An appeal.*) I could protect you. I know karate.

(*Norah laughs.*)

We can't stay stood here for ever.

NORAH: Only till morning. It'll be Easter Sunday. By the rules of the game, as I understand it, I'll be free.

(*A laugh from outside.*)

You see, I'm right.

ROB: Please believe me. I don't know who's out there. I'm not one of them.

(*Noise at the front door. Both react. Rob turning his head to look. The key is pushed out of the lock on to the floor. Then we hear another key being inserted.*

Rob turns back to Norah, wild with fear. The connection is made. Norah lowers the knife.)

NORAH: You're terrified! You're as frightened as I am.

(*At this point, if we can manage to make it credible on televison, Peter comes down the chimney behind her, dropping suddenly as if into the fire.*

He holds the double-headed axe. Rob sees him and gives a cry. Norah swings round.

A frozen moment for everyone to take in what has happened. Then the knife falls out of Norah's hand, and she faints.

Peter steps out of the fire. The front door is opened from outside. Wellbeloved stands there. He steps aside, and indicates that Rob should go out.)

WELLBELOVED (*Gentle*): Come on, Rob boy.

(*Rob does so. Peter follows. Wellbeloved closes the door behind them.*

Camera on Norah. Unconscious on the floor.

A terrible screaming (Rob) heard from outside.

Fade to black. Screaming persists over the fade. Cross-fade sound to a mixed congregation singing cheerfully:)

CONGREGATION (*Heard singing*): Hallelujah!
Hallelujah!
Hallelujah!

(*Meanwhile bring up light to:*)

65

Interior. Living room. Day.

(*The curtains are drawn. Sunshine outside.*

Norah still lies there but the knife has gone. Kitchen door open.

Fade out the singing. Norah opens her eyes.

A moment, then we hear, from the kitchen, the sound of the waste-disposal unit.

Norah sits up.)

66

Interior. Kitchen. Day.

(*Mrs Vigo, dressed for church, is at the sink, running water into the waste-disposal unit.*

Norah appears from the living room. Mrs Vigo shuts off the unit.)

NORAH: What are you doing here?

MRS VIGO (*Turns to her*): Come to take you to church, haven't I?

NORAH: Like before.

MRS VIGO: I brought a hat.

NORAH: What happened last night?

MRS VIGO: Nothing to remember. Just a game we'm about sometimes.

NORAH: I was . . . I was very frightened.

MRS VIGO: Stupid!

NORAH: I thought . . .

MRS VIGO: No call for that. Stupid thinking that. What good would a woman's blood be for the land?

(*Norah is staring at her, unable to take it in.*)

We bear, my dear; we'm give birth; that am our work. It takes a man for the other. (*She begins to leave the room.*) Your spare part for your car come yesterday. Fisher'm bringing it up after morning service.

(*Telephone rings.*)

67

Interior. Living room. Day.

(*Mrs Vigo answers the phone.*)

MRS VIGO (*Into phone*): All right then, Grace.

(*She hangs up. Norah has followed.*)

There'll be no more trouble with that. You'm got time for a bath before church.

(*Norah begins to mount the stairs. She turns.*)

NORAH: Where's Rob?

68

Interior. Lounge. Day.

(*Norah is now dressed for her departure. Fisher is with her. Cut in immediate from the preceding scene.*)

FISHER: Gone to Canada, Miss Palmer.

NORAH: Not till next week.

FISHER: Oh dear me, no; I'm sure you're mistaken. He was to leave today. Easter Sunday . . . a most appropriate start to a new life. By train to Liverpool, and then by boat. An assisted passage.

NORAH: Assisted by you.

FISHER: As it happens. He came round last night, as I understand it, to take his leave. You'll be selling the house, I imagine?

NORAH: Yes.

FISHER: Better. Country life cannot suit us all.

NORAH: I meant, 'Yes, he came round last night'.

FISHER: I heard so. We must all wish him luck in his new venture.

(*Peter comes out of the house with Norah's suitcase, and carries it towards the garage.*)

NORAH: What was Peter doing here last night?

FISHER: Peter, too? But *he* would have no occasion to say farewell. The village is his home.

NORAH: He came down the chimney. He had an axe.

(*Pause. Fisher looking at her curiously.*)

FISHER: Yes ... well, that was very naughty of him. Did anyone else see him?

NORAH: Only Rob.

FISHER: Who is no longer with us.

(*Pause.*)

NORAH: Why are you letting me leave, when I could go to the police?

FISHER: About what, Miss Palmer?

NORAH: Mrs Vigo said something rather curious to me this morning. She said, 'What good would a woman's blood be for the land?'

FISHER: No good at all.

NORAH: 'It takes a man.'

FISHER: Indeed, yes.

NORAH: You understand it, then?

FISHER: The study of religions is one of my many interests. I am a reading man, you know.

NORAH: Known for it.

(*Mrs Vigo has come out, and stands in the doorway.*)

FISHER: The goddess of fertility in the old legends was in some ways like yourself, Miss Palmer. Not a married lady, but nevertheless, if you'll excuse the freedom, not a virgin either. In the autumn, she would couple with the young king.

NORAH: King?

FISHER: He would be treated like a king. Served and ... pampered, you might say. And then, of course ...

NORAH: Killed.

FISHER: He would pass away, yes. Assisted to it, one might say. And from his blood, you see, the crops would spring.

NORAH: A Greek legend, Mr Fisher.

FISHER: And Egyptian. Mexican. Many places. You must read a book by Sir James Fraser—*The Golden Bough* in seven volumes.

NORAH: But not an English legend.

FISHER: Robin Hood. Robin of the Dale. Even Robin Redbreast, one of the very birds in your garden. The male robin only lives a year, you know. The female has many partners. Always Robin. Such bounty there was, such fruitfulness, Miss Palmer, from the blood that drained from Robin Hood the old stories say.

(*Norah can't speak: she just stares at him.*)

But they are only stories, of course. If that were all one had to say to the police, how very foolish they would think one.

(*The car is heard starting.*)

239

Your car is ready now.

NORAH: Thank you.

FISHER: There is only one other small matter. You'll forgive me if I offend you. Your ... er ... your little one ... the expected little bundle. Mrs Vigo was afraid you might be modern in your thoughts, but I was sure you would not wish to take a life.

NORAH: What are you saying, Mr Fisher?

FISHER: I have good friends, Miss Palmer, at a local orphanage.

NORAH (*No colour: very flat*): And in twenty years?

FISHER: It would not concern you.

(*Pause.*)

NORAH: No. No, I don't think so, thank you. (*She goes.*)

Telecine 25: (a) Exterior. The road from the cottage. Day.

(*Norah driving her car away up the road. She looks back.*)

Telecine 25: (b) Exterior. Patio. Day.

(*Tableau: Fisher with antlers as Herne the Hunter, Mrs Vigo as the Crone, Hecate. Peter and Wellbeloved in leather aprons with blood on their arms.*)

Fade.

Another Sunday and Sweet F.A.

JACK ROSENTHAL

Preface

JACK ROSENTHAL was born in Manchester in 1931. His television plays include *There's a hole in your dustbin, Delilah*; *Your name's not God—it's Edgar*; *The night before the morning after*; *Compensation Alice*; *Pie in the Sky*; *Green Rub*. His comedy series include *The Lovers* and he has also written scripts for the following: *Coronation Street, Comedy Playhouse, Thirty-Minute Theatre* and *That Was the Week That Was*.

'There's this tradition that every writer has to look worried. A pale-faced perfectionist, neurotic and defensive about his work. Rumour has it he can hardly sign his name on his Writers' Guild membership card, without complaining that he'd have written it better given more time—and would the Chairman like a re-write?

'I feel slightly uncomfortable criticizing a medium that, for eleven years, has been my bread and butter, and often Marmite. But television *is* the cause of its writers' principal worry: His play is seen only *once*. However enthusiastically-praised by the critics, however highly-rated by the public—*a television play has precisely the same life-span as the worst play ever presented in the theatre*. It closes the same night it opens. However long it has taken to write, however much time, money, energy and talent has gone into its production—immediately its end-credits roll, so does its head.

'When ITV began, it wooed potential advertisers by christening its public the perfect misnomer—"The Captive Audience". A television audience could hardly be more free. Any members of it out on parole playing snooker, or on their honeymoon, or reading *Oz*, or watching an alternative channel when a play is on—have missed it for ever.

'Films and stage-plays, of course, have *truly* captive audiences—who've surrendered time and money to sit facing front and watch till the usherettes let them out. And that happens every night—for weeks, at least. Maybe for months. Sometimes for years. A television play is flickering shadows on a coloured screen. And they don't flicker again tomorrow night.

'The play may have taken months to write. And it'll be many more months before another play by the same writer is on the air. Meanwhile the director and actors who gave the play, say, three weeks of their lives move on to the next play. And there only *is* a next play because another writer has spent months in his cocoon for another bedridden butterfly with ninety minutes to live.

'Perhaps there's no realistic alternative. Perpetual turnover, to both television management and audience, is the very strength of the medium. And, of course, there *are* compensations: the writer is well-enough paid to cover his pallor with a St Trop suntan; the production (despite his nailbiting) is probably excellent; and it's seen by millions of people. But, again, it's promptly followed by the *next* excellently-produced programme, or batch of shimmering, superbly-filmed commercials, and the next, and the next—and inevitably just as quickly forgotten.

'The television writer can't hope to achieve the reputation or prestige of the writer for films and theatre—except by a disproportionate output of new plays. He can, of course, multiply his output twenty-fold by writing for series and serials. But that, by its very nature, is self-defeating. The more successful the initial episodes, the more management and audience, quite naturally, want the same again every week. The same—only different. But still the same. Till finally, through familiarity if nothing else, a long run appears *too* long—and the writer has spent the whole time running on the spot.

244

'Of course, just as the television writer envies the advantages of the longevity of stage-plays and films, *their* authors envy the gigantic, albeit very transient, audience that television has.

'Maybe all *is* vanity, after all. But, assuming everyone in television is guilty of it, maybe when the writer stops worrying, it'll be good reason for the others to start.'

JACK ROSENTHAL

Another Sunday and Sweet F.A. was first transmitted by Granada Television on 9 January, 1972*, with the following cast:

REFEREE (Eric Armistead)   *David Swift*

Parker Street Depot XI:
CAPTAIN (Graham)   *Gordon McGrae*
MANAGER (Arthur)   *Fred Feast*
TRAINER (Sam)   *Joe Gladwin*
GOALKEEPER (Stewart)   *David Bradley*
PLAYER (Steve)   *Stephen Bent*
PLAYER   *Alan Erasmus*

Co-op Albion XI:
CAPTAIN   *Freddie Fletcher*
MANAGER (Colin)   *Duggie Brown*
TRAINER (Brian)   *Bert King*
GOALKEEPER   *John Proctor*
PLAYER   *Joey Kaye*

On the touchline:
GWEN   *Clare Kelly*
ROSIE   *Lynne Carol*
SHIRLEY   *Anne Kirkbride*
DENISE   *Clare Sutcliffe*
GIRL-FRIEND (Gina)   *Susan Littler*
NORMAN   *Michael De Freyne*
FIRST BOY   *Bryan Sweeney*
BOY   *Bruce Witt*
BOY   *Dominic Toner*

Produced by Peter Eckersley
Directed by Michael Apted

* It was later transmitted by NRCV Holland and has been sold to television companies in Germany, Sweden and Finland and won the TV critics' Circle Award for the best single play of 1972.

Characters

REFEREE (*Eric Armistead*)

Parker Street Depot XI:
CAPTAIN (Graham)
MANAGER (Arthur)
TRAINER (Sam)
GOALKEEPER (Stewart)
PLAYER (Steve)
PLAYER

Co-op Albion XI:
CAPTAIN
MANAGER (Colin)
TRAINER (Brian)
GOALKEEPER
PLAYER

On the touchline:
GWEN
ROSIE
SHIRLEY
DENISE
GIRL-FRIEND (Gina)
NORMAN
FIRST BOY
BOY
BOY

ACT I

1

Exterior. House. Sunday morning.

The front door opens and Eric emerges. He's about 45 years old, the sort of man usually described as non-descript. He's wearing hat and coat, and carries a brand-new Adidas bag over his shoulder.

Through the opened door, we hear the distant, shrewish voice of his middle-aged wife, Polly.

POLLY (*Out of view*): Other husbands sleep late Sunday morning.

ERIC: Yes, Polly.

POLLY (*Out of view*): Not you, though.

ERIC: No, Polly.

POLLY (*Out of view*): You have to be different, don't you!

ERIC: Yes, Polly.

POLLY (*Out of view*): I don't know what you see in it.

ERIC: No!

(*With sudden ferocity, he yanks the door towards its lock, hard enough to bring the house down on Polly's head. But, at the last second, he checks himself and closes the door gently and quietly.*

He stands for a moment on the doorstep. Yes, all right, he's given way again. Who cares? Fair enough, normal people stand up for themselves, hit back, try to win. Well, let them. Sometimes you can win by losing ... Shows you're strong enough not to have to win. Oh, sod 'em. And her.)

2

(*Two small boys are fighting at the end of the path, rolling each other over from the pavement and blocking Eric's gateway. Their bikes lie on the pavement. Eric approaches down the path.*

Uh, uh, all right, try it gentle but firm.)

ERIC: All right, lads. In your own gateways. Good lads.

(*They ignore him. He tries lifting one leg then the other to climb over them and fails.*

All right, fair enough. Try smiling. Jokey, one of the lads.)

ERIC: Can't you strangle each other at home? That's why your fathers pay rates.

(*They ignore him. At a loss, he suddenly almost panics. . . . Then remembers normal people stand up for themselves. Firmly.*) Right! Move! (*No effect.*) I said *Move!* (*No effect.*) I shan't say it again. (*He does.*) Move! (*Pause. They wrestle. He watches.*) I'll count to five, then that's it. One, two, three, four, five. (*No effect.*) Six. (*Nothing.*) Right!

(*He stands there. They carry on wrestling. He glances at his watch, sighs. Steps on to his garden and clambers awkwardly over the fence on to the pavement. Sod them as well. He makes his way down the street, only eventually beginning to lengthen his stride.*)

3

Exterior. Playing fields car park.

Some of the players are arriving, boots slung around their necks, and carrying grips with their gear in. Two of the players (Ronnie and Alan) have their girl-friends with them (Shirley and Denise).

250

The two teams about to play are CWS Albion 2nd XI and Parker Street Bus Depot. They each have a team-manager-cum-trainer and an assistant.

For the CWS these are Colin and Brian: and for Parker St, Arthur and Sam. (Sam the assistant, is about sixty, little and shrivelled.)

4

(Eric walks through the car park towards the dressing rooms, aloof from the activity and noise around him.)

5

(A few small boys are messing about, half-heartedly, with a light, plastic football, while the players arrive. They ask who's going to win, and are they any good, and conclude that both teams look pathetic.

A couple of players make their way to the dressing rooms, heading a football one to the other. Eric passes through the throng, continuing to ignore everyone and ignored by them.

Suddenly one of the small boys loses control of his plastic ball and it bounces towards Eric. They shout for him to kick it back to them.

He tries to—and miskicks like a big, soft girl. The small boys—and some of the players—jeer.

The jeers hurt—but not as much as the fact that he missed the ball. His fault, though, not theirs. Sod himself, then, stupid sod. Been stupid all his life. Sod everyone.

He walks on towards the dressing room, with attempted dignity. Fooling no one.)

6

(*At the touchline are the groups of supporters perhaps twenty yards apart.*

In the CWS group are Shirley and Denise, Colin and Brian (Brian wearing gumboots to run the line in.)

In the Parker Street Depot group are Arthur and Sam (Sam's trouser-bottoms stuffed into the top of his socks, ready to run the line).

Each group has holdalls containing oranges, water, first-aid kit, etc. Eric approaches them, on his way to the dressing room.)

ERIC (*As he passes*): Morning.

(*They ignore him. He continues on his way.*)

SHIRLEY: Seen who's reffing?

COLIN (*Regretfully.*): Lord Longford.

SHIRLEY: Good god! (*Calling across to the Parker Street Depot group.*) Have you seen who's reffing?

ARTHUR (*Calling back*): It's the same for both sides. He's blind in *both* eyes.

7

(*Intercut between the players communal dressing room and the referee's.*

Dressing room:

The players (late teens, early twenties) singing, shouting raucously and fooling about, while changing.)

8

Referee's room:
(Eric changing, quietly, soberly.)

9

Dressing Room:
(The players treating their clothes, untidily, carelessly, disguising the tension they feel before their private fantasy of playing in the cup final.)

10

Referee's Room:
(Eric folding his clothes, slowly, meticulously.)

11

Dressing room:
(Young athletic, muscular arms, legs and chests, shiny with oil and embrocation.)

12

Referee's room:
(Eric's thin, white, 45-year-old limbs.)

13

Dressing Room:
(A player slips an Indian band round his forehead to

hold down his long hair. Another ruffles the untidy hair of his pal.)

14

Referee's room.

(Eric, immaculately dressed in referee's uniform, standing before the broken mirror, brushing his short hair down with two brushes.)

15

Exterior. Football pitch.

(The two teams make their way on to the pitch in groups of two or three. Some limbering up athletically, others lethargically (still not completely over their Saturday night booze-up), others having a last drag on their cigarettes. There are four or five players out of the twenty-two in odd shirts, only approximately the same colours as their team.)

16

(The last of the players has trotted on to the pitch. The two teams are practising shooting in.)

ARTHUR *(With patent secretiveness)*: Go on, Sam.

SAM: What?

ARTHUR *(Jerking his head backwards towards the dressing rooms)*: You know.

SAM: It doesn't work. Not with Lord Longford.

ARTHUR: It might.

SAM: It never has before.

ARTHUR: It's worth a bloody try!

(*Sam sighs and moves off towards Eric, who now emerges from his dressing room.*)

17

(*Colin, in the CWS group, sees Sam making his way to Eric. He turns to Brian urgently.*)

COLIN: Away you go.

BRIAN: What's the point?

COLIN: I said away you go!

BRIAN: He might report me. He's threatened to before.

COLIN: Threaten him back. Put the fear of Christ up him.

BRIAN: How do I do that?

COLIN: Stare him out.

(*Brian sighs and moves off towards Eric.*)

18

Cut to Eric striding towards the pitch, looking like— and imagining he is—a World Cup referee.

Sam slides ingratiatingly up to him.

SAM: Morning, Mr Armistead.

ERIC (*Walking on*): No, thank you.

SAM (*Trotting to keep up with him*): I haven't offered you one yet.

ERIC: Offered me a what?

SAM: Cigarette. I'd no intention of doing.

ERIC: Good.

SAM: Fancy some chewing gum?

255

ERIC: Good morning.

(*Sam gives up trying to keep pace with Eric's purposeful stride, and now drops back, defeated, and wanders off to rejoin Arthur.*)

19

(*Brian approaches Eric.*)

BRIAN (*Effusively*): Nice to see you again, Mr Armistead!

ERIC (*Walking on*): I've brought my *own* lemon, thank you. And embrocation.

BRIAN: I never said a word! No one offered you a lousy lemon!

ERIC (*Stopping dead*): Would you like to go before the League Committee?

BRIAN: Would you like to go to hell?

ERIC: I've been, laddie. That's what I'm doing *here*. (*He strides on towards the pitch, till he reaches Colin. He nods towards the football Colin is holding.*) Ball!

(*Colin tosses it to him. Eric stands for a moment testing its hardness, then glances at the pitch.*)

No corner flags again, I notice.

COLIN: That's the last time I'll lend anything to the YMCA.

(*Eric sighs in disgust and makes his way to the centre circle.*)

20

The centre circle.

(*Eric blows his whistle, sharply, summoning the two captains to join him. The CWS captain is Stan. The Depot captain is Graham.*

They trot towards him, loosening up arms and shoulders.)

ERIC: Captains, please! Good morning.

(They both grunt, gracelessly.)

ERIC: A few pearls of wisdom. From one who knows.

(Stan and Graham, who've heard it all before, exchange a long-suffering look.)

What we're now about to witness is called a football match. Not the beginning of World War Three. Not the destruction of the human race. A football match. In it, each team will attempt to score more goals than the other.

(Graham is looking at Stan, derisively.)

STAN: What are you looking at?

GRAHAM: Not much.

ERIC: And that will be done by kicking the ball in the net—as opposed to kicking other people in the crutch.

STAN: Right.

GRAHAM: Great.

STAN: Thank you.

GRAHAM: Shall we start—or are we going to stand here and freeze to death?

ERIC: If I see a good, clean exhibition of football skill, you won't know I'm here. If, on the other hand, and acting according to the new Gospel according to Lytham St Annes, there's any foul tackles from behind, shirt pulling, swearing at me or dropping dead with St Vitus' Dance because some other player accidentally looks at you, out comes my little book— and in it goes the name.

(Another long-suffering glance between Stan and Graham.)

Arguing with the referee will naturally not be tolerated.

STAN *(Arguing)*: Well, who the bloody hell's arguing!

ERIC: Are you trying to get your name in the Guinness Book of Records? The only player to be sent off before the game's even started?

GRAHAM: Like a bloody tape recorder.

ERIC: Did you speak?

GRAHAM: No. I was yawning.

(*Stan looks away in disgust. Eric retains his warning look for a few moments longer then takes a coin out of his pocket.*)

ERIC: Heads or tails?

GRAHAM: Tails.

(*Eric tosses the coin, then picks it up, looks at it.*)

ERIC: Heads, it is.

STAN: As we are.

ERIC: May the best team win.

STAN: Why?

(*Eric gives him a look.*)

ERIC: Shake hands.

(*Stan and Graham start shaking hands. While they do so, their faces make no attempt to hide the total, primeval, bitter hatred they're feeling for each other—and promising each other.*

They finish shaking hands. Stan crosses himself, piously, fooling neither God nor Graham. Eric blows his whistle to summon the two teams to take up their positions.)

21

(*Brian and Sam take up their positions on the two touchlines, holding their handkerchiefs which will be used for flags.*)

22

Cut to the CWS contingent.

SHIRLEY: Come on, the Albion!

DENISE (*Chanting*): Co-op Albion! Co-op Albion!

COLIN: Now go for that ball, lads. *Hungry* for it. Play football, the goals'll come. Hungry for that ball.

SHIRLEY: Thump it in the net, Alan!

DENISE: How are you and Alan doing, these days?

SHIRLEY: All right. (*Shouting.*) Get stuck in Alan!

(*Denise gives her an amused, significant look. Shirley does an ' 'ey, Cheeky!' pout back at her.*)

23

(*Eric blows his whistle to start the game, and as the ball is kicked off, an immediate bedlam of noise breaks out—Arthur, Sam, Colin, Brian, Shirley and players shouting instructions to each other.*)

24

DENISE: Come on, Ronnie! (*To Shirley.*) Ronnie's been off it for a week.

SHIRLEY: Off what?

DENISE: You know.

SHIRLEY: Saving his strength for today?

DENISE: So he says. Lousy pig.

(*Colin, watching the match with concentration, suddenly erupts in anger.*)

COLIN: For God's sake, ref! Obstruction! Blatant obstruction!

25

(*Eric blows his whistle for a foul—while Ronnie rolls on the ground in apparent childbirth and the opposing players protest their innocence.*)

26

SHIRLEY: Who's down?

COLIN: Ronnie. Right in the doings.

DENISE (*Alarmed*): What?

(*Colin picks up his trainer's bag and dashes on to the pitch.*)

27

(*Eric, occupied in admonishing the man who fouled (and his team-mates) and telling Ronnie to stop coming the old soldier turns to see Colin racing towards them, water dripping from his magic sponge.*)

He waves Colin away, sternly.)

ERIC: All right. Back you go.

COLIN: He's in bloody agony!

ERIC: Yes. Actress of the Year Award, 1971.

COLIN: The lad's hurt.

ERIC: Childbirth's never pleasant. Off!

COLIN: Be fair, ref . . .

ERIC: I said Off! (*To Ronnie.*) And you can get up now, you've got your free kick. (*To the depot players.*) And you lot get ten yards back. (*Back again to Colin.*) I said off!

COLIN: Yes, I heard you. (*He nevertheless starts attending to the injured Ronnie.*)

(*Graham starts applauding Eric, sarcastically.*)

GRAHAM: Magnificent. Referee's authority. Wonderful sight to see.

ERIC (*To Colin*): I'm warning you.

COLIN (*To Ronnie*): All right, lad?

(*Ronnie nods, and Colin starts back to the touchline.*)

28

DENISE (*Shouting from the touchline*): Dirty foulers! (*To Shirley.*) Kicked him right in my engagement present.

29

(*Eric whistles for the free kick to be taken. The game continues. Eric sprints along the pitch keeping up with the play.*)

BRIAN (*Shouting*): Be fair, ref!

ERIC (*Voice over, to himself, while following play*): Oh, hello. First cuckoo of spring. He got a free kick. What more did he want? The British Empire Medal and a visit to Match of the Day when it's in his area?

BRIAN (*Shouting*): Fair's fair, Ref.

ERIC (*Voice over, resignedly*): Same old song. Second verse same as the first. Bring on the dancing girls.

261

Slice it for a goal kick and scream for a corner. Boot
it into touch and claim a throw in. One day a player'll
come up to me and say—'Excuse me Ref, you probably
didn't see it, busy as you are, but I've just kicked
their striker in the calf. It's preying on my mind so
would you care to take my name? Please.'

30

Exterior. Empty football pitch.
(*Adjacent to the one on which our game is played.*)

(*Norman, a very young, bespectacled man, in overalls
and gumboots, is pushing the trolley-like machine
which lays whitewash in straight lines.*

*He's slowly, painstakingly marking the touchlines in
preparation for an afternoon game.*

Norman walks with a limp.
He's talking to himself, in a low but petulant voice.)

NORMAN: Well, *he's* supposed to be the park keeper!
It's his *job*—not going fishing in Cheshire, with his
bag of worms and dirty books. (*Mimicking.*) 'You do
the pitches, Norman,' he says. 'You can watch the
football.' If I was interested in bloody football, I
wouldn't be a Parks and Gardens Department em-
ployee, would I? I'd be a bloody footballer. (*Checks
mechanism of his whitewash machine.*) Piccadilly
Gardens, that's where I should be. Planting chry-
santhemums. I told 'em that at the Labour Exchange.
No one listens. (*He checks his machine again.*) Damn
thing. (*He fiddles with the mechanism disgustedly.*)
'You can watch the football!' Silly sod. He's scared of
being here, that's what it is. When they try to pinch
the goalposts after the match. (*Mimicking.*) 'Put them
goalposts back! I know what team you play for! I'll
tell the police!' Silly old fool. It was the Police Cadet
team that was pinching 'em ... (*He looks behind him*

at the slightly wavy line he's made.) That's never straight. (*He sighs and continues pushing his machine.*) I'm not *supposed* to be a painter and decorator. Everyone was put on this earth for a purpose. Mine was to grow chrysanths. That's why I've got green fingers. (*He wipes his hand over his forehead. His fingers are covered in whitewash. So now, is his forehead . . .*)

31

Exterior. Football pitch.

(*Tight on Eric, blowing his whistle sharply for a foul.*

Pull back. Stan is the culprit, staring at Eric in wide-eyed innocence.)

STAN: What?

ERIC: 'Calling for the ball, without calling the name of the man in possession.'

STAN: I called his name.

ERIC (*Placing the ball for the free kick*): No arguments.

STAN: I *called* it!!

ERIC: You can go funny with too much imagination you know. You can start wearing ladies' hats in the middle of Market Street.

STAN: I even called the *other* lad's name—before that one got it!

ERIC: Thank you. That's an even bigger offence. *He's* playing for the other bloody side!

STAN (*Coldly, bitterly*): He's not the only one.

(*On hearing the accusation, Eric immediately freezes his entire body into a threatening stance, his index finger pointing at Stan warningly.*

With several players looking at each other, long-sufferingly, he holds his melodramatic pose for several seconds longer than seems humanly possible.)

Any chance of a game of football?

(Eric walks over to him, body still bent forward, finger still pointing.)

ERIC: In Association Football, we have rules. We call them the Rules of Association Football. Being fair doesn't mean being fair to *you*. It means being fair. Understand?

STAN: No.

ERIC: No.

(Too bloody true, he doesn't. Who does?

Eric waves him away, and whistles for one of the Depot players to take the free kick.)

32

(The game continues.
Eric, more than a little incensed, concentrates even more on his job—strutting, running, bending backwards, peering for offences in every tackle.)

33

(Cut to Arthur, standing on the touchline. Nearby is Sam, running the line.)

ARTHUR *(Disgusted at the CWS tackles)*: By hell, they're a rough lot.

SAM: Rough lot aren't they?

ARTHUR: Kick anything that moves.

SAM: They'd kick their own grandmothers.

ARTHUR: Never heard of sportsmanship. (*Suddenly shouting.*) Get him down. Tommy!!! Go for his left knee-cap! The one with the bandage on! Go for his left knee-cap ...

(*Tommy has done. Arthur's satisfied*)

Good lad.

Cut to:

34

The CWS goalmouth.

(*A centre comes across. Graham collects it, brings it under control and shoots—well wide of the goal. Eric whistles for a goal-kick. While the goalkeeper is collecting the ball, Eric trots back upfield alongside Graham. Eric is smiling to himself, genuinely amused. Graham gives him a dirty look.*)

GRAHAM: Something tickling you?

(*Eric smiles.*)

It was a bad bounce. Wasn't my fault.

ERIC: It was a nice shot. Magnificent marksmanship. Wonderful sight to see. (*He starts applauding Graham sarcastically as Graham did to him earlier.*) Another inch to the left, you'd have had it rolling down the M.1.

GRAHAM: Like you could do better?

ERIC: I wish I was your age, laddie, that's all.

GRAHAM: You never *have* been, mate!

ERIC: We had a thing called *skill*. Different game to-day. Different world.

(*We hear Shirley shouting from the touchline.*)

SHIRLEY: Come on, the Albion! Get stuck in!

(The goal-kick is taken. Stay on Eric as he continues running and following the play.

Denise and Shirley emit great whoops of delight at Shirley's rudeness. Eric glances towards them.)

ERIC (*Voice off*): Different world altogether.

35

(He looks back at the two girls, leggy in their hot-pants. Suddenly, there's a yell of protest from a player (Steve) alleging handball.)

36

(Eric, preoccupied with the girls, has missed the incident. He quickly looks away from the girls, and shakes his head at Steve, dismissing the appeal and waving play on.)

STEVE (*Aggrieved*): He handled it!

ERIC (*Tapping his bicep in disagreement*): Play on.

STEVE: He grabbed hold of it!

ERIC: Never.

STEVE: With both bloody hands!!

ERIC: Accidental.

STEVE: Where the hell were you looking?

ERIC: Don't be so crude! I'm old enough to be their father!

(Eric, grim-faced, waves play on. Sod him. Sod the one who handled even more. For one second he happened to glance at girls' legs. A second, that's all. Glancing. Not chatting them up. Not climbing into

*bed with them. Then climbing into bed with another.
Then another. Just glancing.)*

37

Exterior. Playing fields.

*(Taking a Sunday morning stroll, some distance from
our football match are two middle-aged women, Rosie
and Gwen. Rosie has a small, tatty dog with her on
a lead.)*

ROSIE *(Puzzled)*: President Nixon?

GWEN: President Nixon.

ROSIE: But I thought America and China were bitter
enemies?

GWEN: It's what they call ping-pong diplomacy. That's
the expression they use.

ROSIE: And the Russians have got the needle?

GWEN: Well, naturally. They've been daggers drawn
with China ever since Khruschev denounced them at
the 21st Party Conference. For revisionism.

ROSIE: For what?

GWEN: That's the expression they use. 'course they've
been suspicious of the *Western* bloc ever since Yalta.

ROSIE: Since when?

GWEN: Yalta.

ROSIE: Is that another expression?

GWEN: Another conference.

(Pause.)

ROSIE: We seem to be bigger allies with *France* these
days. Since Whatsisname died.

GWEN: And with the advent of the EEC.

ROSIE (*Not understanding*): Mmm. You know what happened in the *First* World War? The French women put poison in the wells. For our soldiers to drink.

GWEN: They were on *our* side!

ROSIE: Not the women. (*To the dog.*) Now, don't tug, sweetheart. Not nice. Nice walkies.

GWEN: Then there's *Japan*, of course. *Very* touchy about him going to China.

ROSIE: Ping-pong's right. Emperor Doodah coming to visit the Queen. Soon forget, don't they?

GWEN: Forget what?

ROSIE: Like Germany. *They're* our allies now. Young lads go for *holidays* there! Wasn't much of a holiday for their *fathers* . . .

GWEN (*Pause*): Born at the wrong time . . .

ROSIE: Ping-pong.

GWEN: My next-door-neighbour's booked for Northern Ireland. (*She glances at the football match.*) Football's not back already, is it?

ROSIE: Oh, I get sick of it.

GWEN: Malcolm Allison wears nice matching shirts and ties.

38

Exterior. The football pitch.

(*Tight on Eric suddenly blowing his whistle. Cut to two opposing players having a ding-dong fight in the middle of the pitch—nowhere near the ball. Eric races up to them, continuing to blow his whistle. Other players separate the two men. On the touchline, the managers, linesmen and supporters voice their anger. Eric stands firmly between the two players.*)

ERIC: All right, that's it. Final. (*He takes his notebook out*.) Next Sunday you can go to Church for the first time in your life—you won't be allowed *near* a football.

CWS PLAYER: He was pulling my shirt!

DEPOT PLAYER: Only retaliation, ref! Subsequent to constant provocation.

(*Eric gives him a look, unimpressed by the jargon.*)

ERIC: Thank you, Bob Wilson.

CWS PLAYER: Another two minutes, he'd have had me down to my jockstrap!

ERIC (*Licking his pencil*): Names?

GRAHAM: Oh, ref! It was the heat of the moment.

STAN: Technical foul, that's all.

ERIC: I am not giving way! Names!

GRAHAM (*To Depot player*): Keep your mouth shut.

STAN (*To CWS player*): Say nothing.

ERIC (*To CWS player*): Did he pull your shirt?

STAN: No.

ERIC: I'm talking to *him*. Did he pull your shirt?

CWS PLAYER: No.

ERIC (*To Depot player*): Were you retaliating to constant provocation?

DEPOT PLAYER: No.

ERIC (*Putting his book and pencil away*): Now, just hear this, the lot of you. If you want to play according to the Law of the Jungle, I'm abandoning the match. Right? Right. Like a couple of orang-outangs fighting over a bloody banana! It's a Collyhurst and District Third Division League Match—not Custer's Last sodding Stand.

ARTHUR: They're only lads, Mr Armistead.

SAM: Just lads, that's all.

ERIC: We live in a civilized society. Even a *two*-year-old knows the difference between right and wrong.

39

Exterior. The dressing rooms.

(The small boys we saw earlier with the plastic football are grouped together behind the dressing rooms, standing beneath a window. The football match is in progress in the background, its sounds slightly muted.

One of the boys, standing at the corner of the dressing rooms, peers round to see if anyone can see them. Satisfied they're safe, he signals to the boy nearest the window. He acknowledges the signal, climbs on to another boy's back and through the window. The boy on look-out follows him, on the other boy's back and through the window. Then a third.)

40

Exterior. Football pitch.

(Eric is still lecturing the assembled players. Various players sigh wearily)

ERIC: We play to rules. We play as a team. With team-work. Team-work and skill.

41

Interior. Dressing room.

(The first boy nods to the other two. They promptly

start rifling the pockets of the players' jackets hanging from pegs on the walls.

They do it swiftly, expertly, with concentration and team-work. Team-work and skill.)

1ST BOY: Always leave at least half of what's in their wallets. If there's *three* quid just nick *one*. Same with any change in their pockets. Then they're not all that sure it's missing.

(*The boys, working methodically from jacket to jacket do as instructed.*)

42

Exterior. Football pitch.

(*Eric, holding the ball, still lecturing the players.*)

ERIC: So we'll have a bounce-up. And don't think I've given way, because I haven't. I'm respecting you as footballers.

(*Various players roll their eyes heavenward.*)

And you just respect the laws of the game. Respect for each other. Respect for the referee. And we'll *all* profit by it.

(*He drops the ball for the bounce-up. Two players hack into each other, going for the ball.*)

43

Interior. Dressing rooms. Eric's room.

(*The first boy drops into the referee's changing room through a fanlight which is above the door separating this room from the players' dressing room. He takes Eric's wallet from the jacket hanging on the wall.*

271

We see the contents: Two pound notes, various bits of paper—and an old, yellowed photograph of Dixie Dean. The photograph is captioned: 'Dixie Dean, Everton and England'.)

1ST BOY (*To himself*): Who the hell's Dizzie Dean? (*He shrugs and puts everything back in the wallet, except one of the pound notes. This, he pockets.*)

44

Exterior. Football pitch.

(*The match in progress. The CWS Albion goalkeeper is collecting the ball for a goal-kick—and very transparently taking his time about it.*

Eric stands, between the edge of the penalty area and the half-way line, hands on hips, lips pursed, watching him with impatience.

The goalie lethargically places the ball. Then strolls back at snail's pace to take his run-up.

Eric blows sharply on his whistle. The goalie looks at him innocently. Eric starts to run towards him.)

45

ARTHUR (*On the touchline*): I don't believe it! He's whistle-mad! (*Shouting*) Hey, Ronnie Ronalde, get on with the game.

46

ERIC (*Voice off as he runs to the goalie*): That's what I'm trying to do, isn't it? That's what I'm doing!

47

SAM (*On the touchline near Arthur*): Whistle-mad, isn't he? Talk about Ronnie Ronalde.

ARTHUR: Ridiculous. Spoiling the game.

SAM: Spoiling the game, isn't he?

48

(*Eric approaches the goalkeeper.*)

GOALIE: What?

ERIC: Are we ever going to have the pleasure of *seeing* you take this goal-kick?

GOALIE: I'm taking it!

ERIC (*Taking his book out*): Name?

GOALIE (*Pleading*): Oh, no, ref! I can't walk fast. I'm injured.

ERIC: Biggest crime of all, time-wasting. More than a crime. A sin. Wishing your days away. And that's more than a caution, laddie. It's a philosophy of life.

(*He puts his book away again, without having entered the goalie's name.*)

GOALIE: Its nearly half-time, anyway.

ERIC: It'll be half-time when I say so. When the forty-five minutes are up. And not before. It's nowhere *near* half-time. (*He glances at his watch, promptly blows his whistle three times, and announces.*) Half-time!

49

(*Cut to the small boys who've been stealing from the dressing rooms. They're leaning casually against the*

*dressing room wall, desultorily clapping the entertain-
ment that's so far been offered.)*

END OF ACT I

ACT II

50

Exterior. Football pitch.

*(The second half of the match is in progress and the
depot team is mounting a series of tremendous attacks
on the CWS goal. Time and again, the CWS defence
is lucky to scramble the ball clear . . . off the line, the
bar, the post, off outstretched limbs.*

The depot forwards are in agonies of frustration.

*Eric, though sympathetic to the perversities of the
game, is as always, being scrupulously fair.)*

51

Empty adjacent football pitch.

*(Norman is now marking the penalty area with his
whitewashing machine. Still talking to himself.)*

NORMAN: Don't see how I *can* do it straight, if I walk
with a rotten limp. Stands to rotten reason. If I didn't
have a gammy leg, I'd do it perfect. And if I *did* it
perfect, they'd say 'Oh, gracious me! We can't have
that. Let's put him on planting chrysanths in Piccadilly
Gardens.' And if I was brilliant at *that*, they'd say,
'Oh, gracious me! He's brilliant at gardening—let's

274

sign him on for Arsenal at centre-forward.' And I'd say 'Stick it, sweetheart. I'm not interested in football. And I'm not. Am I hell-as-like. (*Pause*.) That's how I broke my leg in the *first* place . . .

52

Exterior. The Depot team goalmouth.

(*Stewart, the depot team goalkeeper is standing in his goalmouth, watching his forwards at the other end of the pitch mounting their fruitless attacks, and sharing in their frustration.*

A girl, Gina, approaches from behind the goal, quietly and with some reluctance, head down.

She stands beside the post, glancing from time to time at Stewart, then at her feet again.

Stewart, concentrating on the game, is unaware of her.)

STEWART (*Frustrated at his team's near-misses*): Damn! Hell-fire and damn! Pig's bum is pork!

GINA (*Quietly*): You know I don't like you swearing.

(*He turns and sees her. He promptly becomes tight-lipped.*)

STEWART: Oh, you've come, have you? When the game's half over.

GINA: You told me not to come at all.

STEWART: Because *you said* you wouldn't!

GINA: Only because you told me not to!

STEWART (*Accusingly*): Why have you then! Because you won't do as I say, or because you tell lies?

(*The ball is cleared aimlessly down to his penalty area. He gathers the ball. Bounces it a couple of times, and boots it back upfield. He returns to his goalmouth.*)

STEWART: It was you that was obstinate at the party.

GINA: You'd been obstinate all evening.

STEWART: Only after you'd been obstinate at the party. (*Righteously.*) You should have said you were sorry when you had the chance.

GINA: Well, I'm here now, aren't I, silly?

STEWART: Halfway through the match . . .

GINA: It proves I'm sorry.

(*He looks at her, pityingly, with patiently controlled exasperation.*)

STEWART: Two wrongs don't make a right.

53

Exterior. Football pitch.

(*Another defence splitting attack by the depot team leaves a forward with an open goal.*

His shot hits Rosie's tatty dog which has strayed on to the pitch.

The ball rebounds to safety.

The dog squeals and is recalled by Rosie.)

54

The touchline.

(*Arthur staring in disbelief at his team's ill-luck. Sam, hanky in hand, is a yard or so away.*)

ARTHUR: Everything bar score. It's heartbreaking.

SAM (*Shaking his head*): Breaks your heart doesn't it?

ARTHUR: Outclassing 'em. We should be five up at least.

SAM: Different class altogether. Could be winning five or six none.

55

Exterior. Football pitch.

(*Another shot from a depot forward smacks against the crossbar.*)

56

Exterior. The Depot team goalmouth.

(*Stewart, hands on hips, watching the game. Gina, submissively, scratching her fingernails against the goalpost*).

GINA: Well, are we friends again *now*?

STEWART: Up to you, isn't it? You're the one that's sulking.

GINA: Me? When?

STEWART: You never dance with me like you were with Alan Potter!

GINA: *You* never look at me like you did at that bird wearing no bra!

STEWART: Only because you danced like you did with Alan Potter!

GINA: Well, doesn't that prove something?

STEWART: No.

GINA: It does. It proves . . .

(*Stewart races from his goalmouth to collect a back-pass. He clears the ball upfield and returns to his goal.*)

STEWART: Proves what?

GINA: I can't remember. Are you winning?

STEWART: Why? Are you interested?

GINA: If I wasn't, I wouldn't ask.

STEWART: If you *were*, you'd have asked as soon as you got here. (*Pause. She looks daggers at him*) It's nil-nil.

GINA: I'm not interested.

57

Exterior. Football pitch.

(*On the touchline, Arthur smacks his forehead with the palm of his hand in frustration. As yet another depot attack fails at the last second.*)

ARTHUR (*Incredulously*): *Again*—for God's sake! It's like a mad-house. It's like the world's gone mad.

SAM: Like a flaming mad-house, isn't it?

ARTHUR (*Screaming*): Do you *have* to repeat everything I say?

SAM (*Shocked, quietly*): I don't do.

ARTHUR: All the time. Every syllable.

SAM (*Frightened*): No . . . no, I'm *agreeing* with you, that's all. I share your opinions.

ARTHUR: That's not agreeing. That's sucking up.

(*Sam walks a little farther away, pretending to follow the play along the line. He now seems more shrivelled and pathetic than ever.*

He's always sucked up. All his life.

Perhaps he's got worse as he's got older.

He turns back to Arthur.)

SAM (*Quietly*): I don't suck up to no one. Never have done.

ARTHUR: To me. Every Wednesday night at the training session. Every Friday night at the planning and tactics meeting. Every Sunday morning.

(*Sam watches the football for a few moments, blankly. He turns again to Arthur.*)

SAM: I just said we're outclassing them, that's all. And we should have had five in. And how the world's gone mad.

ARTHUR: Well, that's what *I* said!

SAM: Yes. Agreed. I just happened to say it just after you did, that's all.

(*They both watch the match in silence for a moment.*)

ARTHUR (*Still watching the match while he speaks*): You're an old man, Sam. You're too old for this caper.

SAM: I know my football! I've got an old head on my shoulders.

ARTHUR: You've got old bloody *shoulders*!

SAM: I saw Billy Meredith, I did. Hyde Road. On the wing for City with a toothpick in his mouth. Always played with a toothpick in his mouth.

ARTHUR: What's that got to do with it?

58

(*In the CWS penalty area, Graham takes the ball, weaves past three defenders, draws the goalkeeper, and gently strokes the ball towards goal. It rolls nearer and nearer . . . and stops about two inches from the line. A defender races up and boots it out of play. Graham gets up, wearily. Eric is nearby.)*

GRAHAM: We should have a cricket score ...

ERIC: That's life, lad, isn't it?

GRAHAM (*Frustratedly*): Can't you just *give* us one?

ERIC: And that's wishful thinking.

GRAHAM: I think there's a jinx on that ball!

ERIC: You can't blame that. Blame the Patron Saint of Football.

GRAHAM: Who's that?

ERIC: Mephistopheles.

GRAHAM: Who's that?

59

(Cut to the CWS contingent on the touchline. Shirley and Denise, fed up, sitting on the grass, watching the game, dispiritedly. Colin—sunk in despondency.)

COLIN: One of those days. Just not getting the run of the ball. (*Shouting.*) Come on, the Albion! You've nothing to beat!

SHIRLEY: I didn't know you were a comedian, as well.

COLIN: Eh?

SHIRLEY: They're all over us!

DENISE: They're making us look sick.

COLIN (*Angrily, frustratedly*): Who's side are you on, anyway?

DENISE: Well, they *are*!

COLIN: Why are they?

SHIRLEY: Because they're a better rotten team, aren't they?

COLIN: Two scrubbers who pack tubes of toothpaste all week—what gives *you* the impression that *they're* making *us* look sick?

SHIRLEY (*Angrily*): What's the score, then?

DENISE: Just 'cos there's no goals, doesn't say there shouldn't have been!

(*Colin looks towards the match again, deciding the discussion is beneath him. He promptly looks back at them again, having thought of an excuse.*)

COLIN (*Calmly*): We happen to be playing 4-3-3. It's deliberate tactical strategy. Playing it tight at the back, and relying on the quick break up front.

SHIRLEY: They *must* be quick—I haven't seen one yet!

DENISE: We haven't *had* one yet!

COLIN (*Not so calmly*): We're pacing our bloody selves!

DENISE: You're just biased.

(*He looks at them, gravely.*)

COLIN: You don't know what it's all about, do you?

60

The middle of the pitch.

(*Tight on Eric as we follow him about the field, refereeing with concentration, grimacing, shaking his head, gesticulating.*)

ERIC (*Voice over*): Nice ball, son! Now, *use* it! Be a decent player, that kid, if he wasn't so ... *That's* a foul! Oh, forget it! *He* clobbered *him* a minute ago. Mind you, he deserved it for *calling* him what he did,

but then again he got called it himself in the first half.
Vicious circle. (*Pause.*) So where do you start? Tell
them to play the game? (*Whistles.*) Play to the rules?
Half of them's probably been on the dole for eighteen
months... Find the space, lad. Now *shield* the ball!
Hard luck! Of course they should have a cricket score.
But that *is* life, I wasn't wrong. Not that it ever sinks in.
(*Pause.*) And all you can do is tell them to be fair. It's
never won a football match yet, mind you. It's never
won anything. They might not know Mephistopheles,
but they know *that* all right. Been out of nappies long
enough. (*Pause.*) And what can *they* do? Blame the
ref. Yes lads, I know being fair isn't fair. *Any* day of
the week. That's why we turn out on Sundays—hoping
this time it will be. It never is, but we *hope*. The beauty
of football they used to call it ...

(*Cut to*:)

61

(*Pull back. Another depot attack in progress. There's
a frenetic goalmouth scramble. The ball is half-cleared
to just outside the penalty area. As Graham races up
to shoot, Stan fells him heavily to the ground. Eric
blasts on his whistle and dashes up, dragging Stan
away from Graham. He grabs Stan by the collar.*)

ERIC: One more. Just one more foul like that—and
you go and get dressed. Bingo.

STAN (*Shrugging Eric's grip from his collar*): I went
for the ball.

ERIC: According to the Laws of Football, all you're
liable for is sending off. According to the Law of the
Realm, you'd get five years at least, without remission.

STAN: I accidentally nudged him!

ERIC: Grievous Bodily Harm before any court in the

land. (*He waves the Albion team back.*) Ten yards from the ball.

(*He places the ball for the free kick and waits for the Albion defence to go back ten yards. Meanwhile a depot player quickly takes the free kick, tapping it to a colleague. Eric blows his whistle again.*)

Bring it back here! You take the kick on *my* say-so.

(*The ball is grudgingly kicked back to him. He places it again, then faces the Albion defenders, who are forming a defensive wall just outside the penalty area, hands cupping their crutches.*)

Ten yards back, I said.

(*The wall moves back a foot or so, then creeps slightly forward again. Eric, hands on hips, watches them.*)

For those who are unfortunately deaf as well as daft, I said ten. Not two. Ten!

(*The wall moves back a yard or so. They're now about five yards from the ball.*)

Bit more.

(*They don't move. Eric, starting at the ball, paces out ten yards, until he is standing behind the wall.*)

Where *I* am.

(*The wall moves back very slightly. Eric sniffs.*)

Captain, please.

STAN (*A member of the wall*): Good morning.

ERIC: I want these chorus-girls standing here. Tell them.

STAN: Back a bit, lads.

(*The wall moves back a foot or so, still yards away from Eric. Right. O.K. They want a trial of strength? They've got one.*)

ERIC: Right. (*Calmly.*) If you don't move ten yards from that ball, I abandon the match.

(*Disgusted, amused looks from the members of the defensive wall.*)

I shall count to five, then that's it. One, two, three, four, five. (*Pause.*) Six.

(*Like the two small boys wrestling in his gateway earlier, they ignore him.*)

STAN (*Amused, to his mates*): He won't abandon it.

ERIC: Match abandoned.

(*He picks up the ball and starts striding towards the dressing rooms. Bedlam breaks out. The managers and linesmen race on to the pitch. The players of both teams besiege him—the depot players complaining that they're being victimized, that the CWS team has nothing to lose, that the depot team are being deprived of imminent victory. Eric bundles his way between the players. Stony-faced.*)

STAN: Look! We'll get ten yards back, all right?

ERIC: Too late, sonny boy.

GRAHAM: Oh, ref! If they get ten yards back, ref!

ERIC: We play to the rules of the game—or not at all. I will not have my authority flouted.

STAN: That's *it*, isn't it. It's you that matters. You and your bloody whistle.

(*Eric stops dead in his tracks He just can't believe what he's heard. It's like 1984 come true: Double-think.*)

ERIC: Me.

STAN: You don't give a sod about the football. Just you. Just so's you're the Big Cheese. Showing everybody who's boss.

ERIC (*Slowly, utterly flabbergasted. Zombie-like*): It's

the other way round. (*He looks at the others.*) It's the other way round. It's completely the oth . . . I just want to be fair . . .

STAN: Prove it.

GRAHAM: Prove it.

(*Impasse. Being fair doesn't mean being fair to you . . . it means being fair. But, hang on. If you're the referee, the instrument of fairness—it does mean being fair to you . . . doesn't it? Isn't the fair thing simply to abandon the match? What the hell does it mean?*)

62

Exterior. Playing fields.

(*Rosie and Gwen walking with the tatty dog.*)

ROSIE (*To the dog*): Yes, I know. Nasty ball hurt your tummy. Well, you stay with your mother, sweetheart. Blooming ruffians.

GWEN: Then there was *Cyprus*. A few years back.

ROSIE: Your Mary's Arnold.

GWEN: Killed by terrorists. And Archbishop Makarios —all the cartoonists and everyone making him out another Hitler . . .

ROSIE: He *looked* a villain with that beard.

GWEN: Not now, though. Best of pals. *He* comes visiting the Queen, as well.

ROSIE: Must seem a bit puzzling to your Mary.

GWEN: And a bit late in the day for her Arnold.

ROSIE (*To the dog*): Yes, love. Nasty boys. Poor tummy.

GWEN: Mary's Arnold was under age when he joined up. Joke, isn't it? Altered his birth certificate . . . (*Pause.*) To get a death certificate . . .

63

Exterior. The Depot team goalmouth.

(Gina beside the goalpost. Stewart, on his line, a little apprehensive that he's upset her too much.)

STEWART: Go on, then. I'll accept your apology.

GINA: I have to go now.

STEWART: I was only rotten to you because we're not winning.

GINA: I know.

STEWART: And you *did* come to watch me . . .

GINA: Yes, I did.

STEWART: And you only danced with Alan Potter because I was obstinate.

GINA: Well, *you* say you're sorry, then.

STEWART: I'm sorry, Gina.

GINA: Say it again.

STEWART: I'm sorry.

GINA (*Smiling for the first time*): I accept. (*Starting to move off.*) Well, thanks for some lousy times.

STEWART: Where are you going?

GINA: Roller skating with Alan Potter. (*She flounces off happily*).

(He stares after her.)

64

Exterior. Football pitch.
Eric and the assembled players.
GRAHAM: Well?

286

ERIC (*Sighing, giving way*): Back to your positions. Direct free kick. Defending team ten yards from the ball. And I *mean* ten yards.

STAN: According to the rules, once a match is abandoned, it can't be re-started.

ERIC (*Lying*): I didn't abandon it. I said I *might*.

STAN: You never did!

ERIC: Don't argue with the referee.

(*They run back to their positions. Eric places the ball for the free kick. The defending wall stands about eight yards from the ball. Eric a couple of yards behind them.*)

ERIC: I *kept my* side of the bargain . . .

STAN (*To his colleagues in the wall*): Back a bit lads.

(*They move back till they're level with Eric.*)

ERIC: Thank you!

(*He blows his whistle. As the player taking the free kick runs up to the ball. The defensive wall moves swiftly forward. Blocking the kick. The ball runs loose. Eric shoots a bitter look at Stan. The player who took the free kick yells his protest at Eric. Eric sighs. Lost out again.*)

Play on.

65

(*The game continues. Tight on Eric. Suddenly his expression of bitterness changes to alarm. Pull back to see him doubling up as the ball cannons full-bloodedly into his stomach.*)

PLAYERS: Get out of the bloody way, ref!

(*He straightens up immediately as though it didn't hurt.*)

66

Exterior. Empty adjacent football pitch.

(*Norman is pushing the whitewashing machine, now marking the centre-circle. Talking to himself.*)

NORMAN: Anyway, you do your best. S'all you *can* do. Even painting white lines. With the same love you give to planting chrysanths. And that's the satisfaction. Whitewashing every *other* bugger's mistakes.

(*The ball is suddenly thumped over from the football match—and thuds heavily against Norman's white-washing machine, just as he's turning it round on one wheel. The machine is knocked on its side. A sea of whitewash floods out and all over the carefully painted line. Norman looks at it, expressionlessly.*)

67

Exterior. Playing fields.

(*Rosie, Gwen and the dog. Football match in progress in background.*)

ROSIE: Poor love. See the way he keeps looking at that ball. He's disturbed, you know. It can disturb them for life.

(*Gwen emits a little yelp as the dog goes for her ankle.*)

ROSIE: And leave your Auntie Gwen alone. That's naughty.

GWEN (*Niggled*): It's all right. He was only playing.

ROSIE: Anyway, that's politics, isn't it? Nothing ordinary people can do.

GWEN: Human beings aren't important to them. It's all money. Power.

ROSIE: No feelings.

GWEN: None.

(*The dog snaps at her ankles again.*)

ROSIE: Leave your Auntie Gwen *alone*! He *is* disturbed. (*Resuming conversation.*) What do Governments care about suffering? Nothing.

GWEN: Nothing at all.(*She surreptitiously but viciously kicks the dog. The dog yelps.*)

ROSIE: What's the matter, sweetheart?

GWEN: Probably trod on a stone with his little paw, little love.

68

Exterior. Football pitch.

(*The game in progress. The Depot team mounts yet another dangerous attack. One player slips the ball through to another—who is, unfortunately, several yards offside.*)

69

(*Sam, running the line and in good position to judge. Flags his handkerchief to signal offside.*)

 The CWS players appeal vociferously for offside.

Arthur notices Sam flagging.)

ARTHUR: Don't flag offside, you old fool! He's one of ours!

(*Sam guiltily drops his arm.*)

70

(*Eric, who is also in a good position to judge, is about to blow his whistle, when another player accidentally jostles against him. Eric's whistle is knocked from his lips.*)

71

(*The offside player races on towards goal, round the goalkeeper and slides the ball into the net.*)

72

(*Eric has recovered his whistle and blows sharply.*

The Depot players, thinking Eric has whistled for a goal, leap in the air, victoriously.

The CWS players appeal for offside. Angrily.)

73

(*Arthur has his arms raised, cheering to heaven.*)

74

(*Shirley and Denise are philosophical: Colin racing on to the pitch protesting.*)

75

(*Eric runs to the spot where the player was offside, pointing for a free kick. As he does so, the mob of*

Depot players who are congratulating their goalscorer are running and jumping towards the centre-circle.

Like a great human tank, out of control, they collide with Eric, who is promptly flattened and trodden underfoot by a forest of feet.

As the players move on, we see Eric prostrate and unconscious.)

76

(The angry, protesting CWS players meet the Depot players en route to the centre spot, complaining bitterly about the goal. Much arguing and gesticulating.)

77

(Eric still lies there, unconscious.)

78

(Eventually, one by one, the players notice him and fall silent. They trundle over to him.)

79

(From Eric's point of view we see the circle of faces. (In and out of focus?)

For a few moments—and for the first time—there is absolute silence and stillness.)

80

(Arthur produces his magic sponge, and sponges Eric's face. He gets to his feet. His face seems strangely calm. He's feeling a sort of quiet strength.

Immediately he's up, there's a great babble of voices again, breaking the silence—appealing and counter-appealing to Eric.)

ERIC: Quiet.

(They fall silent.)

How long was I out?

ARTHUR: Few seconds.

ERIC *(Checking his watch)*: I'll add five seconds on.

(The babble of players' voices starts up again.)

ERIC: Quiet.

(They fall silent.)

It was no goal. It was offside.

(The CWS players cheer. The Depot players protest.)

ERIC *(Calmly, slowly, quietly)*: It was no goal. It was offside.

ARTHUR: You *blew* for a goal!!

ERIC: I blew for offside.

GRAHAM: Well, you took your time about it!

ERIC: I was jostled by a player. *(Still calm and quiet.)* I blew as soon as I could. We'll now proceed with the free kick.

ARTHUR *(Bitterly)*: I'm sorry I sponged your face now!

81

(Arthur wanders off back to the touchline. The players straggle off to take up their positions, grumbling or pleased, depending on which team they're in. Graham is kneeling near Eric, re-tieing his bootlace. He gives Eric a dirty look.)

ERIC: What's that for?

GRAHAM: You could've allowed it.

ERIC: An offside goal? Is that how you want to win?

GRAHAM: It's *right*, that's all. If we don't win it's *wrong*.

ERIC: Yes, it is.

GRAHAM: There's no flaming justice . . .

ERIC: The other side's got a free kick. That's justice.

GRAHAM: You know what I mean.

ERIC: Yes, I do.

GRAHAM: I'm bloody sick of football!

ERIC: Then you should hang your boots up. We all should. We shouldn't play. (*Quietly, very soberly.*) Why do you think I turned to refereeing? I had promise, but for the war. Accrington Stanley once wanted me for a trial, 1939. I could've been another Dixie Dean, they said. Once I'd filled out.

(*Graham looks at him, soberly.*)

GRAHAM: Bloody wrong then, weren't they?

(*He lumbers back into position to face the free kick. Eric stands where he is, gravely pondering on what Graham's just said.*

He whistles, abstractly, for the free kick to be taken.)

82

(*It's a bad one and a depot forward collects the ball and runs out with it on to the wing.*)

83

(*Cut back to Eric, still motionless, still grave.*)

84

(The player with the ball beats a CWS defender and makes to centre the ball.)

85

(Cut back to Eric, watching. He suddenly sprints into the CWS penalty area as the ball is centred from the wing. Stan, defending, leaps up to head it away, but the ball soars over his head.

There are no depot forwards in position to take the ball.

As it soars into the goalmouth, Eric reaches the end of his sprint, leaps into the air like a second Dixie Dean and heads the ball like a rocket into the back of the net.

He promptly whistles for a goal, points to the centre-circle and thrusts his arm in the air, momentarily, in a Dennis Law triumphal salute.

The impossible has happened. On a quiet Sunday morning in Manchester, the earth has spun to a stop, hardly pausing even to clear its throat, and started rotating in the opposite direction.

The twenty-two players stare at Eric, dead-eyed, in utter incomprehension. Eric strides back towards the centre-spot, noting the goal in his book and checking the time on his watch.

All the players are standing stock-still: Motionless since the moment Eric headed the goal.)

86

(Eric passes Graham.)

GRAHAM: Er . . .

(*Eric looks at him, enquiringly.*)

Er . . . what er . . .

ERIC: Mmm?

GRAHAM: I don't . . . er . . . exactly . . .

ERIC: Get your team back in your own half, laddie, for the kick-off.

GRAHAM: Er . . . kick-off?

ERIC: We always kick off after a goal has been scored laddie. Otherwise we'd die of exposure.

GRAHAM: A goal has been scored?

ERIC: A goal has been scored.

GRAHAM: Are we winning one-nil?

ERIC: You're winning one-nil.

(*Graham throws his arms in the air and yells his jubilation. His team-mates follow suit and race about congratulating and kissing each other.*)

87

(*On the touchline, Arthur cheers deliriously and Sam throws his hanky in the air in delight.*)

88

(*The CWS players watch their antics for a moment, blankly, then as they realize what's happened, converge on Eric—with Colin and Brian from the touchline—screaming, threatening and pleading their protests.*

They besiege Eric in a jostling, pushing, angry mob. In reply to their claims that it couldn't have been a goal, he calmly repeats that it was.

295

In reply to their screamed accusations that he, the referee, scored it, he takes from his pocket a copy of the F.A. Laws of Football. *He finds the relevant page.*)

ERIC: Law 9, paragraph B of the *Laws of Football*, published by the Council of the Football Association, Patron Her Majesty the Queen, states as follows: (*Very deliberately.*) 'The ball is in play if it rebounds off either the referee or linesman when they are in the field of play.' Satisfied? (*He replaces his booklet.*)

STAN: Are we bloody hell-as-like! It *didn't* rebound off you!

(*The rest of the team angrily yell their agreement with Stan. Eric looks at them calmly.*)

ERIC: Don't argue with the referee, lads. I don't want to send you all off. They'd stroll upfield and tap another in, wouldn't they?

(*Colin tries to control black, murderous thoughts, with difficulty.*)

COLIN: Ref. That ball didn't rebound off you. You jumped up and headed the sodding thing in. Deliberate.

ERIC: No, sir. And *you're* asking for trouble coming on the field, anyway. The ball was centred from the left. I ran up with play, according to my duty, the ball accidentally struck me on the head, as I endeavoured to get out of the way, and rebounded into the net. Law 9, paragraph B, a goal.

STAN: It didn't strike you! *You* struck *it*!

ERIC: There's eleven players over there wouldn't agree with that interpretation. And neither would the referee, acting in accordance with the Rules of the Game. Be fair.

89

(*He walks on towards the centre-circle. Absolutely in command of the situation—and himself.*

The Depot players are waiting in position, patiently, arms folded.

The CWS players bitterly, grudgingly put the ball on the centre-spot. Eric blows his whistle for the kick-off. The CWS centre-forward, indicates his disgust with life, by booting the ball aimlessly into the opposite half of the field.

Eric glances at his watch, then blows three times sharply on his whistle.)

ERIC: Full time!

90

Exterior. The pitch.

(As Eric makes his way from the field, several members of the defeated team form a rough aisle, and boo and catcall Eric as he strides masterfully between them towards the dressing room.

From a few members of the victorious team come chants of 'We are the champions'.

Eric smiles.

Gradually fade up sound of the Wembley crowd at the 1966 World Cup Final, clapping and chanting '1,2,1,2, 3,1,2,3,4, England!'

Mix from Eric's face to a slow-motion re-enactment of Eric's goal: The words 'action replay' superimposed over the picture.

Mix back to Eric's face. At peace.)

91

Exterior. The football pitch.

Sam is leaving the pitch carrying his trainer's bag etc. He calls—breaking Eric from his reverie.

SAM: Excuse me, Mr Armistead?

ERIC: Yes?

SAM: I'm not complaining . . .

ERIC: No.

SAM: But it *wasn't* fair, was it? Our goal.

ERIC: Absolutely legal. Law 9, paragraph B.

SAM: I see.

ERIC: Good morning. (*Starts to move off again.*)

SAM (*Still slightly perplexed*): I still think it was unfair, really . . .

(*Eric, older and wiser, looks sympathetically at the simple sexagenarian.*)

ERIC: Only in the eyes of God, lad. And *He's* needed new glasses for nearly 2,000 years.

(*He walks on.*)

92

Exterior. Dressing rooms.

(*Outside the dressing rooms, the first small boy is nonchalantly standing, tapping the plastic football to and fro his pals. Eric approaches.*)

1ST BOY: Hey, Mister. Are you Dizzie Dean?

ERIC (*Stopping, about to enter dressing room*): Who?

1ST BOY: Footballer. Dizzie Dean.

ERIC: Dixie Dean.

1ST BOY: Him, then.

ERIC: He was very *famous*.

1ST BOY: Aren't *you*?

(*Eric smiles.*)

ERIC: Who told you about him?

1ST BOY: It was in a comic.

(*Eric opens the door to go in.*) I've been guarding this hut.

ERIC (*Turning*): Mmm?

1ST BOY: I've been guarding it. While you've been playing. Case anyone breaks in and pinches anything. You get skinheads round here sometimes.

ERIC (*Kind smile*): Thank you, son. (*He feels in his pocket and finds a 5p piece. He gives it to the boy.*) 5p.

1ST BOY: Ta.

(*He starts to wander away. Eric calls him back.*)

ERIC: Hey, son!

1ST BOY: What?

ERIC (*Giving him another coin*): And another five makes ten.

1ST BOY: What's that for?

ERIC: It's Sunday.

93

Credits.

Slow-motion replay of Eric's goal, freezing frame for each credit.

Follow the Yellow Brick Road

DENNIS POTTER

Preface

DENNIS POTTER was born in the Forest of Dean, Gloucestershire, in 1935. His television plays include: *The Confidence Course, Alice, Vote Vote Vote for Nigel Barton, Stand Up Nigel Barton, Emergency Ward Nine (30'), Where the Buffalo Roam, Message for Posterity, The Bonegrinder, Shaggy Dog, Beast with Two Backs, Son of Man, Moonlight on the Highway, Lay Down Your Arms, Angels are so Few, Paper Roses, Traitor, Six plays about Casanova, Follow the Yellow Brick Road, Only Make Believe.*

'Most people crave distraction: we are, it seems, unable to sit still for very long in a small room as chained dogs must in their kennels. The bright little screen in the corner has been turned by default and by greed into a domestic appliance which caters for such congenital restlessness. Most of what it shows is merely stuff designed to pass the time, a swirl of endless images, soon forgotten, unchallenging, bland and rubber-boned. The once-named "window on the world" of brave old promise (or dishonest prospectus prose) is now much more like a silvered mirror sending back features we already know and do not wish to change. It sells aero-soled reasurrance during the programmes and aero-soled deodorants in between. When the polychromatic picture collapses into a small white dot there cannot be many minds touched with the pale fire of wonder. Tune in tomorrow instead.

'I think I once knew why it was "important" to write for television but now I am by no means quite so sure. Eight years of feeding the insatiable machine have left their wounds. But when I sat down to write my first television play I had almost evangelical notions about the significance of television as one of the great emancipating forces of our society. The audience for any one programme is counted by the million, and thus is likely to include at the same time, sharing the same sequence of argument or emotion, people of widely differing social and educational backgrounds and different levels of expectation, hope and prejudice: "dons and coal-miners" was the easy shorthand formulation, a lazy piece of near-cant which I mistook for something wholly democratic. In part, this was a healthy enough reaction to an élitist education, and a necessary with-drawal from what too often seemed to be the precious timidities of an English literary culture where "only connect" was reduced to an incestuous whisper across chinking tea-cups and sticky honey-pots. I was certainly not alone among my contemporaries in seizing upon television as a process or a platform whereby we could hope to short-circuit the inhibitions, blockages and snobberies of a hierarchical "print" culture and address our fellow citizens more directly and (especially) more intimately than had ever before been possible. To hell with dreaming spires or bells across the damp meadows: after all, there was scarcely a rooftop in sight which did not spike out its aerial, plucking instant electronic dreams out of the air. Who was to provide them?

'Alas, we know the answer to that, and we know what sort of dreams they are peddling. I have inverted some such dreams in *Follow The Yellow Brick Road*, making the lush buttercups-and-sunshine world of the commercials appear a desired purity, even a religious radiance—as well it might to more than just deranged minds. In the early days of ITV they faded out *Hamlet* in order to get a few ads in, but now they are more discreet: margarine or coloured toilet rolls between the acts. The play has changed, too. The commercials are made with more skill and more resources than the majority of the programmes, and they even say more as well.

'Yet still the most popular and pervasive of all the mass media resists most generalization, sour or otherwise. The beloved box is tabloid newspaper, picture book, sports stadium, concert hall, theatre and cinema, mostly diminished, peculiarly crabbed, but also over-whelmingly in the present tense. I forget now what was on either side of this play but it could have been almost anything from a gun battle in Belfast or a pop singer cleaning her teeth with the microphone to a "live" soccer match in Belgrade. Thus, without even trying, television drama achieves what street theatre sets out to do: the traffic all around it has a strident now-ness, an unthinking, unforced, machine-like contemporaneity that is far removed from the manner in which we expect (and need) to address ourselves to the demands of the older and more prestigious arts.

'And so while most of my original reasons for choos-ing to write for television are—if suitably rephrased—still valid, they leave out something crucial: the quality of *response*. Bullets on one side and football on the other do not make an auditorium, and the life of a play so doubly boxed can be sucked away in the sur-rounding flow. Worse, a panel game, a plastic-prairied western, a hard-eyed news bulletin, Wimbledon, a detective melodrama and an original play eventually submerge together into the same *kind* of experience. It is this landscape of indifference, so hotly lit, which in the end defeats the pride and passion of the writer. The single play is one of the last areas of television where the irritating cadences of the individual voice can still be heard. While this is so I am (perhaps perversely) honour bound to submit scripts for the mauling. But I cannot help at times grieving for work that has been swallowed and perhaps even for a talent which is being exhausted. I follow a yellow brick road.'

DENNIS POTTER

305

Follow the Yellow Brick Road was first presented by BBC Television on 4 July, 1972, with the following cast:

JACK BLACK	*Denholm Elliott*
VERONICA	*Michele Dotrice*
COLIN	*Bernard Hepton*
DR BILSON	*Dennis Waterman*
DR WHITMAN	*Richard Vernon*
JUDY	*Billie Whitelaw*
OLD LADY	*Ruth Dunning*

Produced by Alan Bridges
Directed by Roderick Graham

Characters

JACK BLACK, *thirty-five-year-old TV actor*
OLD LADY, *working-class out-patient*
DOCTOR WHITMAN, *elderly psychiatrist*
JUDY BLACK, *thirtyish, wife of Jack*
COLIN SANDS, *forty-year-old-plus, theatrical agent*
VERONICA SANDS, *his eighteen-year-old child bride, cherry ripe*
BILSON, *young psychiatrist*
PEREGRINE, *the fabulous Great Dane*
DWARFIE, *the miniature Poodle*
A NURSE (*with a few lines*)
A NAKED MALE (*who says even less*)
A RADIO DISC JOCKEY *is also heard out of vision as are voices in the crucial television commercials.*

1

Interior. The big out-patients hall of an old London hospital. Day.

Here the patient out-patients wait and wait before going off into one of the little rooms along one side of the hall.

It is a big, barrack-like place with grey radiators, grey faces, red 'No Smoking' notices, black and white tiles one-third the way up the wall.

Tubular-steel chairs are arranged in clusters, presumably according to the disease.

Music from beginning: A lush exuberantly schmaltzy orchestration of 'Somewhere Over the Rainbow'.

After unhurried, coldly lingering establishing shots to set the tone and mood, settle on 35-year-old Jack Black, alone in his small group of chairs.

Two or three yards from him on the end of her particular group of chairs is an old lady—working-class Londoner.

Watch them a moment as 'Somewhere Over the Rainbow' fades.

Superimpose opening titles.

Titles fade. But still no dialogue, no movement.

Then as though overcome by the same irritation the viewers are no doubt on the point of feeling, Jack Black unlocks himself, shifts almost violently in his tubular-steel chair, glares across at the dead-faced old lady, sighs heavily and folds his hands.

JACK (*Snarl*): Not much action, is there? Not much bleed'n action!

(*The old lady surfaces slowly, comically, out of blank reverie.*)

OLD LADY: Beg pardon?

(*Jack snorts and shuffles his feet, inwardly fuming.*)

JACK: Hardly any dialogue at all. Just background noises.

(*A trolley squeaks by, jiggling its bright biochemicals.*

Silence.

The old lady is a bit uncomfortable.)

God Almighty.

OLD LADY: You talking to me?

(*He turns and examines her.*)

Sorry. I thought you was talking to—

JACK: Waiting!

OLD LADY (*Relieved*): All day. *They* don't care.

JACK: They certainly believe in keeping you waiting. Eh?

OLD LADY (*Relieved*): All day. They don't care.

JACK (*Disgruntled*): Holds up the action. People will switch over. Or switch off.

(*But she has not registered his weird, aggressive intensity. She is merely glad to make her own complaint.*)

OLD LADY: It's no skin off their nose. They get their money just the same.

(*He fidgets, aggressively, pulls out his hospital appointment card and examines it.*)

JACK: Eleven o'clock. That's what it says on my card. Eleven o'clock!

OLD LADY: Gone half past now.

(*He flicks at his card, nastily*).

310

JACK: Eleven *p.m.* it'll be at this rate. (*Urgently.*) *What is going to happen to us?*

OLD LADY: They don't take no notice of the time it says on them cards.

(*He fidgets. Looks at his watch. Fidgets. Looks at his watch again.*

JACK: Must be over-running.

OLD LADY: Pardon?

JACK (*Angrily*): The programmes must be running late.

(*She looks at him anxiously.*

Jack looks at his watch. He cannot keep still.)

Wimbledon, is it? Or a Test Match. Make everything else late. Bloody sport.

OLD LADY: I—don't hear so well as I—

JACK (*Interrupting*): Doesn't matter so much to you. You've only got a small part.

OLD LADY (*Bewildered*): Pardon?

JACK: You aren't very important. You haven't got many lines. (*He looks contemptuously all around the hall.*) Shoddy, this set. Some tuppenny-ha'penny designer. Look at it—!

OLD LADY (*Cautiously*): Not very comfortable. Not for waiting. No.

JACK: Battleship grey radiators. Red 'No Smoking' notices. Squeaking medicine trolleys. (*Snort.*) The only colour here is in the biochemicals.

(*Pause.*

Old lady watching him carefully.)

(*Snigger.*) Let bards sing now of barbiturates as bright as violets.

OLD LADY: I have to take red ones.

311

(*He turns and looks at her, steadily.*)

(*Embarrassed.*) Tablets. I have to take little red ones. Butozolodin.

JACK: Oh? It's in the script, is it? The colour of the tablets.

OLD LADY: Pardon?

JACK: You don't get very interesting lines, do you?

OLD LADY: What are you on about, then?

JACK: Boring, your part. All you keep saying is (*Mimics.*) 'Pardon'? like that. 'Pardon'?—with your mouth sagging open.

OLD LADY: Bleed'n sauce!

JACK: That's better. (*Sniff.*) Predictable—but better.

(*She glares at him.*

But his face has changed. He is staring fixedly at the camera.)

(*Soft hiss.*) Stop looking at me.

(*Camera moves in, steadily.*)

(*Louder.*) Stay still!

(*Camera stops.*

He stares out at us belligerently.

Then, the camera not moving, he visibly relaxes.

Fast zoom into big close-up. He flaps at it as though beating away a venomous wasp buzzing at his head.)

(*Panic.*) Get off! Off!

(*Camera retreats, fast.*

He stares out at us.

Pause.

Then bullet-fast zoom right into his eyes.)

312

(*Shout.*) Get away! Get away!

(*Pull out slowly, taking in the wider scene.*)

OLD LADY (*Anxious*): Here—are you all right? What's up with you?

(*He wipes his forehead with the back of his hand, experiencing the genuine terror of paranoia.*)

JACK (*Mutter*): Watching me . . . all the time . . . all the bloody time . . .

OLD LADY: Pardon?

(*He turns to her almost imploring.*)

JACK: I hate it.

OLD LADY: Well—nobody likes waiting here that's for sure.

JACK: No! The cameras. The plot.

OLD LADY (*Fidget*): Plot?

JACK: Load of old tat. *Dirty*, too. Ob-scene.

(*She looks at him cautiously.*

He fidgets, unable to keep still, anxiety pulsing through him like a nerve.)

I don't want to be in this play.

(*Register old lady, mouth sagging with incredulity.*

He looks at his watch again, sucking in his breath.)

Eleven o'clock. That's what it says on my card. Eleven o'clock. (*Suddenly turns to old lady.*) I used to think it was God. Watching me . . .

OLD LADY (*Faintly*): Pardon?

JACK: Don't you get any better lines than that!

OLD LADY: Look—I don't know what you are going on about—!

JACK (*Blank*): Television.

313

(*Fractional pause.*)

OLD LADY: The telly?

JACK: Yeh. (*His lip curls.*) The telly.

(*The old lady's face slowly changes from anxious hostility to a delighted glow: she has recognized him.*

Close-up old lady beaming voraciously.)

OLD LADY: Here! I know you—I've *seen* you on the . . .

(*Sharp cut in mid-sentence.*)

2

Interior. Stairs. Night.

(*TV commercial: thriller-type music crashes in exactly as we jump into the new scene which starts with close-up of bare feet creeping down a darkened stair.*

Thrilling trill of 'B' movie music as we swing up to face of Jack Black, lit from underneath to increase the impression of stealth, of camp 'menace'.

The music slowly fades as he creeps ultra-cautiously in his pyjamas down the stairs.

A stair creaks.

He stiffens. No sounds so, expelling his breath in relief, he continues down the stair.)

WEIRD WHISPER (out of vision): *What does he want? What is he after in the Dead of Night—?*

(*Close-up Jack Black, licking his lips.*)

3

Interior. Hallway. Night.

(*TV commercial continued.*

Music trills out mock menace again as he creeps along dark hallway to dark kitchen.)

WHISPER (out of vision): *What does he want? What? What is he doing?*

4

Interior. Larder. Night.

(*Close-up of his hand groping claw-like for switch inside larder.*

Light comes on with crash music and his face registers total consternation.

Cut back into 'real life'.)

5

Interior. The big out-patients hall of an old London hospital. Day.

(*The cut comes in the middle of the old lady's sentence.*)

OLD LADY (*Eagerly*): . . . and you find that your wife is already there eating them biscuits. Laugh!

(*He is rolling his head from side to side in distress.*)

JACK: Biscuits. God . . . biscuits.

OLD LADY: I like the commercials. Better than the programmes, some of them. What was them biscuits called?

(*Pause.*)

JACK (*Solemn deliberation*): Krispy Krunch. (*Sniff.*) With two K's.

OLD LADY (*Pleased*): That's the ones. Bleed'n horrible they are, and all.

JACK (*Hiss*): Please . . . !

OLD LADY: Is she really your wife?

(*Pause.*)

JACK: What?

OLD LADY: The woman eating them biscuits. Is she *really* your wife—or is that only on the telly?

JACK (*Hollow*): My wife?

OLD LADY: Yeh. The one in the nightgown. *You* know. With the packet in her hand . . . when you put the light on you catch her crunching up the biscuits—(*Laughs, delighted.*)—what a carry on, eh?

JACK: I caught her all right.

OLD LADY: Eating the biscuits, eh?

JACK: I caught her. I caught her. (*He is beginning to rock to and fro in his tubular-steel chair.*)

OLD LADY (*Cackle*): She'd got there before you did— eh?

JACK (*Moan*): I caught her. . . I caught her . . .

(*As he sucks in his breath in anguish—*

Slow, as it were reluctant, mix with same music on mix as in the mock commercial.)

6

Interior. Bedroom in London flat. Night.

(*Door opens in front of us, as in a thriller.*

Judy Black, naked, is on top of a young man in the tumbled big bed. Slowly, fearfully, she looks up and turns to face the door.)

JUDY (*Horrified*): Jack—!

316

(*Silence.*

Nobody moves.)

Cut harshly back to close-up Jack in—

7

Interior. Out-patients hall. Day.

JACK (*Near whisper*): Krispy Krunch.

(*Pull out slowly.*)

OLD LADY: Had her mouth full, didn't she? Really enjoying it and all . . .

(*He makes a tiny choking noise.*)

(*Stupidly.*) Krispy Krunch. That's the ones. Got little patterns on them.

(*He wipes at his eyes with the back of his hand.*

Momentarily out of vision a nurse calls his name:)

NURSE (*Out of vision*): Mr Black, please.

OLD LADY: Fancy *you* having to wait—!

JACK: What?

NURSE (*Out of vision*): Mr Black—?

OLD LADY: Somebody on the telly nearly every night, having to wait. *That's* not right.

JACK: We're on the telly now!

NURSE (*In vision*): Mr Black?

JACK (*Confused*): What?

NURSE: Doctor Whitman is ready for you now—it is Mr Black?

JACK (*Dully*): Yes.

OLD LADY: What do you mean, we're on now?

NURSE (*Impatient*): Come along then, sir. We haven't got all day.

JACK: Been here since ten to eleven . . .

OLD LADY: Now? Are we on *now*?

NURSE: That door over there, please.

(*Like a man in a sick dream he shuffles away towards the door she has indicated.*

The old lady has been looking all around, gobbling like a turkey.)

OLD LADY: Where are the cameras and that, then?

NURSE (*Astounded*): What?

(*The old lady points at Jack, about to go through the door.*)

OLD LADY: That man—look, nurse—*him*. He's on the telly . . .

(*About to scuttle off in the opposite direction, she turns to look.*

Jack momentarily looks back before going through the door.)

NURSE: Oh, yes! So he is! The dog food man.

OLD LADY: Biscuits.

NURSE: Is it?

OLD LADY: Yeh. (*Chuckle.*) He catches his missis at the biscuits.

NURSE: No—I think he's the man who is knocked into the garden pond by the Great Dane.

OLD LADY (*Tetchily*): Biscuits!

NURSE: All the same in the end, isn't it?

OLD LADY: Are they taking our pictures, then?

NURSE: Who?

318

OLD LADY: The telly people.

NURSE: I—what?—No. I don't think so. (*But she puts her hand to her hair*.)

8

Interior. Doctor Whitman's room off the out-patients hall. Day.

(*Whitman, a psychiatrist, with a heavy work-load, is reading a letter or notes from Jack's G.P. as Jack comes in.*

Sitting with him, at one side of the desk, discreetly apart, is a young doctor, Bilson.)

WHITMAN: Ah. Mr Black. Good morning.

(*Jack does not respond. He stands dead still, body stiff with hostility and fear.*)

Yes. (*Gently.*) Do come in, please, and sit down.

JACK: I'd rather stand.

WHITMAN: You'll be more comfortable, I think, if you—

JACK: I'll stand!

(*Whitman looks at him with interest.*)

WHITMAN (*Amiable*): That's up to you, of course. It doesn't really matter. If you'd *rather* stand ...

JACK: I'll sit. Don't make a meal of it. I'll bloody well *sit*. (*He sits, limbs atwitch.*)

WHITMAN: I'm very sorry you were kept waiting. The appointments system gets snarled up ...

JACK: I won't delay you. Just give me the tablets and I'll be away.

WHITMAN: Tablets?

319

JACK: That's what you are for, isn't it? That's what you *dole out*.

WHITMAN: Sometimes.

JACK: Well, then!

WHITMAN: But I'd rather listen to you for a while. What sort of tablets do you think you need?

(*Pause.*

Jack works his face.)

JACK: Tablets to—to—(*He can't finish.*)

WHITMAN: Do you have a headache?

JACK: Yes—*no*—not that sort of ache . . .

WHITMAN: What sort of ache is it? Can you tell me?

(*No response.*

Whitman purses his lips.)

JACK (*Eventually*): I feel . . . I—(*Suddenly angry.*) Look, you're supposed to bloody well diagnose these things. If I came in here with a broken leg you'd ask me what was wrong.

WHITMAN (*Smile*): Yes—in a way. I'd ask you why you broke it.

JACK: Bloody fool.

WHITMAN: All too often, I'm afraid. But you *haven't* got a broken leg, fortunately. You can run and jump and skip. But you don't want to. Do you.

JACK: Why the hell should I want to run and jump and skip?

WHITMAN: To express pleasure. Joy. Exuberance.

(*Pause.*)

JACK (*Flat*): Joy.

WHITMAN: You don't feel it?

JACK: I'm not a child. And I'm not *blind*.

WHITMAN: Yet the world is dark.

(*Jack twists his head away. To deflect the observation he settles on young doctor Bilson.*)

JACK (*Sneer*): Who's this? Your *understudy*?

(*Bilson smiles nervously.*)

WHITMAN: This is Doctor Bilson.

BILSON: Understudy is a good word.

WHITMAN: You are an actor. That is so, isn't it?

JACK (*Sniff*): Yes.

WHITMAN: On the television.

JACK (*Reluctantly*): Yes. Commercials, mostly.

WHITMAN (*Pleased*): I *thought* I had seen you *some-where* before ... you do the one where this man is creeping on tiptoe down the ...

JACK (*Violently*): Yes! Yes!

WHITMAN: Mmm. No doubt you *do* get sick of being—um—yes, but that is not why you are here, is it?

JACK: The commercials are all right. I quite like the commercials. There's nothing wrong with the commercials.

WHITMAN: Not very satisfying for an actor though, surely?

JACK: Better than the plays.

WHITMAN (*Surprised*): Oh? I would have thought that ...

JACK (*Interrupting*): You don't know anything about it, do you!

(*Pause.*)

WHITMAN (*Mildly*): No. I suppose I don't.

JACK: The commercials are *clean*.

WHITMAN: Clean?

JACK (*Not listening*): They have happy families in the commercials. Husbands and wives who *love* each other . . .

WHITMAN: But not *real* husbands and *real* wives, surely? You can't expect—you don't really think that love is so simple or—

JACK (*Interrupting*): There's laughter and, and, and sunshine and kids playing in the meadows. Nobody mocks the finest human aspirations. There's no deliberate wallowing in vice and evil and and—(*Breaks off.*) No. There's nothing wrong with the commercials. Nothing at all!

WHITMAN (*Gently*): They offer a processed or edited prototype of a certain kind of contentment. But—look, you know and I know that the real world is not so easy to live in. We can't actually buy a ring of confidence— can we? Not you. Not me.

(*Pause.*)

JACK (*Half plea*): But there are *tablets* . . .

WHITMAN: Yes. They can help. I *will* be able to help in that way. But listen to me, I—

JACK (*Swift*): Nothing wrong! Nothing! It's the *plays* that do all the damage. The plays.

WHITMAN: I'm not sure I understand what you mean . . .

JACK (*Hiss*): The plays nowadays—they—(*He looks round furtively.*)

WHITMAN: Go on.

JACK: I have to be very careful what I say.

WHITMAN: Everything you say here stays here. You can say exactly what you want to say.

322

JACK: Why do you wear a *red tie*?

WHITMAN: Oh. Is it red? I just put on the nearest one at hand.

(*Pause.*

Jack examines him.)

JACK: They are all *socialists*, you see. Trotskyites to be more precise.

WHITMAN: Who are?

JACK (*Cunning*): Never you mind. But I know what I'm talking about. I've been in a good many of these plays.

WHITMAN: And you don't like acting any more?

JACK: I've been given scripts that—(*He stops, reluctant.*)

WHITMAN: Please go on.

JACK: They are dirty and corrupt! I've been given parts which would make Satan himself throw up. You have *no idea* the sort of things that go on nowadays. Talk about paddling in the sewers! Ach!

WHITMAN: Do you want to stop acting?

JACK: Do *you*?

WHITMAN: If I can. But we all act a bit—we have to.

JACK (*Aggressive*): You mustn't think you know it all, you know.

WHITMAN: No.

JACK: Be quiet then!

WHITMAN (*Sigh*): Yes.

(*Pause.*)

JACK: I have no wish to be rude.

(*Pause.*

Whitman waits patiently.)

Paddling in sewers.

WHITMAN: Sewers?

JACK: Yes! Switch on the set and you'll see! Despair. Violence. Filth. Sadism. Adultery.

WHITMAN: And party political broadcasts.

JACK: These writers and directors—they are not content with driving themselves mad. They want to drive *us* mad as well.

WHITMAN: Possibly so.

JACK: Filth—that's what *oozes* out of these plays. Filth of all kinds to mock virtue and to encourage doubt. They turn gold into hay, these people. Angels into whores. Love into a s-s-sticky slime—and Jesus Christ into an imbecile bleeding and screaming on a cross. God! I hate them. I bloody hate them, and their rotten, festering, suppurating scabs of ideas!

WHITMAN (*Mildly*): Steady up, there.

JACK: Whatsoever things are false, whatsover things are debased, whatsoever things are evil, whatsoever things are impure, adulterated, perverse, grossly s-s-sensual—ugly—bizarre—kinky—(*He sucks in his breath.*) Wallow in all that, wash your hands and face in shit, and you'll get *plenty* of work. Oh, yes! The director will mince his way down from the gallery in his beard and his brown suede boots and say 'Mar-vell-ous ducky'. I know all about it. The dirty sods.

(*Silence.*)

WHITMAN: Mmm.

JACK (*Aggressive*): What?

WHITMAN: I—ah—well, I can't say I have time to watch all that much tel . . .

JACK (*Interrupting*): The truly amazing thing is that

these people keep crapping on about 'Integrity'. They trot it out of their dirty mouths almost every other word. Integrity! Like a raddled old whore talking about chastity.

WHITMAN: 'They'?

JACK (*Blink*): What?

WHITMAN: 'They'—who are they, Mr Black?

JACK (*Suspicious*): Don't you *know*?

WHITMAN: The word tends to—ah—mean different things at different times in different places. I think I know what you mean, but I want to be quite sure I understand you.

(*Pause.*

Jack, suddenly cautious, works his mouth.)

JACK: I could give you a list as long as my arm.

WHITMAN: A list of what?

JACK: Names.

(*Deadlock.*

They examine each other.)

WHITMAN (*Quietly*): The conspiracy?

(*Jack's eyes shift round the room.*)

JACK: I—(*He stops.*)

WHITMAN: Yes?

JACK (*Embarrassed*): I don't want to sound paranoid or anything like that ... (*Again he stops, as furtive as a petty crook.*)

WHITMAN: But as *you* see it ...?

JACK (*Rising tone*): As I see it if there is a conspiracy there's no point in calling it something else. Is there?

WHITMAN: No. Not if there is one.

JACK: Oh man, there *is* one all right!

WHITMAN: To what end? A conspiracy for what?

JACK: A conspiracy to corrupt and degrade and confuse people.

WHITMAN: I see.

JACK: They all know each other, these people. They go to Trotskyite meetings. They sleep with the same women. They pass on the clap to each other like it was a relay baton. They talk about alienation and worker's control and the pill and—and—ach, they make me sick to my stomach. If they have an affair with some equally promiscuous woman that lasts *all of three weeks* they get worried about it feeling so (*Jeers.*) perm-a-nent.

(*Whitman is amused despite himself. He straightens his face.*)

WHITMAN: Would you say they were—obsessed—with —um—(*He offers the word like a lump of sugar.*)—*sex*?

JACK (*Eagerly*): Obsessed? I'll say they are bloody obsessed. They see it everywhere. They interpret it in every gesture, every aside, every silence. The whole world can be reduced to a hairy lump between a woman's legs. (*Hiss.*) *That* stinking hole! All of them are obsessed with somebody else's loins. They all ought to live in Rutland.

WHITMAN (*Confused*): Rutland?

JACK (*Sweeping on*): They talk about sex over their cornflakes. They discuss it over their coffee. They snigger about in the corridors. They chew it over the bar. And they all end up in each other's beds and ... (*He falters.*) Looking at ... looking at dirty pictures and ... (*He closes his eyes.*)

WHITMAN: So you don't get on with your—what is the right word—your colleagues ...

JACK (*Derisive*): Colleagues!

326

WHITMAN: I mean the people you work with, or used to work with. Am I right in assuming that recently you have not been able to get work?

(*Jack fidgets and shuffles.*)

JACK: I did biscuits.

WHITMAN: Yes. That's the one. Where you—um— creep down the stairs . . .

JACK: And I did Waggytail Din-Din.

WHITMAN: Pardon?

JACK: Dog food. All heart and kidney.

WHITMAN: Oh.

JACK: I did it with a Great Dane. He was called Peregrine.

WHITMAN: Didn't see that one. But of course there are so many . . .

JACK (*Helplessly*): A nice dog, Peregrine. Upstaged me something cruel. But he was a n . . . nice d . . . d—

(*He covers his face with his hands, in extreme distress.*)

(*Young Bilson seems about to speak, but Whitman motions him to silence.*)

WHITMAN: Great Danes can be very lovable, I know. Particularly when they are called Peregrine. Did it really eat (*Pulls a face.*) Waggytail Din-Din?

JACK (*Recovering*): No. It was given—(*Starts to laugh.*) —it was . . .

WHITMAN (*Smiling*): Yes?

JACK: Half a sheep. Half a bloody sheep.

(*They both laugh. It lowers the emotional pressure. Whitman sits back.*)

WHITMAN: Well, it's very pleasant to chat about dog food and biscuits but I fear the clock is against us. You

327

didn't really come to talk about these things, did you? Mmm?

JACK (*Hollow*): No.

WHITMAN: What did you come to talk about?

(*Silence.*)

It is quite possible that I can be of some real help to you. But you must go some way to meeting me. . . . What?

(*He breaks off in astonishment.*

Close up Jack.

Camera pans slowly round the room and Jack, eyes fixed on the lens, swivels his head round with it.

Pull out. It looks ludicrous.)

(*Sharp.*) Mr Black. What precisely are you doing?

(*Close up Jack again.*)

JACK (*Hiss*): Stop *looking* at me all the time.

(*Fast zoom at Jack.*)

(*Desperate.*) Get out! Get out!

(*Pull back fast.*)

WHITMAN: Mr Black.

JACK: I'm sick of it.

(*Pause.*)

WHITMAN: What on earth were you—

JACK: The camera!

(*Pause.*)

WHITMAN (*Gathering himself*): I am afraid I'm not with you . . .

JACK: I don't like this play. I don't like the things that go on in it. Dirty things. Things best forgotten.

328

WHITMAN (*Anxious*): Play?

JACK (*Incredulous*): Are you trying to tell me you don't know we are in a play?

(*Silence.*)

WHITMAN: Mr Black, now listen to me. . . .

JACK (*Snort*): The one thing that is true about this play is that we are *in it*. That is *demonstrably* the case.

(*Silence.*)

WHITMAN: If you could explain a bit more clearly for me . . .?

(*Jack peers at him, cautiously.*)

JACK (*Patiently*): The play I am in. The play you are in. (*Indicates Bilson.*) The play that deaf mute there is in.

BILSON: Thank you.

JACK: The play Judy is in.

WHITMAN: Judy?

(*Jack nods, dumb with pain.*)

(*Floundering.*) Who is Judy?

JACK (*Whisper*): She . . . she . . .

WHITMAN (*Rising tone*): Yes?

JACK: She's my wife. In the play, that is. Only in the play, of course.

WHITMAN: I see.

JACK: Do you?

WHITMAN (*Sadly*): I think so.

JACK (*With relief*): Not many people do, you know. They are totally unable to discern the true nature of their predicament. They are locked up in the lines of a script and they do not even know it. That's why they feel so *helpless*.

329

WHITMAN: Who is the—The Author then?

(*Silence.*)

If there is a script—well, then, somebody wrote it. Yes?

JACK (*Defensive*): I—well, I haven't worked all this out yet. Not to my own satisfaction.

WHITMAN (*Gently*): Listen—I follow what you say. All of us at some time or another feel that we are being manipulated. And indeed we *are*.

(*Jack interrupts savagely.*)

JACK: Do you deny that you are an actor in a play? Do you?

WHITMAN: Well, in a sense we all are . . .

JACK (*Quietly*): I used to think it was God who— *arranged* things.

WHITMAN: Yes. A lot of people think God writes the script—(*Sigh.*) to use *your* language.

(*Jack is not listening to him. He has too much of his own to get out.*)

JACK: When I was a boy I—When I was little. I thought God was watching me all the time, every minute of the day. I could never ever escape his attention, not in the lavatory, not on the football field, not eating my dinner. He was there all the time—

WHITMAN (*Quickly*): Malevolently?

JACK (*Angry*): God I said! Not the Devil.

WHITMAN (*Apologetically*): Yes, there is a difference. I'm sorry I interrupted.

JACK: You couldn't help it.

WHITMAN: No.

JACK: It was in the script. It was all set out beforehand.

WHITMAN: I'm sorry I interrupted you. God, you said.

(*Jack looks at him aggressively, then decides to continue.*)

JACK: I remember once—when I was—oh, seven, eight years old, not more—I was riding this tricycle down a hill near where we used to live—riding it in the middle of the road, jingling the bell—it had a nice, hard sound, that bell—when I—The clouds massed up in great banks over the valley down below took on this—this—(*Searches for the word.*) radiance.

(*Silence, neither of them moves, nor the camera.*)

I got off my trike as quickly as I could. I ran to the grass bank at the side of the road. I ran and I stood there, trembling. Trembling like a leaf. I left my trike in the middle of the road.

(*Silence.*)

WHITMAN: Now why did you do that?

JACK (*Simply*): Because God was *too near.*

WHITMAN: So—all your life you've felt—watched. Observed.

(*Jack nods, dumbly.*)

And do you still believe in God?

(*Silence.*

The word is, as it were, dragged out of him. It sounds strangled, or peculiarly reluctant.)

JACK: No.

WHITMAN: I think perhaps you do. I think you *want* to . . .

JACK (*Shout*): *He isn't there!*

WHITMAN (*Sadly*): No.

JACK (*Distressed*): For years and years I hadn't thought about it, hadn't considered it. I just—assumed—somehow—that he—it—was—there, still there, still

331

watching, still *present*—Then—then . . . (*He stops. And rocks gently. It seems a long time before he tries again.*) Then one morning—daybreak—I—well, I'd been up all night. Couldn't think. Couldn't sleep. Couldn't sit. Couldn't stand. She—(*Abrupt change.*) I was alone. I could see light in a chink through the curtains. First light. Half-past four in the morning and —Oh, birds. They were singing. Mad chatter of them. A dog was barking, somewhere across acres of concrete. Empty yearning. First light. First sounds of the day. (*Bitter laugh.*) New Every Morning. I thought— I stopped in the middle of the room—I thought it's been *like this* since the world began. Light pushing back dark. Birds jabbering. New day starting. What for? What *for*? So—so I tried to—for the first time in years and years I—it seemed—(*Rush.*) I got down on my knees and I closed my eyes and I put my hands together and I said to myself I won't ask for anything, won't ask, *won't ask*, not even for . . . (*Stop.*) I'll just let *you* come. I'll just see if you are there if you are still there still there—I'll wait. I'll wait for—(*Gets it out.*)—the word.

(*Silence. He works his face, remembering, reliving it.*

Whitman purses his lips.)

I waited. I waited and waited. I just wanted the word to drop into my mind. I was open for it. *Ready* for it. In my mind I got off my tricycle again and ran to the side, ran to the grass bank—(*He stops.*)

WHITMAN (*Quietly*): You mustn't expect childhood exp—

(*Jack interrupts with a near shout.*)

JACK: Slime!

WHITMAN (*Blink*): What?

JACK: That was the word! Slime. That was the message I got. No God. On my knees with my eyes shut I got this one word or feeling or impression or—I don't know—but there it was, long slippery strands of it—slime—nothing else but slime. (*Chokes.*) And dirt and —stinking slime contaminating everything. All over my hands. All over my face. In my mouth. In my eyes.

(*He is shuddering now in revulsion.*)

WHITMAN (*Alarmed*): Hey! Stop! Come on, stop it!

(*But Jack's whole body is contorting in disgust. He looks as though he is going to retch. He speaks as though at any moment his stomach is going to boil up into his mouth.*)

JACK: I was kneeling in a s—a s—in a s—in a sewer—yuk—lumps of—yuk—swirling all over all over all over every—yuk—everything—(*He puts his hand to his mouth, retching.*)

WHITMAN (*To Bilson*): Quickly! Get the staff nurse!

(*Bilson rushes anxiously from the room.*)

JACK (*Choke*): Help me. Hel . . .

(*Jack lurches to his feet hand over his mouth. Whitman scurries round the desk to grip him by the arm.*)

WHITMAN: Hold on! There's a good chap . . .

JACK (*Shout*): Slime!

(*He shakes himself free and bolts from the room, spewing into his hands. Whitman is left standing, helpless. He sighs heavily and then sits down on the edge of the desk.*)

WHITMAN (*Moved*): Dear God. Why do we suffer so?

Telecine 1: Exterior. Outside Hospital. Day.

(*Judy Black sits waiting in an open sports car, hands on the steering wheel, eyes fixed on the hospital gates. She stiffens as Jack comes running out.*

333

He stands for a minute, holding some railings, gasping for air, trying to recover.

She edges the car forward.)

JUDY: Jack.

(Holding on to the rails, still, he turns slowly and stares at her. Balefully.)

(Hesitant): Are you—are you all right?

(Silence.)

Jack?

JACK: Go away.

JUDY: Jack—For God's sake—look, get in. Please get in.

JACK: Go away!

(She hits both hands on the wheel in frustration.)

JUDY: Fool! Fool! *(She stops banging on the wheel.)* Why don't you *talk*? Why don't you listen to me? Why don't you face things, Jack? Please.

JACK: How did you know I was coming here?

(Pause.)

JUDY: Get in, Jack. Please get in.

JACK: Dr Barber, I suppose. I'll get him struck off.

JUDY: Please, Jack. Please, please get in. I'll drive you anywhere . . . wherever you want to go . . .

(He looks all round him, cautiously. He is looking for his imaginary 'camera'.)

What are you doing? What are you looking for . . . ?

JACK *(Quickly):* Nothing.

JUDY: I want to talk to you. I want us to get things in perspective . . .

JACK: Into focus.

334

JUDY: **What?**

JACK: Get the picture into focus.

JUDY: Right! But we can't do that if we don't talk to each other . . . Come on. Don't be so stubborn . . . Get into the car.

JACK: It stinks.

JUDY: What . . . ?

JACK: The car stinks. The street stinks.

JUDY: Jack—?

JACK: A bitch on heat. You can't mistake it. Follows you round, that particular stench.

JUDY (*Choke*): Oh, Jack—

JACK: A rutting bitch! Yuk!

(*She looks at him a moment in helpless despair.*

He shrugs, almost in compassion.

Then walks away along the pavement.

Let him go out of shot.

Watch Judy her face dead with paralysed emotion. She sighs, we are moving in slowly to a big close-up.)

JUDY (*To herself*): Go, then. Bloody well go.

(*Still big close-up. Her face changes.*

Pulling out, we see why: Jack is turning back, fifty yards away. He saunters along the pavement smiling.)

JACK (*Warmly*): All right, Judy. Sorry I was—rude.

JUDY (*Hesitant*): Jack . . . ?

(*Jack spreads his arms, smiling.*)

JACK: I'm the Krispy Krunch man. And the Waggytail Din-Din man.

(*She looks at him steadily. And unbelievingly. He drops his arms, and stops grinning like a fool.*)

I don't know what to do. I don't know where to go.

(*She leans across and opens the car door.*)

JUDY: Get in.

(*He hesitates.*)

Come on, Jack. We'll—go for a drive, anything. Get in.

(*He does so.*)

Home?

JACK: No.

JUDY: Jack ...

JACK: Let's—hey, let's go to Barnes Common. Over the bridge. Walk a bit. Or something.

JUDY (*Surprised*): All right.

(*And off they go, Jack smiling idiotically, Judy a bit thoughtful.*

Let sports car sweep away into middle distance. Start music—'It's a lovely day today'. (Without words.)

Slow mix, retaining music, to:)

Telecine: Extract from mock commercial.

(*Music continuing. In a buttery meadow a huge dog is running with a stick in its mouth.*)

JACK (*Out of vision*): Heah boy, Waggytail Din-Dinnn!

(*The powerful great dane drops the stick, turns in a full loping circle and races away in the opposite direction—towards the voice.*

Close up of running dog with huge, slavering jaws. Slow mix (music continuing) to:)

Interior/Exterior. Inside the car.

(*Big close-up of Jack in the car, working his mouth. Eyes blazing.*

Pull out.

The car radio is on. The 'Vocal' takes over:)

D.J. (*On radio*): Remember that one? *Call me Madam.* Only don't wilya? (*Snigger.*) It was a lovely day on Tuesday, too. Went for a walk. Saw this man ambling along a busy street with a crocodile under his arm. The croc snapping at everybody in sight. 'Hey,' I said, 'Why don't you take that thing to the Zoo!' 'I took him to the zoo yesterday,' the man said. 'Today I'm taking him to the cinema.' Oops! While you wince, try this one . . .

(*Judy switches it off.*)

JACK: Hey! I like that.

JUDY: Oh, Jack!

JACK: Well, perhaps not.

(*Silence.*)

JUDY (*Hesitant, but determined*): Jack—why were you at the hospital?

JACK: Why were you at the hospital?

JUDY: Because I want to talk to you. Because I went to—find out what's wrong with you . . .

JACK: Wrong with me?

JUDY: Where are you living? Why don't you come home?

JACK: Because I don't like coming in and finding my wife being screwed in my own bed.

JUDY: Will you listen to me? Will you really listen?

JACK: I got in the car, didn't I?

337

JUDY: We can't just let things . . .

(*He interrupts, loudly.*)

JACK: The psychiatrist was a religious maniac.

JUDY (*Startled*): What?

JACK: Kept talking about God. Kept on about God watching him. All the time, watching, watching. I think I'll take the Bible along next time. Except there won't be a next time. Turn off here—park the car over there . . . we'll walk on the grass . . .

JUDY: Are we allowed? The car, I mean.

JACK: Who cares. Just park it over there.

(*She pulls off the road, and parks on the grass of the common.*

They sit in the open car, staring straight ahead, embarrassed by each other.)

JUDY (*Gently*): Jack. I love you, Jack.

(*Pause.*)

JACK: Yeh. (*Pause.*) I'll bet you think about me even with somebody else on top of you. Ta.

(*Face set, she gets out of the car. He watches her carefully. There is menace about him.*)

JUDY: It was the only time.

(*Silence. He turns his head away. She holds on to the door of the sports car.*)

I regret it. I regret it very, very much.

(*He turns, and his face is wet.*)

JACK: Then why, Judy? Judy?

JUDY: Walk with me, please?

(*Pause. He seems about to refuse, then swings out of the car. suddenly manic.*)

338

JACK: Sure. Why not? Walk and talk with the lovely lady. (*Flings up arms.*) Waggytail Din-Dinn!

(*She laughs nervously.*)

Exterior. Barnes Common. Day.

JACK: We shot it here, you know. Barnes Common. The first bit. The dog knocked me into the pond in the studio. Rotten beast. (*He grabs hold of her hand, tightly, too tightly.*)

JUDY: Ow!

JACK: There were cameras all over the common. Cameras cameras cameras.

JUDY: Jack—are you all right . . . ?

JACK: I could see them then.

(*They are walking. He is swinging at her arm.*)

JUDY: See what?

JACK: Cameras. (*He stops swinging her arm. But still holds her hand.*)

JUDY: What are you talking about?

(*He walks on with her, looking at the ground, self-absorbed.*)

JUDY: Jack?

(*He looks up, and at her, frowning.*)

JACK: Judy—do you ever . . . ?

(*He stops and looks down again. They almost stop walking.*)

JUDY: Yes?

JACK: Do you ever feel you're—being—watched?

(*They stop walking. She faces him.*)

339

JUDY (*Quietly*): How do you mean that?

JACK: Do—(*Shyly.*)—do you ever feel that—well, that you are playing a—playing a scene in a play?

JUDY: Well . . .

JACK (*Eagerly*): Do you?

JUDY (*Little laugh*): In a way. Sometimes. Yes, I suppose I do.

(*He grabs at her arm, imploringly.*)

JACK: How? Judy? How do you feel it?

JUDY (*Alarmed laugh*): Hey!

JACK: Tell me! Tell me!

JUDY: It's nothing to get worked up about. It's quite an ordinary sort of feeling, I should think . . .

JACK: Is it?

JUDY: Jack . . . ?

JACK (*Choke*): Please tell me . . .

(*She shrugs, confused.*)

JUDY: When I say 'ordinary'—well, I mean it's not unusual—it's like thinking that what you are now saying or now doing you have said or done before . . . I mean, we see so many films and plays and stories of one sort or another we're bound to be . . . influenced.

JACK (*Sour*): Influenced?

JUDY: Why does this matter so much?

JACK: Influenced! Is that all you mean . . .

JUDY: Not quite—look, what are we talking about? Oh, it's a vague, very vague, feeling somewhere way out on the edge of your minds, our minds, that things have some shape or pattern or meaning—can't get the right word . . .

JACK (*Interrupting*): A script, you mean. A script.

JUDY: Well, not exactly. Jack?

JACK: Oh God, Judy. Dear God. (*He starts to cry.*)

(*She touches his face, tender, but also obscurely frightened.*)

JUDY: I—please—?

(*He wipes at his face with his knuckles, and tries to smile.*)

JACK: Do you remember when—when we used to come here?

(*She nods, nearly in tears herself.*)

Seven years ago. Or eight.

JUDY: Eight.

(*He reaches for her hand.*)

JACK: They put down plastic buttercups on the grass.

JUDY: What?

JACK: When we did the dog food thing. Plastic buttercups!

(*She laughs, beginning to relax. Hand in hand they start to walk again across the tufty grass.*)

JUDY: Hand in hand across the tufty grass. A bit like a commercial itself.

JACK: Happy Days are Here Again.

JUDY: Not quite.

JACK: A Lover and His Lass. (*The hard edge is coming back into his voice.*)

JUDY (*Steadily*): No, Jack. That was half the trouble. That was all the trouble.

JACK: Hey Nonny No.

JUDY: 'Lover' is not quite the right word. Is it Jack?

341

(*He does not answer, but keeps walking, eyes to the ground.*)

Is it?

JACK (*Mock snigger*): Plastic buttercups. As yellow as plastic butter.

JUDY (*Bitterly*): Good old Jack.

(*He stops walking.*)

JACK: What?

JUDY: Never listen. Never face up to things.

JACK: Some things I don't want to face up to!

JUDY: Like what?

JACK (*Shout*): Like you in bed with . . .

JUDY (*Scream*): Shut up!

(*Silence. They face each other, eye to eye.*)

(*Quietly*): Yes. Me in bed with a self-satisfied ram.

JACK (*Shudder*): Yuk.

JUDY: Why would I Jack? Why?

(*He rolls his head from side to side.*)

Because you couldn't or wouldn't or—

JACK (*Anguished*): Please don't Judy, please, please, please don't.

(*Pause.*)

JUDY: It happened once before. With somebody else.

JACK (*Spit*): You said—!

JUDY: I know what I said. But now it's time to—yes, I went to bed with your agent when you . . .

JACK (*Incredulously*): Colin!

JUDY (*Nodding*): When you were doing the . . . (*She*

doesn't know whether to laugh or to cry.) . . . filming the Waggytail Din-Din thing . . .

(He stands still, just staring at her, wild eyed.)

(Hiss.) The bastard!

JACK *(Thickly)*: Judy?

JUDY *(Cold)*: Well, aren't you going to do what you did before?

JACK *(Faintly)*: Wh-what?

JUDY: Aren't you going to hit me?

JACK *(Whisper)*: No.

(He covers his face. She moves into him and, with vicious suddenness, he slaps her to the grass.)

(She lies there without a word, looking up at him.)

JACK: You filthy mucking whore.

(He stands above her, horribly menacing. She just lies there.)

JACK *(Monotone)*: You cheap sex sodden little slut.

(And he drives his boot into her.

She moans softly.

And he kicks again, she sobs out.)

JUDY: Jack . . . !

(And he is beside her on the grass.)

JACK *(Choked)*: No—no—Judy—please—no—

JUDY: Jack . . . ?

(He is kissing her, hungry and sick. She responds, passionately.

Then suddenly he pulls away.

343

Silence.)

JACK (*Cold*): Tell me about it. You've got to tell me all about it. Otherwise . . . (*He stops*.)

JUDY (*Panting*): Otherwise . . .

JACK: I'll walk down the road to Hammersmith Bridge. And I'll wait for the camera. And then I'll jump in the stinking, garbage polluted river. That's what I'll do. That's what I'll do.

(*Silence*.)

JUDY: Camera?

(*He grabs at her and, as the graphic phrase has it, shakes her until her teeth rattle*.)

JACK: Tell me about it! Tell me! Tell me!

(*Cut into next scene from his angry face, not hers*.)

9

Interior. Colin Sands's flat. London. Evening.

(*Sands is forty-plus, with a Mex moustache. He is Jack's agent.*

The room is almost as trendy as a new boutique except that not all the things in it are tat. There is a mineral collection, for example, all the stones mounted in blocks of Perspex or legs of stainless steel.

He is finishing a telephone conversation as Judy comes into the room.)

COLIN (*On phone*): So that's it, then, is it? You want a dwarf with a German accent? (*He grimaces a greeting to Judy*.) I'll have a look see. Yep. Only send me the script, O.K.? Bye, love. (*Puts phone down*.) Judy, beautiful Judy.

JUDY (*Smiling*): Follow The Yellow Brick Road.

SANDS: What's that?

JUDY: This room, Colin.

SANDS: This room—?

JUDY: I always think it belongs to the Land of Oz.

SANDS (*Blink*): Richard Neville's Oz?

JUDY: Judy Garland's Oz. You know—follow the yellow brick road. All the little dwarfs sing it to her.

SANDS: A dwarf I need—yes. Sit down. But, hey, the Wizard of Oz was a *fraud*.

JUDY: Neville's Oz?

SANDS (*Laugh*): Garland's Oz. He was a sad, watery-eyed old impostor.

JUDY: Exactly.

SANDS: Ooch. O.K. sweet tongue, what's your drink?

JUDY: Scotch. Neat. No ice.

SANDS: Hello, hello.

JUDY: What do you mean?

(*Pouring drink, he winks at her in parody.*)

SANDS: The pretty lady is steeling herself to make a pass at the handsome gentleman.

JUDY (*Mock coy*): Och, Mr Sands.

(*He gives her the drink and sits beside her, wearily.*)

SANDS: Oof.

JUDY: Tired?

SANDS: No. Just disillusioned.

(*She laughs, drinks hard, and shudders involuntarily.*)

Hey!

JUDY: First of the day. Almost.

SANDS: Mmm. Not bad. It's nearly eight o'clock. Where's Jack?

(*She pulls a face.*)

JUDY: Waggytail Din-Din.

SANDS: Oh, yes, with the Fabulous Great Dane.

(*They both laugh.*)

JUDY: And where's your child bride, Colin?

SANDS: I don't know how to say this, but . . .

JUDY (*Apprehensive*): What's wrong?

(*Sands drains it out. He looks at her solemnly, then looks down at his glass, sloshing the Scotch around as though under stress.*)

SANDS: She . . . she's gone to buy a poodle.

(*Judy glares at him. He roars with laughter. Then, without quite knowing why, she does, too.*)

JUDY: Oh, Colin! Shut up!

SANDS (*Grinning*): No—really she has—a bloody poodle . . . apparently you can almost get it in a matchbox. Rare sort. There's an ad in *The Times* today. Some dotty lady with a title out in Beaconsfield or some such place. Veronica phoned, oohed and aahed, and shot out of here as though she had discovered a coelacanth.

JUDY (*Amused*): But why would she want one of those yappy little beasts?

SANDS: You did say *child* bride.

(*The sharpness of this last remark hangs on the air.*)

JUDY: Oh, well. I suppose poodles are no worse than (*She indicates the nearest.*) your collection of minerals.

(*His tone is immediately lighter again.*)

346

SANDS (*Laugh*): That's exactly what she said.

JUDY: Quite right, too.

(*She drinks again. A lot. He watches her, speculative.*)

SANDS: If you *can* get it into a matchbox, that is what I intend to do with it.

(*She doesn't laugh. But drinks again.*)

(*Gentle.*) You won't get yours into a bottle though.

JUDY: What?

SANDS: Troubles. They never did fit into a whisky bottle, Judy.

(*She twirls her glass.*)

JUDY: There's no trouble, Colin.

SANDS: No, no. The world's a hip-hap-happy place.

(*He gets up and switches on an electric fire with his foot, turns, and beams at her.*)

JUDY: You really *believe* that though, don't you?

SANDS: Doesn't everybody?

(*Looking at him, she takes a smaller sip.*)

Don't they?

JUDY: No. Not everybody, Colin.

(*This is the precise moment when he senses that he can have her, So he stands stock still, very alert.*

His silence makes her speak when she otherwise might not have.)

Some people think *pleasure* is a—is a sort of disease, a dislocation ... (*She drinks.*)

SANDS (*Softly*): But you don't, do you, Judy?

(*She looks at him, steadily.*)

JUDY: No.

(*Pause.*)

SANDS : Jack does.

JUDY (*Quick*) : I didn't say that.

SANDS : Look—I've known you and Jack for—what?
—four, five years?

JUDY : Five.

SANDS : Right. So Jack, I know.

(*Pause. They are looking at each other, tensely.*)

I like him, of course.

JUDY : What's that stone there, Colin?

(*He snorts, then controls himself. He picks up a huge
chunk of malachite set in a slab of clear Perspex.*)

SANDS : This? Malachite.

JUDY (*Strained*) : It's lovely.

SANDS : Better than poodles. (*He hands it to her, a
tender gesture.*)

JUDY : Difficult to say precisely what colour it is.

SANDS : Difficult to say precisely what anything is. But
that—well, its shadowy greeny blue or bluey green,
misty as mist, yet solid as stone. Earth and sky in one.

JUDY : Yes. Misty, greeny blue.

SANDS : Like your eyes.

JUDY : Aw, come on!

(*He hides behind a laugh.*)

SANDS : Solid as stone, I meant. Drink?

JUDY : Yes. All right.

(*He gets her one. Eyes on her, at her, all the time.*)

SANDS : Keep it if you want.

JUDY : The malachite?

SANDS: It's yours.

(*She puts it down.*)

JUDY: No, Colin. Spoil your collection.

SANDS: Or *add* to it?

(*Pause.*)

JUDY: No, Colin.

(*He sits, giving her the drink.*)

SANDS: Cheers for the Permissive Society.

JUDY: And Waggytail Din-Din.

(*He laughs, but his eyes are still too bright.*)

SANDS: I think I've got some more work for Jack.

JUDY: Oh?

SANDS: Not sure yet. But there's a new series in the offing. BBC.

JUDY: What about me?

SANDS: Well—you know what it's like.

JUDY (*Sigh*): I know. What's the series.

SANDS (*Wrinkling nose*): Parson's Pleasure. That's the working title. About a young prig of a clergyman trying to hot gospel in an East End parish. I'm putting Jack up for it. (*Joke.*) Between him and Cliff Richard, I'd say.

(*Judy, helplessly, lets out a sudden whirl of near-contempt.*)

JUDY: That'll suit him right down to the ground!

(*Pause.*

Tentatively he runs his finger down her arm.)

SANDS: Lovely Judy.

JUDY: Don't Colin.

349

(*He doesn't stop.*)

SANDS: Troubles, Judy?

(*She shuts her eyes and nods. He stops the moving finger and clasps her hand.*)

Shoot. As small English boys say.

JUDY: I love Jack.

SANDS: Of—course.

JUDY (*Fierce*): I do!

SANDS: But—?

(*Pause.*)

JUDY: But—oh, God—

(*Sands waits, pretending to look concerned.*)

Parson's Pleasure, you say?

SANDS: Working title.

(*Pause.*)

JUDY (*Savage abruptness*): Jack can't do it. Or *won't*.

SANDS (*Cautiously*): The part?

(*In infinite distress she gives her head a quick shake.*

He stares at her, then strokes her hand.)

JUDY: He—(*Quick turn to him.*)—Oh, Colin, this is just between us, this is j—

SANDS: Shh! Shh! You don't have to say it.

JUDY: Sex—it's—

SANDS: It's lovely!

JUDY: Don't Colin—no—

SANDS: Sorry. Just trying to—lower the—just want to help.

(*Judy puts her other hand on top of his, apparently grateful.*)

350

JUDY: He—starts all right. Like it used to be. But then—

(*She stops, he waits.*)

It's as though he's *transfigured* with—with—(*Voice breaks.*) disgust . . .

SANDS (*Shocked*): Disgust?

JUDY: The only word I can think of. Jack's going through a bad spell. I can't get to him. He says—one night he said that everything was—to *him*—everything was the colour of rain on old slate. Everything.

SANDS (*Purr*): Poor Judy . . .

JUDY: Poor Jack!

SANDS (*Briskly*): Get him to a doctor. He probably needs some anti-depressants. Like half the people in this business.

JUDY: You think so?

SANDS: I'm sure so.

JUDY: He—well—

SANDS: You can't stop now.

(*She looks at him.*)

JUDY: He says love is more than just *a sticky slime.*

(*Sands is genuinely shocked. His face is so astounded that, despite herself, she almost laughs.*)

Oh, Colin. Your face!

SANDS: Bloo-dy hell!

JUDY: I know. I know.

(*Pause.*)

SANDS: Poor Judy . . .

JUDY: Don't keep saying that!

(*He starts to stroke her.*)

351

SANDS: Poor Judy ... poor Judy ...

(*She clenches herself.*)

JUDY (*Faint*): No ...

SANDS: Malachite ... Judy. Judy?

(*And he envelopes her.*

The most perfunctory of struggles.

Don't pan away to the Malachite, whatever else.

Slow mix through to:)

Telecine 2: Exterior. Barnes Common. Day.

(*Judy and Jack on the grass.*)

JUDY: By the time sweet—little—Veronica was back with her weeny poodle your agent had had his ten per cent and more.

(*She is being deliberately brutal. He sucks in his breath, as from a blow.*)

JACK: Oh, Judy—(*He is almost too deeply humiliated to speak.*)

JUDY (*Savagely*): You sick, sick, sick creature!

(*He recoils.*)

JACK: Ah, no!

(*Silence, except for a distant ice-cream bell. 'Greensleeves' no less.*)

(*Hesitant*) Judy—?

(*She does not answer.*)

Do you?—

(*Silence.*)

JUDY (*Fierce*): What? Do I *what*?

JACK: Do—(*Gabble*)—do you want an ice cream?

(*It ought to be ludicrous. But it mustn't be.*

She looks at him nearly tender. Then shakes her head.)

No. Suppose not.

JUDY (*Dull*): My side hurts.

JACK: Pardon?

JUDY: Where you kicked me.

(*He hangs his head.*)

JACK: I didn't m— it wasn't really me . . .

JUDY (*Snort*): *Felt* like it!

JACK (*Mumble*): Made to do it. Made to.

(*She stares at him.*)

None of this is real. None of it. None of it.

JUDY: Jack—!

JACK: Plastic buttercups.

JUDY (*Frowning*): What?

JACK: All in the script. One stage direction and I can— I can lie down and die. That's all it needs. A few strokes of the pen.

JUDY: *What did you go to the hospital for?*

(*He starts to rock again, like a disturbed child.*)

JACK: In the script. In the script.

(*She scrambles to her feet, looking down at him.*)

JUDY (*Shrill*): *Jack.* What are you saying?

(*He looks up with wide, vacant eyes. Wordless.*

She shakes at his shoulder.)

Stop it! Stop it, do you hear?

JACK: That series never did get off the ground, did it?

JUDY (*Bewildered*): What series?

JACK: Parson's Pleasure. (*He starts to laugh.*)

JUDY: No. It didn't. Colin probably made it all up.

JACK: I got landed with this lot instead. Eh, Judy?

(*She looks down at him thoughtfully.*

The ice cream chimes ching out again, very much nearer.

Follow her eye-line. The van is on the cross-common sideroad, near to them. She seems to make up her mind about something.)

JUDY (*Falsely bright*): O.K. We'll have an ice cream.

JACK: Pardon?

(*She starts to walk to the van.*)

Oh. (*Pleased.*) A cornet.

(*And he gets up. She half waits.*)

JUDY: Got any money?

JACK: Yes. A pocketful of dreams.

(*They walk towards the van, not talking.*

Then he stops.)

JUDY: What it is?

(*Slow zoom to Jack, who puts his hand to his face.*

Fast pull back.

Jack tries to control his panic.)

JACK: A wasp. Something—

JUDY: Don't think so.

(*He looks about him, stiff, anxious.*)

JACK: N-no. Maybe not. (*He begins to relax.*)

(*Bullet-fast zoom into Jack.*)

354

Get off! Off!

JUDY: Jack!

(Like a man retreating from a swarm of hornets he cuts and runs towards the sports car.

Pull out so that we see Judy watching him, utterly astounded, calling his name.

Go with him so that she goes out of shot.

Running, he is making weird half-sobbing, half-panting noises, those of a hunted Man.)

Exterior. Car/Common.

(He clambers into the car.

Zoom in fast.

In driver's seat he frantically 'beats off' the camera, which pulls back again.

He looks cautiously, fearfully all round. Relaxes.

Then notices the ignition key, still in the car.

He freezes.)

JACK (*Hiss*): In the script. It's in the script. (*But he waits, breathing hard. Muttering.*) Has to be. Has to be. All written down . . .

(He presses the radio button.

On comes a well-syncopated version of 'Anything Goes'.

He listens, smiling.)

Music to kill adulterers. (*Sniff.*) Background music.

(And the car—spilling out its music—moves slowly forward on the grass, like a leashed panther.

Slowly he manoeuvres it into position, until we see Judy in the middle distance through the windscreen.

Car accelerating now. Music still splaying out.

Faster and faster over the bumpy grass.

(Everybody loves 'B' movies.)

Judy suddenly realizes that he is going to drive straight at her.

As the sports car hurtles towards her we see her (through windscreen) run in a terrified zig zag.

From another, wider angle the car is almost on top of her.

She flails her arms in screaming panic, loses her shoe, trips and falls.

Close up of advancing bumper and headlights—music very loud.

Cut into:)

End of Waggytail Din-Din Commercial.

(Peregrine, the fabulous great dane almost at the end of his loping, jaw-slavering run.

In front of him, standing on the edge of a lily-embellished garden pool, is Jack Black, holding up for all to see a can labelled 'Waggytail Din-din'.

The dog, with one leap at the can, paws on Jack's shoulder, knocks him flying into the pond.

Splash!

Jack surfaces, blowing out water. A comedian.)

JACK: I haven't even opened the tin yet!

(But Peregrine trots off happily, the can in his mouth.)

VOICE (*Out of vision*): Dogs can't wait for it. Dogs can't live without it. *Waggytail Din-Din* makes a splash!

(*Close up Jack blowing out pond water.*)

10

Interior. Sands's flat. Night.

(*So-called 'child bride', the beautiful Veronica, is alone in the flat, alone with the miniature poodle and the mineral collection.*

She is sitting on the huge leather settee, the dog on her lap. She is about eighteen or nineteen years old, an age at which it is easier than ever to be both stupid and brutal.

Unlikely though it is, I would like her to be attempting to feed the wretched beast with 'After dinner chocolate mints', the ones in the little envelopes.)

VERONICA (*Discarding 'envelope'*): Comesy on then, ickle Dwarfie. Eat it up. Eat it up then.

(*Pause for viewers to be sick. Dwarfie, not being able to read ads, doesn't want any of it.*)

(*Pout.*) Oh, Dwarfie! Don't you like them? Eh? Come on—try. (*She puts one at or into his mouth.*) Itsby bitsy minty for itsy bitsy Dwarfie.

(*The dog bites her finger.*)

Ow! (*She pushes Dwarfie off her lap.*) Nasty little bastard!

(*The bell goes. She is pleased, fed up with being on her own. She goes to the front door. Standing there, glowering, is Jack.*)

Why, Jack!

JACK (*Snarl*): Where is he?

VERONICA: Colin? Not here. But come on in and cheer me up.

(*Jack strides in glowering all around.*)

JACK: Where's he gone—where is he?

VERONICA: Hey—what's the matter with you?

JACK: Not you, too!

VERONICA: What?

JACK (*Mimics*): 'What's the matter with you?' That's all people seem to say to me nowadays. 'What's the matter with you?' Have I got fungus on my cheeks or something?

VERONICA (*Soothingly*): Drink?

JACK: Drink? (*He glares round the big room again.*)

VERONICA (*Laugh*): Jack! You look as though you've come to *kill* somebody.

JACK: Where is he, Veronica. Where's my bloody agent?

VERONICA: At the Centre. One of his writers has got a play being taped. Or something.

JACK: Another bucket of filth I suppose.

VERONICA: It's about an old age pensioner who inter-feres with little boys in the Natural History Museum. So Colin says.

JACK: Typical!

VERONICA: This one's a bit different, apparently. The old-age pensioner is a woman. Scotch?

JACK: What? Oh. Yes. All right.

VERONICA: You don't *have* to, you know.

(*He looks at her, the aggression ebbing away.*)

JACK: Sorry. I—

(*Veronica smiles at him, pours him a drink.*)

VERONICA: Well *I* didn't want to go, anyway. So I'm glad you came.

(*He takes his drink, stays standing.*

She sits, swinging her leg.)

JACK (*Suddenly awkward*): What's this play called?

VERONICA: Pterodactyl. Part of a trilogy.

(*They look at each other. Then laugh.*)

JACK: Oh well. Better than Brontosaurus I suppose. If that's not Part Two.

(*She pats the settee. Next to her.*)

VERONICA: Sit down, Jack.

(*But he sits opposite her, peculiarly stiff, like someone at an interview.*)

Was Colin expecting you tonight?

JACK (*Flat*): No.

(*Silence. He is staring into his glass.*)

VERONICA: Do you like my little dog?

JACK (*Dully*): Yes. Very nice.

(*Silence. She shifts uncomfortably.*)

VERONICA: I think I'd rather have a cat, though.

(*Silence. She re-crosses her legs in irritation.*

Jack still stares into his glass.)

Stimulating.

JACK: Pardon?

VERONICA (*Edge*): I said I thought this conversation was stimulating. Exciting, even.

(*He looks at her, owl-eyed.*)

JACK: Sorry, Veronica.

VERONICA: Doesn't matter.

JACK (*Stirring himself*): Flat patch of dialogue. Often like that.

VERONICA: No point in saying anything if there's nothing to say.

JACK: That rules out *half* the plays one sees for a start!

(*Silence. It's getting boring.*)

VERONICA: Well, everybody *I* know seems to talk with his head in his hands. (*Pause.*) Or a gleam in his eye.

(*Jack smiles at her shyly.*)

You're the head-in-hands type.

JACK: Yes. That's me.

VERONICA: Colin is the gleam-in-the-eye breed.

JACK (*Suddenly*): I'd like to break his bloody neck!

(*Silence.*)

VERONICA: I see. *His* head in your hands. What's he done?

(*He doesn't smile. He looks fierce.*)

JACK: I'm going to need a new agent, that's for sure.

VERONICA (*Brightly*): I'm stuck with him.

(*He examines her.*)

JACK: Ten months? Eleven months?

VERONICA: What?

JACK: Since you got married.

VERONICA: Mmm. About that. Feels longer.

(*He still examines her. She smiles.*)

JACK (*Dry mouthed*): You—

VERONICA: Yes?

JACK (*Rush*): Do you ever feel you are in—in a—*play*?

(*She blinks.*)

(*Flailing.*) I mean, do you—oh, forget it.

VERONICA (*Amused*): I feel I'm in the Black and White Minstrel Show more often than not.

(*He is staring down into his glass. Then he looks up, wistfully.*)

JACK: I haven't known you very long.

(*She catches the change of tone; the yearning, almost.*)

VERONICA (*Soft*): No, Jack. Not very.

(*Pause. He is looking at her body, her face, hungrily.*)

JACK: You—

(*She waits, relaxed.*)

You've always seemed to me—well—so, so . . .

VERONICA (*Encouragingly*): Yes?

JACK (*Gulp*): Pure.

(*She swallows a shout of hilarity.*)

VERONICA: H-how do you mean that Jack. *Racially?*

(*He stares at her, face hung in grief.*)

Sorry. (*But from now on she wants to laugh.*)

JACK: I sometimes use—antique words. I know I do.

VERONICA: Nothing wrong with that. Soon be quite trendy . . .

JACK: I remember when I first met you. It was at Nigel's champagne and strawberry party. Two years ago, almost.

VERONICA: Was it?

JACK: On the lawn. By the rose trellis.

(*She still wants to laugh.*)

VERONICA: Goodness.

JACK: Some things stay in your mind. And they grow there. The first sight, the first picture, is the blossom. And the memory is the fruit.

(*She smiles, not displeased.*)

VERONICA: You're not drinking.

JACK: No. (*And he gulps some down.*)

VERONICA: What are you angry about Colin for?

JACK (*Clenching*): Never mind.

VERONICA: I don't remember that party. *Rose* trellis?

JACK: Yes. And you sitting near it in a—on a white garden chair. I had a—(*Smiles.*) sudden nursery-book picture of Snow White as I looked at you. You couldn't have been much more than sixteen, seventeen.

VERONICA: And pure.

JACK: Yes!

VERONICA (*Mock prole*): Blimey.

JACK: Everybody was talking. Yakkety yak. All the usual bilge. All the usual sniggery innuendoes and camp asides *aerosoling* out of their mouths like insecticide spray—

VERONICA: Who listens, anyway.

JACK: Right! Who listens. Who thinks. Who cares.

VERONICA: My, my, we *are* gloomy aren't we?

JACK: Chatter, chatter. All except you. *You* were quiet.

VERONICA: Probably because I couldn't think of anything to say.

JACK (*Insistent*): You were more than quiet. You were —*still*.

VERONICA: Oh.

JACK: Gracious, graceful lady.

(*Silence. He begins a circuitous approach.*)

When I was a boy, I was riding my bike down a long hill near my home and suddenly spread out, *laid* out, in front of me I could see the whole great bounce of the landscape in a—a—trembling sort of haze of light. It *reached out* to me. I was outside it and then *inside* it— part of the grass, the road, the hill—even the handle- bars and the bell. Gleaming. Singing. Yet also silent. Even the—you know, I could *see* my own face as though all the air itself had a new sheen—a p-p-polish . . . I—Radiance! A sort of impossible clarity or, or—(*He stops, stops struggling, and almost snaps out the conclusion, disconcertingly abrupt.*) *Love is like that.* ˑ

VERONICA (*Edge*): Is it?

(*He nods.*)

JACK: And a secret love—forever unspoken love—that is the most brave and—and—the most *illuminating* love of all. You can guard it like God guards us . . . (*Sudden twist of head.*) If He was there. If He existed, if He cared.

VERONICA: Jack—?

JACK: We don't know the meaning of the word any more. Love. It's a lost word.

(*Silence. His voice has become thick with emotion.*

She fondles the poodle, strained, half-amused, greatly puzzled.

He tries to surface out of a black lake of pain.)

There was a man walking down the street with a crocodile on a lead.

VERONICA (*Gape*): Pardon?

363

JACK: Crocodile. It was snapping at everybody in sight, trying to tear pieces out of them. 'Ere—' said a pedestrian—'why don't you take that thing to the Zoo'? 'I took him to the Zoo yesterday' the man said—'today I'm taking him to the pictures.'

(*Silence.*)

VERONICA: I never understand jokes.

JACK: I never tell them.

(*Silence.*)

VERONICA: Jack—?

JACK: I think I'd better go. (*Sniff.*) Colin's bigger than I am anyway. In one sense.

VERONICA (*Bright deliberation*): There's no hurry.

(*He twists his head from side to side.*)

JACK (*Thickly*): Oh, Veronica . . .

VERONICA: What is it? What can't you say?

(*He looks all around the room.*)

JACK: I don't like this set.

VERONICA: Set . . .?

JACK (*Sneer*): Trendy.

(*She coos at the poodle for want of better.*

But his eyes now fix on her, bright.)

And then I didn't see you for months and months.

VERONICA: Itsy bitsy Dwarfie . . .

JACK: He goes out, I come in. You go out, she comes in. It's all too bloody neat.

VERONICA: Jack—you are talking to yourself.

(*He passes his hand in front of his face, wearily.*)

JACK: I suppose so.

VERONICA: This little dog won't eat after-dinner mints.

JACK: Dogs can upstage you something rotten. They don't know the camera is looking at them, you see. They have no sense of . . . of . . . (*Angrily.*) Why the hell should it eat after-dinner mints?

VERONICA: Because they taste nice.

(*Fractional pause. His eyes bright.*)

JACK: It was winter time before I saw you again.

(*She looks up questioningly.*)

You were walking down Kensington Church Street.

VERONICA: Was I?

(*He nods, too vigorously.*)

JACK: Words spoil things.

VERONICA: Come again?

(*He runs his tongue out along his dry lips.*)

JACK: Words. They—words are second hand. *Soiled*.

VERONICA (*Frown*): Don't get you.

(*His body jerks with the old passion.*)

JACK: Soiled! Words are grubby. You don't know where they've been. Some dirty sod puts them in your mouth.

VERONICA: How's Judy?

JACK (*Snap*): She's fine! Fine! (*Pause. Soft.*) Snow Queen!

(*She laughs nervously.*)

Pure. You are *pure*.

VERONICA (*Shakily*): Now, Jack—

JACK: I've always felt that. Whenever I've seen you I've felt that.

365

VERONICA: Well, I knew you fancied me but . . .

(*He isn't listening. He has to build another picture.*)

JACK (*Rising tone*): Pure and clean and honest!

(*Close up Veronica, mouth gaping in comic incredulity.*)

Two years I've kept that thought. Two years, a secret, sustaining *clean* idea—so that no matter what pain, what distress, no matter what *dirt* was crunching under my feet there was always within me this pulse, so sacred to me, which takes its beat from you, from images of you . . .

(*Dead still.*)

(*Simply.*) Pardon me.

VERONICA: I don't mind . . .

JACK (*Swift*): I wrote to you. Lots of times . . .

VERONICA: *Wrote* to me—?

JACK: But I ripped them up. The letters. You wouldn't have understood them . . .

VERONICA: You don't know that.

JACK: I ripped them up. Every time your name came out on the page it danced and danced on the end of my pen. Things I had no right to say.

VERONICA: Tell me them now.

JACK (*Gulp*): Pardon?

(*She smiles, enjoying herself.*)

VERONICA: Tell me what danced and danced on the end of your pen, Jack.

(*There is a hidden cruelty not gentleness in the invitation. He doesn't sense it, of course.*

He stares at her, trying to speak. It takes time.)

366

JACK: It—I—the syllables of your name (*Little anxious laugh.*) Ver—on—ic—a. Veronica. I just liked writing down the name. When I couldn't sleep—when the— the nasty things, the corrupt things, debased things, were moving the curtains at the bedroom window— (*Swallow.*) Well, then I used to come down the stairs to write my s-s—secret letters, my secret cry of— (*Cut in middle sentence.*)

11

Interior. Repeat of scenes 2, 3 and 4.
Krispy-Krunch Biscuit Commercial.

(*The thriller-type music crashing in exactly as we jump into the new scene.*

Starts with close-up of bare feet creeping down a darkened stair.

Thrilling trill of 'B' movie music as we swing up to face of Jack Black, lit from beneath to increase the impression of stealth, of camp 'menace'.

The music slowly fades as he creeps ultra-cautiously in his pyjamas down the stairs. A stair creaks. He stiffens. No sounds, so expelling his breath in relief, he continues down the stair.)

WEIRD WHISPER (*Out of vision*): *What does he want? What is he after in the dead of night?*

(*Close-up of Jack Black licking his lips.*

Music trills out mock menace again as he creeps along dark hallway towards dark kitchen.)

What does he want? What? What is he doing?

(*Close-up of his hand groping claw-like for switch inside larder.*

Light comes on with a crash of music.)

367

12

Interior. Back in Sands's flat with Veronica.

(*And as light comes on, so to speak, it is Veronica's face we see, absorbed on the very brink of laughter and yet also, just possibly, just implausibly, moved too, by the odd man opposite.*)

VERONICA : And you never posted one of them. Not one.

(*He hangs his head.*)

JACK : No.

(*Veronica makes a theatrical sigh.*)

VERONICA : So I'll never ever know what it was you wrote to me.

(*Jack flaps his hand helplessly.*)

JACK : No.

VERONICA : I think that's very *rude*.

(*He stares at her.*)

JACK : R—rude?

VERONICA : If you write to someone you should post it. You should let them know what you have said.

JACK : I was writing to myself.

VERONICA (*Mockingly*) : Are you called Ver—on—ic—a then?

JACK : I was writing to God.

(*This shuts her up.*)

I was writing to Judy. (*He starts to cry, oddly, like a baby animal.*)

VERONICA (*Helplessly*) : Jack—?

JACK : It's all right—all r—all right . . . (*Pause. Then claws back to control.*)

VERONICA: Do you want an after-dinner mint?

JACK (*Faint*): What?

VERONICA: Dwarfie doesn't like them.

(*Pause, a comic pause.*)

JACK: I think he's peed on the carpet.

VERONICA: Oh, he's always doing that. Naughty Dwarfie!

(*Pause. A comic pause.*)

JACK: I want to be sick all the time. I want to cry and I want to be sick and I don't know why and I wish the dirt wish wish the dirt would go away go away go go away.

(*They examine each other like hapless stand-up comedians who have forgotten their lines.*)

VERONICA: I'll clean it up. It's only a weeny little puddle.

JACK: I wish you would . . . *could* clean it up . . .

VERONICA: The puddle?

JACK (*Choke*): The world.

VERONICA: Pardon?

JACK (*Gabble*): Up against the rose trellis. Silent in all the smutty chatter. Look at you—clean—pure—so, so —so *divine*.

VERONICA: Cor!

JACK: No, no—listen! Listen to me—no—

VERONICA: I'm listening. Nothing could stop me listening now!

JACK: Sometimes . . .

VERONICA: *Go on*, then.

JACK: Sometimes a person can illuminate, can—oh,

369

God, sometimes you can be *visited* by images, soft images, petal soft—petal p- p-

VERONICA: Petal, Yes.

JACK (*Gulp*): Images that keep falling back into your mind—my mind—pictures no c-camera can *get at* ... (*He looks cautiously round the room, not sure this is altogether true.*)

VERONICA (*Impatient*): Don't you like the colour of the walls or something?

(*He looks at her again, churning.*)

JACK: Rain on old slate.

VERONICA: Jesus Christ, Jack—What *are* you talking about?

JACK: I—Veronica—I was trying to—to ...

VERONICA: I know what you're trying to do, Jack.

JACK: No. Yes. No. I mean—

VERONICA: Anyone would think I was going to bite your head off.

JACK: You? Oh no! Not you Veronica ...

VERONICA: Don't be so timid then.

JACK (*Swallow*): No. It's just—*I* was trying—there's a way, you see, in which those images, those pictures about a mile and a half deep into your head—my head—were all of—of ...

VERONICA: Of what?

JACK (*Whisper*): of you.

(*Silence.*)

(*Suddenly.*) Barnes Common is full of used contraceptives. Dribbling out rancid juice on the poisoned grass!

VERONICA: Jack!

JACK: I love you. (*Pause.*) I love you. I love, love, love you.

370

(*She looks at him steadily, making a decision.*)

VERONICA: O.K. We've got an hour.

JACK: Who—?

(*She gets up, holding out her hand.*)

VERONICA: We've got all of an hour before the man with the moustache gets back.

(*He looks up at her, bewildered, frightened.*)

JACK (*Flat*): Moustache?...

VERONICA: Colin—who else? Come on, then.

JACK: Wh—where?

(*Veronica pushes her fingers through his hair.*)

VERONICA: Bed. Where else, waggytail?

(*Jack gets up, panic all over him.*

She turns her back to him with a smiling swirl.)

VERONICA: Unzip me, Jack.

Telecine 3: Part of Waggytail Din-Din Commercial.

(*Peregrine the fabulous great dane knocks Jack flying into the pond.*

Splash!

Jack surfaces, blowing out water. A comedian.)

JACK: *I haven't even opened the tin yet!*

13

Interior. Sands's flat (as at the end of Scene 12)

(*She turns her back to him with a smiling swirl.*)

VERONICA: Unzip me, Jack.

Telecine 4: Part of Waggytail Din-Din Commercial.

(*Peregrine trotting off happily, the can in his mouth.*)

VOICE (*Out of vision*): Dogs can't wait for it. Dogs can't live without it.

Waggytail Din-Din makes a splash!
Close up of Jack blowing out Pond water.

14

Interior. The consulting room at the hospital. Day.

(*Whitman is absent. A slightly edgy Dr Bilson has taken his place.*)

BILSON: No, no. Don't apologize. Dr Whitman expected you back or hoped you'd come back and . . .

JACK: But you're his stooge!

BILSON: Understudy.

JACK: Stooge!

BILSON: I caught your dog food thing on the box last night.

JACK: It's on all the time.

BILSON: I have a cat myself. Still—(*He shuffles through his papers. A benign smile on his face.*)

JACK: Forgot your lines?

BILSON: Dr Whitman made notes. Now where were we?

JACK (*Sigh*): I said there was nothing wrong with the commercials.

BILSON: Quite so. Quite so.

(*Jack glares at him.*)

JACK: Nothing wrong with them at all. It's the stuff in between which stinks. (*Deadly mimic.*) *Unzip me . . .*

BILSON: Unzip me?

JACK: Unzip yourself, mate.

(*Pause.*)

BILSON: I—um—I've rather lost track . . .

JACK: You young actors! Lost all sense of profession-alism. Learn your lines!

BILSON (*Hopefully*): Commercials. We were talking about comm . . .

JACK: It's the stuff in between that is full of pain.

BILSON: Pain. Yes.

JACK (*Snarl*): Don't keep saying what I say!

BILSON: I beg your pardon.

JACK: You dried up old dog's turd!

(*Bilson sits back and examines him with raised eye-brows.*

Jack passes his hand in front of his face in what has by now become a familiar gesture.)

Dear God—the lines I have to deliver . . .

BILSON (*Hurriedly*): Well, Mr Black, what have you been up to since yesterday—mmm?

(*Jack works his mouth.*)

JACK: Unzip me . . . unzip.

(*Bilson decides to ignore this.*)

BILSON: A beautiful sunny day, wasn't it? What did you do?

JACK: Barnes.

BILSON: What?

(*Jack shifts in his chair.*)

JACK: Went to Barnes Common.

BILSON (*Pleased*): Oh, really? Nice place. What a very sensible thing to do.

JACK: Plastic buttercups.

BILSON: I haven't been there since I was a kid. Things *do* change, of course.

JACK: And ice-cream vans playing Greensleeves.

BILSON: Honestly?

JACK: And dog shit on the grass.

BILSON: Yes. Filthy beasts.

JACK: And French letters hanging on the bushes. Like punctured balloons.

BILSON (*Frown*): Mmm.

JACK: And butterflies copulating with each other in mid-air.

BILSON: Still, it can be very pleasant there. All that nice grass, all those little bushes. (*Laugh.*) Well, you know what I mean . . .

JACK: I used to walk there with my wife. Before we got married.

BILSON: Ah.

JACK: Ah?

BILSON: Nice place to walk with a girl.

JACK: Used to be. It was nice when I walked there with my wife. (*Changes tone.*) I refer, needless to say, to my television wife. My screen partner.

BILSON: Ah.

JACK: Ah?

BILSON: I'm not with you.

JACK (*Savagely*): You are, mate. You're with me, all right!

BILSON (*Amiable smile*): I'm sitting opposite you, yes.

JACK: For a while. (*Looks at his watch.*) A little while.

BILSON: Well, we haven't got all the time in the world, that's true. Not with the National Health being what it is. We're inundated these days with people under— um—stress or . . .

JACK (*Cackle*): Like half the bloody audience. At least half, munching away on their telly snacks, rolling the monosodium glutumate round in their mouths. Zombies. Corrupted zombies, all of them.

(*Bilson examines him again.*)

BILSON: Dr Whitman wrote you a prescription yesterday. I've since had it made up. I think you will find it more than helpful. Really.

(*But we are drifting into close up of Jack.*)

JACK (*Whisper*): *I am in close up again.*

BILSON (*Out of vision*): Listen to me! Please listen!

JACK (*Fearful*): A million or so people looking right into my head right into my head right into my— head . . .

(*Silence. Hold this close shot.*)

(*Hiss.*) Not going to run. I am not going to get off my trike. (*Sob.*) I'm not going to run. No!

(*Slowly pulling out.*)

BILSON (*Coming into shot*): These tablets—they *will* help. I'm quite sure of that.

JACK: See! I didn't run! I didn't.

BILSON: No. Well done. I—look, take one of these things now, eh? It'll calm you. *And* me . . . (*He starts to pour water into a small tumbler from a carafe on his big desk.*)

JACK: Tablets.

BILSON: They are very new. Very good. Mogabrium.

JACK (*Dull*): Mogabrium.

BILSON: We are making considerable advances in bio-chemistry these days. I have myself been privileged to witness the remarkable manner in which even grossly schizophrenic behaviour was dissipated within forty-six hours following quite small dosage of a new drug.

JACK (*Suspiciously*): Schizophrenic behaviour? Who was it?

BILSON (*A joke*): Someone who'd been to see *Family Life*.

JACK (*Horrified*): Dear God!

BILSON: Quite. But he's better now. Much, much better. He's settled for Julie Andrews.

(*They look at each other, smiling.*)

JACK: A spoonful of mogabrium helps the sewage go down?

(*Laughing, Bilson shakes out a blue, red and green capsule into the palm of his hand.*)

BILSON: Very pretty, aren't they?

JACK (*Rocking*): Mogabrium. Mogabrium.

BILSON: Take one. Please.

(*Jack hesitates, then grabs at the capsule, stuffs it in his mouth and swallows. Hard.*)

No water?

JACK: No! It doesn't look very clean to me . . .

BILSON (*Little smile*): No matter, no matter. The crucial thing to realize is that there is absolutely no need to walk around burdened with a sense of disgust. No man should carry *that* sort of cross nowadays.

(*Bilson, suddenly realizing what he has said, emits a happy little chuckle.*)

JACK (*Hostile*): What are you sniggering about *now*?

BILSON: Cross.

JACK: What?

BILSON: If Mogabrium had been available two thousand years ago—well, I can think of at least one wild man who would have stuck to carpentry.

JACK: I don't like you. I don't like you one little bit. Bloody *stooge*.

BILSON: I understand. There's no reason why you should.

JACK: No?

BILSON: Not really.

JACK (*Deflated*): Oh.

BILSON: Listen, you will be a much—well—'happier' man by the day after tomorrow. I want you to take one of these capsules when you go to bed and another when you get up. Will you?

JACK: Can't I offer them round to my friends? This Mogabrium stuff.

BILSON (*Smile*): I would like to give it to all people who feel too oppressed by their surroundings or their interpersonal environment. There is no need to endure that sort of thing. No need at all.

JACK: Now the camera is on you. Right on your mouth, clever dick.

BILSON (*Rising tone*): Disgust, or alienation as some people call it, will soon be as old fashioned as—as—diabolism or witchcraft . . .

JACK: Or fidelity?

BILSON (*Sweeping on*): Disgust is a purely medical phenomenon. At least—in its darkest and bleakest form. I know I sound like—an evangelist.

377

JACK (*Sneer*): Don't shift about in your seat, turd face. You understudies always overdo it when you get your big chance.

(*Bilson, however, is in full flight, aflame with evangelical fervour.*)

BILSON: Everybody should *strive* to be more or less at peace with themselves. And such a state is easier to reach with the right sort of treatment. It's sheer *waste* to wake up and feel that the world is ugly or twisted or deformed or that life itself is intolerable—waste of yourself, waste of the good all around you.

JACK: I hope you get a better bleed'n script next time.

(*Bilson stops, smiles, and hands Jack a long tube of bright capsules.*)

BILSON: One in the morning. One at night.

JACK: Peace of mind?

BILSON: Peace of mind? Well—a little more, hopefully.

JACK: Like the ads?

BILSON (*Sigh*): In a way. Yes.

(*Jack shakes the tube like a baby's rattle.*)

JACK: No more muck in between?

BILSON: There's always muck in between. We can't escape that—but we don't have to *eat* it, do we?

(*Jack gets up, clutching the tube.*)

JACK: Dogs can't wait for it.

BILSON: Twice a day, Mr Black.

JACK: Sure, sure. (*He half hesitates, shrugs, walks away.*)

BILSON: Good luck. (*He watches Jack go to the door. Then he pours himself a glass of water, shakes a different lot of tablets into his hands, swallows them, and shudders slightly.*)

(*To himself.*) The muck in between.

(*Silence.*

Then Bilson looks steadily at the camera. The faint smile on his face slowly, slowly fades.

We are looking now at a face off-guard. A face heavy with misery.

Swirl up lush, over romantic orchestration of 'Somewhere Over the Rainbow'.

Slow mix, music carrying over to:)

15

Interior. Out-patients hall. Day.

(*Alone in the big, big room the old lady sitting in her tubular-steel chair.*

We get the feeling she has been sitting there, waiting and waiting, since the beginning of the play.

Her chin falls slowly as she nods off to sleep.

Music swelling up.

Her eyes suddenly pop open. She looks frightened.)

OLD LADY: Nurse! Nurse!

(*Slow mix, music carrying over, but fading to:*)

16

Interior. Colin Sands's flat. Day.

(*Colin on the telephone, in the middle of a conversation. Music fading fast.*)

COLIN: No, no, it's not that at all. The problem is not finding a dwarf, duckie. It's getting hold of one who can actually *act*. Yes. And this play badly needs a dwarf good enough to be— (*Snigger.*) Well, a pocket Hamlet.

What? I mean when he plays that long scene in the disused abattoir with the fashion model after she's had her nipple cut off by that guitar player in the subway he's got to have—ooh, *compassion.* Yeh. Tenderness. All that stuff—none of your glycerine tears. Sebastian isn't that sort of dwarf at all. He's only played circus before, hanging on to a horse's tail or something. Yes— quite true—he was in pantomime last year—but oh Gawd! No—sorry, my love. Just isn't on. I've got a much better suggestion if you'll listen a minute . . .

17

Interior. Out-patients hall. Day.

(Old lady still sitting.

Hold.

Bring up 'Somewhere Over the Rainbow'.

Gently.

She nods off.

Mix from her face to:)

Telecine 5: Exterior. Outside the hospital. Day.

(The face of Judy, waiting again in the open sports car.

Music continuing.

Pull out.

She sees, we see, Jack coming out through the hospital gate.

He holds on to the rails for a moment.

Judy slowly edges the car: Intercut between their faces. Yearning.

380

She leans across and opens the door for him.

'Somewhere Over the Rainbow' swelling up louder now.

He hesitates. Then shrugs. Then rattles his tube of capsules.

Then climbs in.

She accelerates away, vroom.)

Exterior. Car.

('Somewhere Over the Rainbow' given full, schmaltzy value now, this time with the vocal—the original Judy Garland vocal if possible.

Judy's hair blowing wild in the wind machine.

And like in Top of the Pops or Previn's TV music or a million, million ads, back projection totally encapsulates the seemingly speeding car with glorious corn-flake packet colours.

Red

Blue

Green

Blue

Red

And, inaudible against the loud, loud music, Jack and Judy, heads back, hair blowing, laugh and laugh like the happy cretins in a TV commercial.)

Until at last the car is in mid-air, swallowed up in glorious blue. Smaller and smaller goes the car. Until just blue. No more music left.

Silence.

Iris out for final commercial.

381

18

Interior. TV commercial type lab.

(*Jack, in white coat and earnest spectacles, holds up his pretty phial of capsules. He speaks from the Epistle to the Philippians with the eye-snapping, hard-sell telly-ad voice known to us all.*)

JACK (*Brisk*): Whatsoever things are true, whatsoever things are honest, whatsoever things are just, whatsoever things are lovely ... (*He shakes out the pretty capsules into the palm of his hand, like a man showing us the blue specks in a washing powder.*

Close-shot of capsules.) Whatsoever things are of good report, if there be any virtue, and if there be any ... (*He dries.*) Oh, shit! Sorry everybody!

19

Whole studio.

(*Pull out. We are in the television studio, seeing at least one camera. Sounds of studio.*)

VOICE FROM GALLERY (*Out of vision*): Never mind, Jack. Try it again. Keep it punchy! *Quiet studio—we're still recording.*

(*Jack recomposes himself to start again.*)

JACK: Whatsoever things are *true.* (*Happy grin.*) Whatsoever things are *honest.* (*Grin.*) Whatsoever things are *just.* (*Grin.*) Whatsoever things are *lovely.*

(*Pull right away, losing his words, looking right down on all the disconcerting electronic mess.*

Final credits over this shambling ironmongery. 'Thank you very much studio!)

Fade.